Praise for *You* ...

"The ultimate career guide to help you discover your path in the workforce."
—Daymond John, *New York Times*
bestselling author of *The Power of Broke*

"Whether you want to advance in the career you are already in, change directions, or you haven't decided what profession you want to embark on, this is the book for you. In her inspiring and brilliant book, *You Turn*, Ashley shares all her tips, wisdom and strategies on how to move forward and create the successes you desire in your professional life. It is an infusion of fuel to move forward towards your fulfillment."
—Agapi Stassinopolous, author of *Wake Up to the Joy of You*

"Success begins with looking within yourself, figuring out what you want, and deciding how you want to achieve it. Ashley Stahl's *You Turn* is here to help."
—Alex Banayan, #1 international bestselling author of *The Third Door*

"*You Turn* is the most important book you could read if you want confidence and success in your career. This book is so practical and powerful that it will change your life."
—Dr. Benjamin Hardy, author of *Personality Isn't Permanent*

"*You Turn* is meant for anyone striving to find real clarity on their dream career, and figure out the exact steps to getting there! Stahl's stories are gripping (I couldn't put this book down), and her insights are sharp and unique."
—Natalie Ellis, cofounder of BossBabe

"This book is unlike any career book I've ever read—a soul drenched blend of inspiration, strategy and actionable advice to get clear on your vision, while making sure you are doing what truly fulfills you."
—Lori Harder, founder of Drink Lite Pink and
host of the *Earn Your Happy* podcast

"*You Turn* is a much needed guide in today's workforce to help so many get clear on WHO they are, what natural talents they have, and what work they're truly meant to do!"
—Sahara Rose, creator of Rose Gold Goddesses
and host of the *Highest Self* podcast

"Stahl brings the emotional depth, introspectivity, and genuine story to the pursuit of finding fulfillment in work. This book will revolutionize the way we think about work."
—Samantha Skelly, founder and author of *Hungry for Happiness*

YOU
turn

YOU ↑
turn

GET UNSTUCK, DISCOVER YOUR DIRECTION, DESIGN YOUR DREAM CAREER

ASHLEY STAHL

BENBELLA

BenBella Books, Inc.
Dallas, Texas

BenBella

BenBella Books, Inc.
10440 N. Central Expressway
Suite 800
Dallas, TX 75231
www.benbellabooks.com
Send feedback to feedback@benbellabooks.com

BenBella is a federally registered trademark.

Printed in the United States of America
10 9 8 7 6 5 4 3 2 1

Library of Congress Cataloging-in-Publication Data

Names: Stahl, Ashley, 1987- author.
Title: You turn : get unstuck, discover your direction, and design your
   dream career / Ashley Stahl.
Description: Dallas, TX : BenBella Books, [2021] | Includes bibliographical
   references. | Summary: "From Ashley Stahl, counterterrorism professional
   turned career coach, You Turn is a guide to help people redirect their
   career path toward a role where they thrive and let their passions
   shine-rather than feeling stuck"-- Provided by publisher.
Identifiers: LCCN 2020039264 (print) | LCCN 2020039265 (ebook) | ISBN
   9781950665693 (paperback) | ISBN 9781950665747 (ebook)
Subjects: LCSH: Career changes. | Career development. | Job satisfaction. |
   Self-realization.
Classification: LCC HF5384 .S73 2021 (print) | LCC HF5384 (ebook) | DDC
   650.1—dc23
LC record available at https://lccn.loc.gov/2020039264
LC ebook record available at https://lccn.loc.gov/2020039265

Editing by Greg Brown
Copyediting by Michael Fedison
Proofreading by Sarah Vostok
   and Laura Cherkas

Text design and composition by
   PerfecType, Nashville, TN
Cover design by Jessica Lynn
Printed by Lake Book Manufacturing

Distributed to the trade by Two Rivers Distribution, an Ingram brand
www.tworiversdistribution.com

Special discounts for bulk sales are available. Please contact
bulkorders@benbellabooks.com.

To those in pursuit of a career that lights them up:
who you are is so much bigger than the title on your business card
or the number in your bank account.

CONTENTS

PART *three* REROUTING

PART *four* THE HIGHWAY TO HAPPINESS

INTRODUCTION

START HERE

When I was five, I knew I was supposed to be a writer. I'll never forget walking up to the microphone onstage at my preschool graduation after the principal encouraged each of us kids to tell the audience "what we want to be when we grow up."

Loaded question for a five-year-old, right?

So there I was, waiting my turn, listening to *all* the answers you'd expect: a fireman, police officer, astronaut, doctor, singer, athlete . . . None of them fit the blueprint of who I wanted to become.

I took the microphone out of the principal's hand and squinted into the bright stage lights.

"I am going to be a mom, an author . . . and a poet," I stated.

I don't know what I was expecting. Loud cheers or clapping from the audience, maybe? But all I heard was silence. Deafening silence. Not really knowing what to do, I raised the microphone and spoke into the black void: "Thank you, ladies and gentlemen."

My voice echoed as I walked offstage.

Ladies and gentlemen . . . Who did I think I was?

I'll tell you exactly who: a five-year-old girl who got kicked out of preschool for headbutting, that's who. I'm not joking. For whatever reason, I'd walk up to little kids on the playground, appearing as though I were going to hug them, and then bang my head into theirs.

I've always felt like my body didn't have enough space to hold all my energy, all my creativity, or all my thoughts about the future. That energy needed to go *somewhere*. Some people expel their energy through expressing certain emotions, such as laughter or anger. Others perhaps expel their energy through physical activity, such as exercise, art, or dance. I chose to write.

This book is a place for me to release my failures, understand my successes, and use them to support you in finding your chosen career path. So welcome to my *You Turn* . . . and yours as well.

What's a You Turn? It's that critical moment of transformation when you become honest with yourself about some core area of your life that isn't working. It's that moment where you realize the only thing worse than stepping into the unknown is staying stuck where you are. This could be in any area of your life, be it love, work, or friendships, to name a few. More than anything, it's that moment when you finally stop letting fear drive you, and you suddenly choose to listen to that quiet yet wise voice inside of you that's begging to be heard. For once, instead of muffling it, you honor it. You surrender to all the inconveniences this could bring into your life, and you decide—*decide*—to make a change, jumping off the road you've been traveling and going in a new, unknown direction. In doing so, your whole life is about to become better, but often that doesn't come until you've allowed it to unravel. Instead of making a U-Turn and going back to where you may have started, or questioning yourself when the drive feels rough on the roads of life, why not instead get more intentional and see that lack of alignment as an opportunity to go deeper and connect to your heart, making it more of a *You Turn*?

I know this all too well because I've stepped into the unknown more times than I can count. In fact, the loneliest places I've ever been were at the tip-top of my successes and the rock bottom of my failures.

I am writing this book as a career coach, keynote speaker, and CEO of my own company with hundreds of thousands of email subscribers, a successful podcast, thousands of clients, a snazzy book deal, and all that jazz. To say I'm not scared would be a lie. The truth is, I'm terrified and don't *really* feel like I know what I'm doing. Nonetheless, I've learned over the years to make friends with this fear and embrace it because I know it's just the mind trying to play tricks on me.

This book is written in twelve chapters and segmented into four parts. Each chapter (except the final one) will come with an action step you can take in my *Eleven-Step You Turn Formula*, which is designed to help you discover your dream career path. This means a career aligned with your most innate skill set, your core values, and your purpose in the world.

To get started, here's an outline of my *Eleven-Step You Turn Formula*. We'll explore one step in each chapter.

1. Know your CORE NATURE.
2. Discover your CORE SKILL SET.
3. Unlock your MONEY BLUEPRINT.
4. Determine your CORE VALUES.
5. Learn how to BEFRIEND YOUR BLOCKS.
6. Be sure to ASSESS YOUR CORE INTERESTS.
7. Learn how to TURN CONVERSATIONS INTO OPPORTUNITIES.
8. Discover how to CRAFT THE PERFECT ELEVATOR PITCH.
9. STOP APPLYING FOR JOBS, AND START NETWORKING.
10. Take steps to CREATE YOUR PERSONAL BRAND.
11. Know your primary and secondary CORE MOTIVATORS.

PART I is called *The You Turn*, the act one must choose to make that lies at the heart of this book. Chapters one and two will cover the biggest *You Turn* I ever made in my career: quitting my "dream job" in counterterrorism for the Pentagon in Washington, DC. This part of the book is focused on helping you answer the age-old question of when to stay in your career path or job versus when to go. It will help you understand what I like to call your CORE NATURE, based on how people experience you, and it will help you discover your CORE SKILL SET, which is key for clarifying your best job options. By understanding these two aspects of yourself, your most ideal career path becomes clear.

PART II is called *TURN SIGNALS*. Here, in chapters three through six, we'll look at the moments in your life when you may not have been paying attention to your TURN SIGNALS, instinctual or experiential indicators letting you know that you may be off course from the kind of career you actually want. We'll discuss your mindset about money and how to upgrade the belief system you picked up as a child. We'll also unlock your top five CORE VALUES, the primary principles rooted in the core of who you really are. Part of this means looking at who you're not, which is often a result of your limiting beliefs; we'll look at healing those as well. A final career topic in this section covers the difference between pursuing a career you're passionate about versus one you're simply interested in. I don't believe you should just "do what you love" when it comes to making a career decision; I believe you should do what you *are*.

PART III is called *Rerouting*. We can only reroute once we notice the TURN SIGNALS we've been ignoring in our lives and decide to come home to our true selves, the ultimate *You Turn*. Chapters seven through eleven are about committing to the career you were always meant for. Tools you'll learn in this part of the book focus on taking action through networking, crafting an effective ELEVATOR PITCH, and BUILDING A PERSONAL BRAND. I'll then walk you through the job-hunting formula I've taught thousands of my students in my flagship course, the Job Offer Academy. While all of these steps will take your career to the next level, none of it would be possible without exploring what motivates you at work, which I call your CORE MOTIVATOR.

PART IV is called *The Highway to Happiness*. Here, in chapter twelve, I'll share my most recent, and most meaningful, *You Turn*: returning to the work my soul was meant to do after hitting rock bottom. If you've ever thought about reinventing yourself, or doing work that speaks to your heart, this chapter is for you. Since writing this chapter, I have stepped into an energetic harmony with the world around me, and I want that for you, too.

At the end of each chapter, we'll do an even deeper dive into your world, applying the principles of the *You Turn Formula* to what's going on in your career *right now*. So get your pen ready.

Along your journey through this book, remember this: fear is friendly. It's an indicator that you're pushing toward a personal edge and rising into a new level. The discomfort is a reminder that you're going somewhere new—and new is good. Remember, too, that I'm just like you. The challenges we face are truly the same. My spiritual teacher, Ron Hulnick, inspired me to see life through a more neutral lens, often saying that "we're all just souls, having a human experience."

Have you ever considered what your past experiences have done to shape the person you are today? One reason I wrote this book was to ultimately help people sift through the noise of life and see who they really are. Not who they want to be. Not who they should be. But who they actually are. We all know the truth can hurt, but as the saying goes, the truth will also set you free. What I've come to notice about this whole "personal power" or "personal truth" thing, though, is that it's always there . . . waiting for you to see it, realize it, and, if you're truly inspired, embody it. Choosing not to look at the truth can energetically feel like trying to push a beach ball under the ocean. It might stay there for a little while, but sure as shit, it will explode back to the surface.

Facing the truth is like ripping off a Band-Aid. Yes, it's going to hurt, but dreading the inevitable or denying it only prolongs your pain. So you get to decide: face the truth and cry over it this year, or face the truth next year, and cry then . . . This is why I have developed the inner muscles to "grip it and rip it."

The lessons and mindsets I discuss will help you step into more power and purpose in your career. I'm so grateful my stories and lessons have supported thousands in getting clarity on their careers, developing their best skill sets, and harnessing those skills. I'm so grateful they will help you now, too. More than anything, I encourage my clients to stand in their worthiness, regardless of their present outside circumstances. This means connecting to who you *can* be, not necessarily who you are now, and trusting that vision even when your life hasn't yet realized it.

That's where my *You Turn Formula* comes in, and why I want to help you make a *You Turn* into your power. Before we do that, we need to take an honest look at your life. What's working for you? What isn't? Then we'll look at how some of your decisions today are really motivated by the past.

My human experience has been a cocktail of joy and heartbreak, all of which have led me here, into your hands as you read this book. My journey may not be exactly like yours. I've been in some very unexpected roles in the workforce, and yet I've learned as a career coach that it doesn't matter what our highs or lows look like, because a high or low feels the same to anyone going through one.

We're going to look at what you're avoiding in your life and career, so that we can help you see who you really are and what you actually want. We're going to craft a life vision that lights you up and won't burn out.

Ultimately, this book will get you out of the trap of holding on to a career plan just for the sake of having one. That means you'll start asking bigger life questions that take you out of autopilot, so you can courageously admit when it's time to come home to yourself and make a *You Turn*. When you operate from this place of knowing, you will be able to lock into a career path and a life you can lean into and feel inspired by.

If you opt for denial, life is eventually going to respond by smacking you with a two-by-four to wake you up, be it through anxiety, divorce, illness, debt, dead-end jobs, low self-esteem, or a good old-fashioned midlife crisis. As you cultivate a willingness to lean into these moments, you will notice that they're an opening—a spiritual awakening. After all, ignorance is not bliss. The state of ignorance is simply a state of hiding from the truth. The truth has taught me that happiness isn't for the faint of heart. And happiness is for the spiritual warriors who are willing to look in the mirror and admit when something sucks or doesn't work for them anymore. The truth is meant for those who are willing to look at any situation and muster the courage to step away from it, knowing that their future greatness is available *only* if they make the space for it.

By the end of this book, you will come to understand these truths deeply: You are not your parents. You are your own person with your own dreams, your own hopes, and your own organic abilities. You are not your circumstances or your appearances—from your bank account, to your job title, to the friends you associate with. Where you are in life on a random Friday can be totally different by Monday, but only if you choose for it to be.

You will also learn how catchphrases like "follow your passion" or "do what you love" are a one-way ticket to nowhere. If you aren't sure about what to do with your career, you'll realize that you don't actually need clarity; you just need to connect to yourself and what's true for you right now, what's lighting you up here, in this moment.

It's time we join together to trust that same intelligence that holds the stars in the sky at night. Thank you for being here with me. I'm honored. More importantly, thank you for learning how to be here with *you*. When you choose to be who you are, the sky smiles down on you. It's painful to wake up, ask the big life questions, and dig inside of yourself more deeply for those answers. But you've got this. You're a warrior.

As the previously-mentioned Ron Hulnick has said, a conscious world begins with conscious people.[1]

Cheers to your awakening.

PART *one*
THE YOU TURN

You can't numb the sadness and think you're going to feel this amazing joy and enthusiasm in life. It's one pipe that all the emotions go in and out of, so if you try to numb one, you will numb them all.

—You Turn Podcast
Episode 28: "How to Have More Fun While You're Achieving"
with Jason Goldberg, Business Mentor

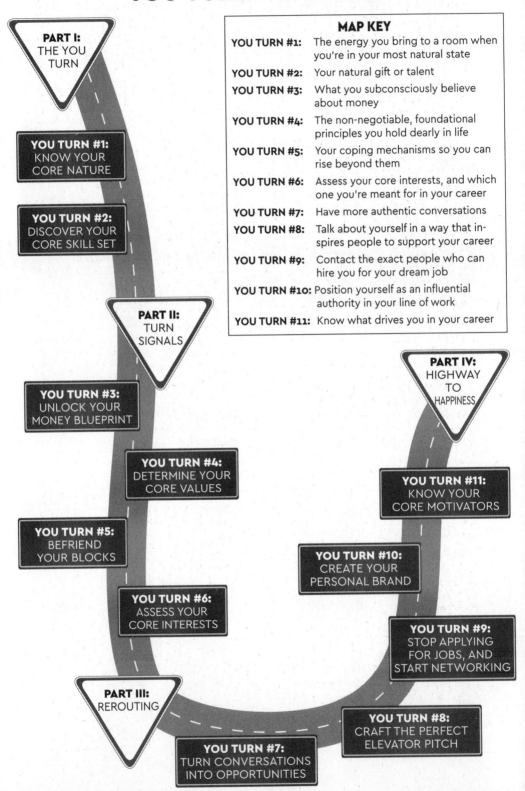

Chapter One

Don't Do What You Love, Do What You Are

OCTOBER 1, 2011

Deep down, I knew it was coming because I couldn't shake the feeling of being out of sync. With myself. With my life. With . . . everything. It was as if everything felt like an itchy sweater. Have you ever felt like that? Not the sweater, but that feeling of being trapped in your own life with no way out? What I didn't realize at the time was that I should have leaned in to that feeling and gotten curious about it, rather than feeding it with a constant flow of resistance.

What you resist gets louder. I found that out the hard way.

I knew my life needed to change, but I wasn't sure how it would happen or if I even wanted to face it. It wasn't until I found myself holding a loaded .45 caliber handgun that the *it* finally happened. It wasn't a dream, or some runaway fantasy of a better life, either. It was an awareness, a newfound realization that my life was about to change forever. And like a seed that eventually has no choice but to burst open and turn

5

into a flower, my moment came. With that pistol in my hand, I had no choice but to grow.

One of the biggest *You Turns* I've ever made was in my career. The year was 2011, and I was twenty-four years old. Being a young person in the workforce, I constantly found myself questioning what society would tell me: that I'd have to start my career out fetching coffee, work my way up the ladder, or take jobs for no other reason than to get my foot in the door. I yearned for more. Something in my heart told me I could just work hard and grow quickly in my career. I *lived* in that mindset of possibility despite the results I saw in front of me, trusting that perhaps there was more. Then, one day, there was. Just weeks after leaving my job as an administrative assistant in Los Angeles making minimum wage, I became the shiny new supervisor for a coveted training program at the Pentagon. I went from an assistant at an advertising agency in LA to being in charge of a high-level training curriculum preparing seasoned US government civilian workers for risky new assignments in Afghanistan. I'd stepped into a rare opportunity to start my career in a management role, and I couldn't believe I'd networked my way into this job. I was excited to learn from senior staff who could mentor me.

Rumor on the street was that this job was previously filled by a slew of smart senior military officials who weren't good fits for it. In fact, the last person in my role had been a sixty-five-year-old colonel. Why didn't they work out in the position? Because the military taught them to delegate to a large team, and while they did it brilliantly, this job required someone who was alert, energized, and hungry to do the work herself. In a military world committed to ranking order and climbing the ladder, I somehow became the exception to the rule. Knowing I wouldn't have to work my way up, I was giddy at the thought of stepping into leadership at such a young age. I was also scared shitless and unsure whether this was even my path. In fact, I was unsure of who I really was at that time.

My first day on the job started oddly to say the least. One of my colleagues led me down a gray hallway. As I followed this guy walking in front of me, all I heard was the out-of-place sound of *clickity-clack* from my high heels, echoing across the concrete floor. There wasn't any kind of small talk, or even a "hey, congrats on the new job" or "welcome to the team." I wasn't sure if it was his choice to show dominance, or the fact that I was just a woman in a man's military world, but there he was, three steps ahead, leading me down the halls of the Pentagon as if I were a lost puppy trying to find a home. I had a fake smile plastered on my face; beneath it were worry, panic, and an extraordinary fear of failure. Do you ever smile at people at work when you're actually petrified?

My escort was head of the Republican club at his college in the Northeast, played on the varsity golf team, and served as a former White House intern for the Bush administration. I would later find out he was also getting $17,000 a year more than I was for doing the exact same job. The realization was painful, and left me wondering what I possibly could have done to better advocate for myself. Have you ever found out someone's getting paid more than you for the same job? It's painful.

I looked around the room and realized there were no windows. My fancy new job, the one I'd worked so hard to get, began inside a bunker-style basement. It was exactly how it sounds: cold floors, battleship-gray walls, and no windows or heat to speak of. *Welcome to government work*, I thought to myself as I adjusted my coat to fend off the chilly air wafting throughout the room. It was the middle of December in Washington, DC, and there wasn't a jacket in the world that could save me. In fact, I wore one coat every day that friends lovingly referred to as "the sleeping bag."

I was shown to a large desk in the far corner of the basement, also known as my new office. Don't get me wrong, I was grateful for the opportunity. To be twenty-four years old making nearly six figures in a management job—that blew my mind—and working for the Pentagon, no less (more on that *You Turn* later). Nonetheless, I was still totally thrown off as I looked down at the red glow of the space heater clearly struggling to do its job against the cold leaking through the walls.

I said to myself, *I'm a sweater girl, I can work with this. As long as my feet are warm, I can bundle up and make it work.* Next, the guy turned around and said, "So this is my desk . . . and over there, that's yours."

I turned and saw an isolated chair in the opposite corner. There was no desk, no table, just a chair. I smiled and thought, *Is this some sort of joke?* I even wondered if my new colleagues had a dark sense of humor, pulling me into some sort of welcome prank, but the guy didn't even blink.

"Where's my desk?" I turned around, offering a curious smile. His response made my lungs pop like little balloons: "This is just like Afghanistan. Girls come second to men," he said, finally looking in my direction. And through his smirk, he continued: "One day, we'll give you a desk, but you're going to have to earn it first."

I remember thinking to myself, *Is this guy stuck in the 1800s? How am I supposed to write pages upon pages of intelligence reports if I can't put my laptop on a desk?* I wish I could tell you that I stood up for myself and called Sheryl Sandberg, Susan B. Anthony, and Gloria Steinem to organize a feminist march with me in the basement, or that at least I commented on his sexism and reported him to HR, but I didn't. Instead, I went to the bathroom and cried. Of course, I wept quietly, silencing my whimpers with paper towels, because hey, I was rolling with the military now, and there wasn't space for me to complain. I wasn't aware then how low my confidence was, despite being someone friends knew to stand up for a cause.

I had a master's degree from King's College London (a top foreign affairs graduate program worldwide), and a triple major in government, history, and French, which represented years of study, achieving fluency in French, and producing a dissertation on Al Qaeda in the Islamic Maghreb. All for what? To deal with unequal pay while working out of a dungeon in the dead of winter? Really?

After three days of balancing my laptop on my knees in my single chair, I found an empty two-drawer filing cabinet gathering dust in a storage closet down the hall. It wasn't a desk, but I made it work. After a couple of weeks of working alongside Mr. Misogyny, and living my single-chair existence, I was saved by an angel.

DISCOVER YOUR CORE NATURE

My angel came in the form of a sweet, curvy southern woman named Janette (her name, like many names in this book, has been changed to keep privacy intact). She was a single mom from Louisiana and had moved to DC after her son, a marine, got stationed there. She was always bringing baked goods into the office like a grandma I saw in the movies, and best of all, she insisted that I have a desk close by her.

"He didn't give you a *desk*?" Janette said to me one day, outraged. "Girl, why didn't you show him *who you are*?"

I looked at her and repeated her words with curiosity. "Who I am? Maybe I don't know who I am, Janette."

She laughed and said words I'd never forget. "You've just been here a few weeks, and let me tell you, the room changes for all of us when you walk in. You're communicative, wise, joyful, bold, curious, and funny . . . You gotta use those God-given skills you got to get what you want."

I stared at her, not registering that these six words—communicative, wise, joyful, bold, curious, and funny—represented a career-coaching term I'd eventually coin, my CORE NATURE. Your CORE NATURE is all about the energy you bring to the room when you're in your most natural state and a reflection of how people experience you. Usually it's about four to six words that sum your energy up.

"Here," Janette exclaimed unapologetically, walking toward me with a small desk in her hands.

Have you ever had someone advocate for you at work? They change *everything*, right? I stood up with a smile on my face. My back straightened, and unexpected tears filled my eyes. With a desk of my own, I felt like I was finally seen as a true professional. She reminded me of the worthiness that's always been inside me, a sense of self-value that's necessary for making a *You Turn*. More often than not, even when we're in the darkest of places, our pain cracks us open for change. In this sort of fragile state, we tend to come across these rays of light that shine into us.

Janette was my ray of light in a world that felt very heavy to me—she was a fierce, motherly presence in a masculine building—and her way of being in the world inspired me. Her light also reminded me of my own light, my CORE NATURE, as those six words she'd spoken would become the foundation I'd eventually build my career upon.

Here's the thing about being a twenty-four-year-old woman working among military men: I received a lot of attention—the wrong kind of attention. I'm sure it had a lot to do with the fact that, other than Janette, I was one of the only women in sight. It didn't matter if they were married or single; it was as though I was in one of those cartoons where you see a small sheep innocently frolicking around in a herd of hungry wolves. Later, I heard someone refer to me as "civilian eye candy." It was a spotlight I wanted no part of, and I had bigger dreams for myself.

All this dehumanization and objectification led me to start reflecting on what inspired me to join the government in the first place—the opportunity to learn foreign languages and work toward my dream of eventually becoming an intelligence officer for the Central Intelligence Agency. That means a person willing to travel the world and use her people skills as a tool to build foreign relationships, with the hope of turning people against their own state in order to collect information for the US government.

Looking back, I'd grown up in a house where the news was always on, and I was always curious about the happenings of the world. Part of my CORE NATURE, curiosity, was noticeable at a young age. Plus, my extended family was on the East Coast and was very impacted by 9/11. So there I was, young, sitting at dinner parties, listening to my parents argue over politics with my uncles. Early on, I told myself that joining the government would be a service to the world—to keep people safe. Being bold was a part of my CORE NATURE, and I thought perhaps I could use it for this purpose. What do you notice about your energy now that you also carried with you at a young age?

THOUGHTS ON THE PASSION MYTH

Leading up to college, I was often told: "Follow your passion," or "Do what you love." Sound familiar to you, too? I loved studying politics in college, but what I didn't realize then is that there's a big difference between *what you love* and *who you are*. In fact, I love a lot of things. I love cupcakes, five-star hotels, and massages. But let me tell you, I'd be a shitty cupcake baker, a horrendous concierge, and a nightmare of a masseuse . . . Ask any of my ex-boyfriends about that.

A lot of us think passion should dictate the work we choose to do. I learned the hard way that there's a huge difference between being a *consumer* and a *producer*. Just because I love buying clothes as a *consumer* doesn't mean I should become a fashion designer, the *producer* of the clothes. A happy consumer does not always translate into a happy producer.

I walked into my new job filled with a passion for wanting to help people. I don't think the intention was wrong, but I quickly realized I needed more than just passion to be successful or fulfilled. I needed to consider my CORE NATURE, my CORE SKILL SET, my CORE VALUES, and so much more. I didn't know all this because I wasn't yet a career coach, but we'll examine these concepts as they relate to your career throughout this book. Look, every field comes with its own challenges. You can try to change them, but more often than not, your success will come from how you work with them.

THOUGHTS ON THE EXPERIENCE MYTH

I also learned early on in my career that your natural, innate talents can always outmaneuver years of experience. Do you get caught in thinking you don't have enough experience to land the job of your dreams?

Look, we live in a workforce that prizes years of experience, climbing the ladder, and unnecessary corporate degrees, but the truth of the matter is that *who you are—your natural gifts—always wins* at work. That's why we'll also talk about your CORE SKILL SET in the next chapter.

Take me, for example. Why did I land such a powerful role at the Pentagon? Because of my ability to communicate. So there I was, in my CORE NATURE—communicative, wise, joyful, bold, curious, and funny—which really came across as happy, chatty, and ready to take the job by the reins.

"You've got lots of energy," my future boss had commented in my initial days in my new position, "so I'm going to offer you this leadership role . . . It's gonna take a lot out of you, so buckle up."

I'd cried then with excitement and shock, especially given how recently I'd been working as an administrative assistant. Guess what kind of job I would have gotten if I bought into the belief that I needed more experience? Perhaps another administrative assistant job. But not this time. This time, I realized my experience had nothing to do with my capability, that I wanted to be more, have more, and do more. And so I did.

When I started working for the Department of Defense, I thought I would be working with a group of like-minded individuals committed to helping the world. In the military, though, I'd learn that, as a civilian without direct military experience, you're rarely seen as a valuable contributor. I quickly found out the soldiers were more interested in discovering who the "new girl" was. I was often asked about my life story, which felt more like an agenda for the military men to gauge whether I was single, or old enough to be doing my job.

To make matters worse, I was younger than virtually everyone working on the base, so people often confused me with an administrative assistant or secretary who'd fetch their coffee. I quickly hatched an expert plan to handle their assumptions. Instead of saying, *Get your own damn coffee*, something I wanted to say, I would play it off like they were asking *me* if I wanted a cup of coffee: "Oh! So sweet of you to offer. No thanks, no coffee for me, I'm trying to cut down." Have you ever been treated like an assistant when you're in a leadership role? For young women in the workforce, it's all too easy to internalize that messaging around who we are.

The average age of an American employee is forty-two,[1] but in industries like technology and media, that number is dramatically lower. In fact, a recent *Harvard Business Review* survey[2] showed that the average age of private company founders with a valuation of more than $1 billion is thirty-one, not to mention the average age of their CEOs is forty-one. Interesting, right? I've heard all too often that young professionals don't want to take leaps in their career because they think they have "little experience," but that's a story many of us buy in to in order to stay small. Though younger workers have proven time and again to be just as knowledgeable, committed, and talented as their older counterparts, it's easy to feel like the new kid in school . . . every single day. We live in a workplace culture of proving yourself. In fact, have you ever acted in a certain way at work to make sure your "superiors" know that you're working hard or creating results? This scarcity is getting old, right? And this culture of "proving ourselves" keeps us from really doing our best work, let alone discovering who we are at work, and our CORE NATURE.

THE NUMBERS DON'T LIE

Working in national security brought me face-to-face with these challenges and my own belief systems as a young woman working in a male-dominated world. As women, we are not only up against institutionalized ideas on age; we also have to battle millennia-old ideas about women's equality, or the lack thereof. More than 40 percent of the 53.5 million young people in the workforce today are women. Yet, only 26 percent of executives or senior managers, and less than 5 percent of CEOs, are women.[3] The numbers don't lie. And don't get me started with politics, where roughly 20 percent of the 535 seats in Congress are held by women.[4]

Until there is a balance in gender representation, our age and beauty will have an undeniable impact on our salaries. In fact, what we look like, how we dress, and whether the men around us deem us attractive (and it's not fun either way) influence our opportunity to succeed and thrive in the workplace. According to research published in *Psychological Science*, the general population perceives competence based on how attractive, confident, and masculine a person appears.[5] Despite our progress, it's an uphill battle toward the glass ceiling.

Over time, the "guys" on the base got the message, but one in particular couldn't take a hint that I wasn't there to land a husband. His name was Farhad, and he served as a diplomatic liaison between the Pentagon and the Afghan government, which meant that he was military royalty in Afghanistan. Farhad was nice enough, but man, the guy was a hugger. Now, I have no problem with huggers. In fact, I *am* one. But Farhad's hugs had a way of lasting a little too long. Because of his diplomatic status and the escalating conflict as NATO was withdrawing from Afghanistan, Farhad was always in the office. As a result, he would make a point to be in my department, walk past my desk when I was working late, and give me one of his intense embraces.

One afternoon, Janette looked over after Farhad left with his bodyguards and said in a bad accent, "*Great to zee you, Ashley.*" I immediately felt the need to defend myself, to make sure she and everyone else knew there was nothing going on between Farhad and me, but Janette beat me to the punch.

"Girrrrrl, you just a honey trap," she said, rolling her eyes and returning to her hum of southern church melodies. "Mmm, you ain't nothin' but trouble."

I stopped typing midway through a briefing on US foreign policy objectives in Afghanistan, lowered my Harry Potter–looking eyeglasses, and asked, "Wait, what's a honey trap?"

I could hear the intelligence analysts behind me cracking up. Before Janette had a chance to answer my question, her phone rang. "Saved by the bell," she said with a smirk as she picked up the receiver.

THOUGHTS ON EFFECTIVE COMMUNICATION

A mentor once told me that in any given communication exchange, we're either adding value or taking up space. More often than not, I felt like a burden when I asked questions. Do you ever feel like that—that if you ask a question, you're in the way?

Despite my fears, I'd muster the confidence to ask away. Sometimes I'd fall on my face and make a mockery of myself. But other times I'd save the room by asking something that would have otherwise slipped beneath the radar, something so necessary that it would add extraordinary value. We've been taught to interpret fear as a signal meaning "don't do this"—but what I learned working for the Pentagon was about courage: when you feel fear in a situation that's otherwise good for your growth, do it anyway. It's a muscle you build.

In the counterterrorism world, the term "honey trap" signifies a pretty girl who goes out into the field and seduces men as a way to collect intelligence. Based on my career trajectory, I guess Janette was right. I was working to eventually become that honey trap she spoke of, traveling to some of the darkest corners of the world. Not because I wanted to become some sort of seductress (in fact, that was the darkest thing I'd heard as a possibility of this job), but because I wanted to make an impact. What drives you in your career?

As the laughter from my colleagues finally died down and Janette was still on the phone, I received an email that would instigate my transformational *You Turn* out of government work. The subject line of the email read INSIDER ATTACKS ON THE RISE. One of the civilians I had trained months prior had been killed by a single gunshot to the head from his Afghan counterpart in the capital city of Kabul. To this day, that email still haunts me.

It was the first time in my short stint working for the Department of Defense that someone I knew personally—someone I befriended and supported through my work—was killed. The experience had a profound effect on my life outlook and the work we were trying to accomplish in the region. His death, while tragic, didn't come as a surprise. I was keenly aware of the rise in what the media referred to as "insider attacks."

An insider attack is when your foreign counterpart, the one you were working alongside in whatever job you were assigned to, suddenly becomes your enemy, brings a gun to work, and shoots you, likely in the face. I know it sounds harsh and overdramatic to include it here in the pages of this book, but that was the world I lived in then. That was my new reality. People I had trained were getting murdered.

With this trend on the rise, the deploying civilians became more fearful and curious about the prospect of bringing a weapon into the country to protect themselves. At first I didn't know what to say, though the request made perfect sense to me. After all, heading into a danger zone without a weapon is like skydiving without a parachute. While having a gun sounded reasonable, the truth was that none of our deploying civilians knew how to use one. This needed a solution, which meant it was time for me to change their curriculum and ensure they got the proper training.

Implementing this was really a gift to myself. After all, I never again wanted to feel that pain of getting an email about a colleague being killed. Do you ever get too attached to the people you work with?

The deploying civilians would often tell me about their families, their impressive government careers, and their aspirations to do something great for their country. We would travel together from DC to various military bases to undergo all sorts of confidential training. Dropping them off at the airport for their final deployment was always a challenge for me because they felt like my second family. How could I not care about them or worry about their safety?

My passion was a double-edged sword. It fueled my commitment to the work, but also devastated me when the job got too tough. Some people could shake off civilian deaths with ease, but I took every fatality to heart.

I don't know about you, but one of the biggest challenges I faced when I entered the workforce was managing my professional identity while honoring my personal feelings. These were honorable people trying to do something good for their country. To think once they were deployed to Afghanistan, they could show up to work and get shot in the face weighed heavy on my heart. It was a loss that I couldn't chalk up to being "part of the job." I mean, if this was part of my job, it was something I would never be okay with. That's just not how I'm wired.

THOUGHTS ON BOUNDARIES AT WORK

As Sigmund Freud says, "Love and work . . . work and love, that's all there is." Your career should be a vehicle for your self-expression, an art form that helps you be you in the world. There's something beautiful about that. Work is also a place where I rose to the challenge of creating boundaries—what I'd later start to see as the highest form of self-love.

Your boundaries are where you decide what's healthy for you—not just what you want to do, but what you need to do. You decide in advance how you will show up in the world to honor them. In my case, boundaries included: never engaging in shit-talking, listening without talking if I felt uncomfortable, and telling people I'd get back to them if they had a great question I couldn't answer. Do you ever get uneasy when people are talking smack at work? Stay neutral at all costs. And, most of all, know that one of the worst things you can do in the workforce is bullshit your answer to any question. There is an art to being an excellent bullshitter, but a danger to speaking beyond the capacity of your current knowledge.

The ability to compartmentalize one's life in that way was never going to be one of my strong suits. To me, that was okay. I was great in other areas. I did, however, begin to keep my head down, do my job, and emotionally divest myself from getting too close to the people I was in charge of training. The thought of the risks they would face when they landed in Kabul was just too painful for me to imagine.

I found myself constantly wondering, How do I balance the art of professionalism while still softening into human connection? After all, we're hardwired for human connection—especially me. I learned not to judge myself for feeling emotional toward my work and the people I worked with.

In the following weeks, I pitched the idea for a civilian weapons training program and asked that it be included in our current training curriculum. Without some kind of weapons training, I argued, a civilian advisor with a gun was more of a threat to himself than anyone else. My immediate supervisor agreed. Two weeks later, the program had been implemented and our civilians were deploying with a gun in their hands.

All this was happening when it was already a really tense time in DC and overseas. My civilian trainees were preparing for their deployments, insider attacks were at an all-time high in Afghanistan, President Obama was cutting down the number of troops we were sending into the country, and the search for Osama bin Laden intensified. Amidst all this, I was lost on who I truly was and more disconnected from my CORE NATURE than ever before. Sometimes this disconnect happens when we focus more on what we're interested in, or our passions, than who we are and our gifts. It also happens when we forget to leave blank space in our calendars for our own sanity, for our being. Other times it happens when we don't slow down and question the goals we're setting for ourselves. Perhaps you have great goals, but do you *truly* want to reach them? Are they *actually* meant for you?

I started splitting my time between DC and a military base in Indiana. My mornings in the Pentagon were a whirlwind of meetings with high-level Afghan government officials and endless news briefings that turned into late-night sessions of drafting intelligence reports that I couldn't write quickly enough. More often than not, the political situation would change by the time I'd email them out.

In the months that followed, I saw less and less of Janette as I spent more time at the thousand-acre military base in rural Indiana. This base was used to train civilian first responders, as well as marines, for military urban warfare. It was also home to the National Guard Patriot Academy, which is a program that gives potential recruits the chance to earn a high school diploma.

In many ways, life on the base was a long way from my life in DC, and the only thing that felt familiar about Indiana was the cold. As I drove away from the Indianapolis airport, I braced myself, knowing that the training center would be eerie; in fact, it used to be a psych ward back in the 1980s. There was a creepiness to it all. The hallways had a palpable air of insanity. The doors to my bedroom didn't have a lock, and in some of the rooms there were no windows at all. Like I said, creepy . . . horror-movie creepy.

Every day, I would wonder: *Why am I doing this? And who am I, really?* I had wanted a job where I got to help people. I was certainly fulfilling that mission. Yet I felt utterly empty. I knew that if I was going to be doing a job, any job, but especially one where I worked more than sixty hours a week, it should be filling me up, not gutting me. I realized that we don't just work for passion, and we don't just work to fulfill a mission. We work as a way to express ourselves in the world . . . and I felt suppressed.

My responsibilities intensified, which was fine because there was nothing else to do in the area, and I found myself working later at my desk every night. The joy of the approaching weekends began to give way to working seven days a week. It probably was due to the fact that I was in the middle of nowhere and it was freezing outside, but free time had lost its value to me. Saturday and Sunday became just another couple of days at the office. My health was in decline and my diet, or lack thereof, was in complete disarray. Twinkies for lunch? Yes, please.

On some nights, actually *most* nights, I worked right through dinner and forgot to eat. If you're thinking it was because I was trying some new fad diet my friends in LA were raving about, it wasn't. It had everything to do with a work ethic I was taught growing up. A limiting belief I held from a young age—which I later would question—is that the more you work, the more valuable you become. While that sounds great on paper or as advice from a parent to a child, the stack of security reports sitting on my desk kept growing no matter how long I was at the office or how hard I worked.

I now realize that the value I added wasn't always tied to the amount of hours I worked. Sure, I was filing more reports than most of my colleagues and building a reputation as someone who could both train and support new recruits, all while managing all the logistics on the back end. I was slowly gaining the respect of both my superiors and my peers (even Mr. Captain Golf Republican). On the outside, I was successful in my job, but that's the thing about a *You Turn*—financial success is not enough to keep you where you are. Fulfillment is truly an art, whereas success is often just a science, a step-by-step formula, if you will. In fact, as I quickly realized, success could become a treadmill to nowhere.

I kept working to feel like I was worthy, or like I deserved to be there. Do you work hard just to show yourself that you're capable of something? That was me at the Pentagon.

"You look LA-skinny," my girlfriends would say over the phone. To help me feel less disconnected in the middle of Bumfuck, Indiana, I would send them selfies. The pictures ranged from me sitting inside the office to the snow on the ground outside.

"I'm just depressed, I think," I would often reply. My no-dinner diet went on for a couple of weeks, until one of the worst nights of my life arrived. But depending on how you look at the journey of life, the yin and the yang, the ups and downs of our experiences, perhaps that night was the *best* night of my life. I say that because it turned out to be a catalyst for my career *You Turn*, and the inspiration for this book. Chances are that you can reframe any issue into a blessing if you're willing to see it that way. More often than not, our painful experiences can and will serve as trampolines, launching us into our next level in life.

RESISTANCE IS FUTILE

Did you know that a rocket often uses almost half its fuel just for takeoff?[6]

Similarly, getting started is perhaps the toughest part of any goal. For years, I tended to feel consistent nudges to make some sort of change in my life before I'd finally listen to them. But why? Why do we choose to ignore those whispers? Because we've been taught that "fine" is just fine. But it's not. When was the last time you said something was fine? Was it *really* actually okay for you?

As a coach, I've found that people who say they're fine usually just aren't in touch with their pain. I've come to learn that lukewarm feelings about anything, be it in my career or otherwise, are an indicator that it's time for me to do a self-audit and take an honest look at my life. No matter how much you love that job, relationship, or pair of comfy jeans, we tend to outgrow the things that once felt like home to us. It's almost like we suddenly wake up and our old tactics or ways of being don't seem to work for us anymore, but that's a good thing as we are being forced to find a new way. This is growth.

In the words of Carl Jung, "what you resist not only persists but will grow in size." Typically, when you're resisting your reality, you're only giving it more energy. Think of all the sauciest love stories: Romeo and Juliet, Bonnie and Clyde, and so on. They eventually gave in to their desires because resistance is painful and tiring. In fact, sometimes it can become a full-time job to ignore it, because your energy tacitly becomes focused on *not* coming to terms with whatever it is you're resisting. So not only do you squander precious energy in seeking to bypass what's still lurking inside you, but the effort itself is useless. The irony, huh? And here's the truth: once we become willing to confront whatever we're up against, the rest becomes a lot easier.

In my case, that force was a six-foot-three-inch drill sergeant.

It was well past 10 PM, and I, once again, had worked through dinner. For the past few hours, I had been the only one in the office while I was in the groove of writing my reports. I didn't realize that I'd pushed right through my hunger pangs until the words on the intelligence report I was writing began to blur on the page. It was time for a break and a proper meal, so I stopped typing, grabbed my coat, and walked to the base cafeteria.

It was early February and the snow from three days prior crunched under my hiking boots like a bed of saltine crackers. As I walked across the quad, I noticed the lights in the cafeteria were off. Looking around,

I saw most of the buildings in the complex were dark as well. When I glanced down to check my watch, thinking I might have worked past midnight (closing time for the cafeteria), something hit me. It was a violent, concussive blow to the back of my head, and it threw me to the ground. Hard. My face was pushed into the packed snow. I was disoriented and for some reason couldn't move. Something or someone was assaulting me.

Instinctively, I tried to fight back, but all I heard were screaming voices amid the violence I found myself in: "Don't move! Shut your mouth." I was ripped to my feet with such force, I felt like my arms were about to pull from their sockets. Before my eyes could adjust to identify my attackers, a bag was placed over my head and its drawstrings cinched tight around my neck, almost cutting off my airflow. I could hardly breathe. Somehow, the whole thing reminded me of an episode of the TV series *Homeland*: foreign assets being grabbed and stuffed into an awaiting van. The entire thing was fast, violent, and precise.

Then it hit me. This was a mistake. It was my mistake. When I felt myself slammed into a waiting Hummer truck, I remembered the direct orders from my superior that very morning: "Ashley, make sure to stay in your barracks tonight after 10 PM. The marines are conducting capture-and-kill training exercises on the base. If you're outside after 10 PM, you're fair game."

"This is a mistake! Let me go!" I began screaming. "I'm the supervisor for the civilian training program! Let me go! I know you guys are training and I shouldn't be out here! I forgot. *Fuck!* Just let me go."

I thrashed about, giving these guys a run for their money. *Okay, probably not a run for their money*, but at least I got in a few shots here and there before my face was slammed into their Hummer seat. The hood covering my face was ripped off and a series of flashlights immediately blinded me. There I was, in the wrong kind of spotlight, again.

"Show me your credentials!" a large, bearded man with horrible breath yelled at me like a drill sergeant. With a nod from the drill sergeant to the two muscled-up marines holding me up, I was able to dig my ID from my coat pocket. After he gave my ID a quick and rather skeptical glance, I was released. In my own move of authority, feigning self-confidence, I snatched my credentials from the scary, bearded man, and shot back my own cold glare. I stepped through the crowd of marines who began appearing from the shadows and walked away.

"You're rolling with the military now, so it's about time you start listening to orders. Do you understand me?" he barked. I paused, hoping to find some sort of smart-ass comeback, but I didn't. I simply kept walking before another snarl came from the bearded man: "Next time, girl, you're in for a wild ride."

This time, I didn't stop walking. I didn't answer. I just headed straight to my room and cried. With every tear falling down my face, I felt more out of place than ever before. The next morning, I opened my eyes to the sounds of birds chirping outside my window. It was 6:45 AM, and last night's kidnapping felt like nothing more than a nightmare. That is, until I tried to sit up to turn off my alarm. I wouldn't say my head hurt from the initial takedown or the knee of the bearded man digging into my lower back, and I wouldn't even say my arms hurt after they dragged me across the quad. It was my entire body. Everything hurt.

That being said, I think my pride hurt the most. I had made a thoughtless mistake and I knew it the minute I hit the ground. Plus, the military didn't have room for mistakes—unless you wanted to end up with a bag over your head. That's how life is sometimes. A bag over your head, suffocating from the life you thought was the one you were supposed to live. Welcome to *You Turn*: a place that will scare the shit out of you, but serve you in the long run.

The question now is, Are you ready?

YOU TURN #1:
KNOW YOUR *core nature*

Let's face it. Our natural state is love. That's how we're born, and yet, over time, we're taught fear, which is a necessary inner alarm system for us to survive in the physical world. *We learn* to look both ways when crossing the street. *We learn* to be afraid of talking to strangers. *We learn* not to touch the stove when it's hot. Along the way, we get hurt, we stop taking risks, and we become afraid.

People often call themselves "practical" or "realistic" for making choices that feel "responsible." They buy into limitations about what's possible because they're scared of putting themselves out there. After all, if we stop hiding, we're vulnerable to criticism and pain. But if we're being honest with ourselves, some part of us knows that people who call themselves "realists" are often just dreamers who've gotten their hearts broken somewhere along the way. So how do you make a *You Turn*? How do you reconnect to yourself and figure out what you really want?

You come home to yourself, returning to your CORE NATURE. Knowing your true nature means knowing how you feel when you're in your most natural and honest state; it means knowing how people experience you when you're in a room with them.

I can't tell you how many clients have come into my coaching practice telling me that they want clarity, as if it's something they can quickly order at a Starbucks. But as a career coach, when I hear someone saying that they're stuck or they need clarity, I immediately get curious. Here's the truth of the matter: clarity comes easily when you're connected to yourself. That's why clarity isn't usually the problem . . . The problem is disconnection. In fact, according to research, we're the loneliest generation yet, despite being surrounded more than ever by people who statistically and economically look just like we do.[7] I wanted to solve this disconnection, which is why I created the Career Clarity Lab, an online course to help you access your most ideal and aligned career options and the clarity that already exists within you.

So why do we feel so disconnected from people whose data, income, education, and lifestyle look so much like ours? Because we're not actually being ourselves. When you're not connected to yourself, or owning who you really are, it's tough to know what you like, what you dislike, or what you're truly interested in. That's why finding out who you are, your true nature, is first a game of realizing who you're not.

What does it mean to come home to yourself and own your true nature? And why is your nature so powerful to know when it comes to living your calling?

This isn't just about me, a girl who felt she'd landed her dream job, only to find out it wasn't what she thought; it's about how all of us tend to lose sight of our natural state and the energy we're in when we are our best selves, our CORE NATURE, when we start making career and life decisions. We choose autopilot. We start prioritizing light and fleeting interests, and not who we are. We eventually become scared of the vulnerability that comes with being ourselves at our core, and as a result, we become someone we're not. This is poison for our careers.

WHAT I KNOW NOW

Discovering your CORE NATURE requires two commitments:

1. Asking for feedback from friends and family, the people who know you best and really see you for who you are.
2. Looking at the fears, blocks, or limitations you've bought into about who you should be in your life and career. Those are what keep us from the truth of who we are and the fulfillment we really want.

So let's start with asking for feedback. I've noticed that after I have guests on my show, the *You Turn Podcast*, they tend to give me feedback about my interview skills. They consistently tell me things like, *Wow, you're such a people person*, or *Wow, you have great insight, you're really easy to talk to*. Compliments like this are key for you to pay attention to, because they point to your CORE NATURE.

Just look at Janette's feedback when I was at the Pentagon. It was pretty consistent with the feedback I get from friends and family on my CORE NATURE: communicative, wise, joyful, bold, curious, and funny.

Then it's about asking yourself: What career paths demand this kind of energy? What kind of careers are built upon my CORE NATURE? I thought about talent agents, real estate agents, speakers, authors, teachers, comedians, communications managers, poets . . . you name it.

One of the biggest mistakes I often see people making in their careers is in limiting themselves to one or two basic job titles, versus realizing that their nature is expansive, and that many career paths will suit them.

USE THIS NOW

Exercise 1: Questions to ask in order to collect feedback on your CORE NATURE from friends, family, or colleagues.

1. When have you seen me at my best?
2. How does the room feel different when I walk in?

Exercise 2: Examining the blocks that keep you from your CORE NATURE.

1. What was the conversation like in your household about career success or fulfillment? How did your parents or your caretakers relate to their careers?
2. What is your first memory of success, or more importantly, what is your first memory of failure as it relates to the topic of career? This could come from an experience you saw your parents have, or it could come from an experience you yourself had.
   a. Ask yourself: What did I make that moment or situation mean about life or the world around me? And what did I make that moment mean about me?
3. Fill in the blank: *I'm not where I want to be in my career because I'm not* _____.
   a. So what is it? What do you believe is keeping you from where you want to be? More often than not, whatever you put in the blank is simply a limiting belief or mindset you've been buying into for a very long time. And it's these sorts of beliefs that tend to block us from our nature. They typically come from a

memory or experience that sat with you. After all, trauma is not always about having something big happen to you—it's about how you relate to it, and what you decide to believe about it.

CONCLUSION

The good news for me was I got clarity that holding a .45 caliber gun wasn't connected to my CORE NATURE. Apparently, neither were subzero weather, starvation diets, or misogyny. My CORE NATURE is one of joy, and, needless to say, that didn't work in a military environment where we were living in constant fear. This realization would later morph me into an author and speaker. But, remember, it takes courage to step into your CORE NATURE when your career isn't working for you, and sometimes that means giving yourself permission to leave where you are.

Chapter Two

The Worst Kind of Betrayal (Is the Kind You Inflict on Yourself)

JANUARY 17, 2012

In the moment of my takedown in Indiana by the Bearded Man and his team of marines, it struck me that my life was out of sync, that I was sleepwalking through my career. And yet, I remembered: I'm human. Knowing that mistakes are such a fundamental part of our human experience and growth, I wondered why we beat ourselves up over them.

My hard military base workouts reminded me of how pain often serves as a one-way ticket to growth. In fact, there is research on this. Did you know that after grueling exercise, when you feel tired and exhausted, you are actually changing the very chemistry of your muscle fibers? You are literally making yourself strong from breaking yourself apart.[1] Similarly, I'd eventually learn that success is often what happens only after a series of failures and that failure is simply part of the alchemy we use to create success. I came to believe failure was neutral, just information rerouting us back to our destiny. Other times, I saw failure as feedback that we're leaning into a challenge or personal edge. Most importantly, I knew I was so much bigger than any success or failure.

We have a tendency, as human beings, to live our lives on a pendulum of judgment: I'm nice. I'm mean. I'm fat. I'm skinny. I'm smart. I'm stupid. I'm successful. I'm failing. Through it all, we forget the vastness of who we truly are: souls who are here on the planet having a human experience.

In truth, life is all about these dualities. In order to understand your greatness, you need to have sat within your smallness. In order to become masterful, you must have, at one point, been a beginner. A big part of awakenings is understanding and accepting these dichotomies.

The Bearded Man saw me as small, but I didn't want to buy into his limited experience of me. Deep down, some part of me (not all of me) knew I had access to a greatness that was living inside of me, one that had always been there. Oddly, we often tend to miss what's great about ourselves because it's so obvious. We overlook our natural gifts and talents, especially our fundamental and most natural CORE SKILL SET, which we take with us everywhere we go in our career. In my case, I didn't realize my CORE SKILL SET was all about *words* — speaking them, writing them, or just using them as a tool in general. It was too . . . obvious.

Far too often, we drive through life looking through a mucky windshield. This muck, our own limiting beliefs, hinders our vision of the road ahead, and the possibilities of it all. This muck makes for a journey rife with judgments, fears, doubts, limiting beliefs, and worries that take us out of the truth of who we really are. As a career coach, I've had many clients step into my office having subscribed to the belief that they don't have clarity and need to find their purpose in life, or in the workforce.

That couldn't be further from the truth. What they really need, what we all need, is to clean up our windshield. This means taking a look at the muck: the judgments about ourselves and others, the limitations in

our thinking about what's possible for us, and the stories we tell ourselves, particularly the ones that keep us in our smallness. It's here where
we see the problem we face isn't a lack of clarity—it's being disconnected from ourselves.

As I stepped outside to walk to the showers on the military base, I
was mentally preparing for the first day of introducing the new weapons
training program. I got a good look at myself in the mirror. The circles
beneath my eyes were darker than they had ever been. My skin was
pale, and my cheekbones were hollow. My eyes were puffy from crying
myself to sleep. Breathing felt like work. Turning, I saw a softball-sized
bruise in the middle of my back. This was, no doubt, courtesy of the
Bearded Man's knee in my back during my nightmare of Capture and
Kill. I tried to tell myself I was okay, but looking back at myself in the
mirror, I knew I wasn't. Not even close. I was more tired than I had ever
been in my life. It wasn't the type of tired that could be solved with a
good night's sleep, either. This was an emotional kind of tired, and hard
to explain unless you've been there. It was an emptiness. I missed my
family, my friends, and the semblance of a normal life.

As the warm water fell onto my skin, I thought about my life before
all of this, perhaps as an attempt to cathartically put things into perspective or find some moment I could hold on to for comfort. I found myself
wondering about the choices we make in life and how they lead to our
day-to-day. I wondered about my friends back home in LA. I imagined
how, in a few hours, they'd wake up, put on makeup, and decide what
fashion statement to make today. Would they all be hanging out in the
evening, talking about life and in community—something I missed so
deeply? They would climb into their cars and stop at Starbucks before
a nice drive down Sunset Boulevard on their way downtown for their
creative marketing jobs. This trip down memory lane wasn't working.
This mental exercise seemed only to make me sad. No matter how hard
I tried, there was no hiding the fact that I was sore, embarrassed, and
feeling more alone than ever.

THOUGHTS ON FEELING LONELY VERSUS ALONE

There had been times in my life when I felt the sensation of loneliness, but I'd never felt completely alone. Until now. I realized there's a big difference between feeling lonely and feeling alone. When I felt lonely in the past, I still had an awareness of the fact that there were people in my life who loved me, but I felt as though they couldn't understand me or what I was going through.

However, when I felt *alone*, it was as though there was a big gap between me and the rest of the world. My aloneness felt like being in a sea of people and feeling invisible. It reminded me of that feeling you get when you have an epic head cold and it's hard to hear. You feel slow, as though everyone else is walking past you too quickly. Lonely I could handle, but alone felt dark.

I got dressed, pulled on my boots, and headed out for the weapons training. I should have felt a sense of pride for the days I'd spent in DC creating this program. I wasn't proud of myself, and I wasn't standing tall. I was just devastated. I felt spiritually sick, like a deep void was penetrating every cell in my body. This spiritual sickness was like an existential crisis—not knowing why I was here, not knowing my purpose in the world or even if I had one. The worst part about all of this wasn't feeling disconnected in my job; it was in the hopelessness of not having clarity on where to go next in my career. This sort of hopelessness is an indicator that it's time to come back to the truth of who you are, that it's time to make a *You Turn*.

THOUGHTS ON YOUR CORE SKILL SET

When people are "failing" in their careers, it just means they're operating out of alignment with their CORE SKILL SET, their most natural and ingrained talent or gift in the world.

When we face "failure" in our careers, usually through getting fired or being passed over for a promotion, we tell ourselves something's wrong with us, or that we're not capable. That's just not the case. The reality is that this sort of "failure" is just feedback telling us it's time to reconnect to our core and make a *You Turn*. In fact, it's often so natural and easy for each of us to use our own unique CORE SKILL SET that we don't even notice how special it is or how masterful we are. I used to think it was cheesy when college professors told me that everyone had a special gift to offer the world, but as a career expert, I've come to see that was actually true. I believe most people who haven't gotten clarity on their purpose at work haven't done so for one of two reasons: because they're buying into the belief that there's no other option and they have to keep pushing along the path they're on, or because they haven't truly committed to their own self-discovery.

THOUGHTS ON LIMITING BELIEFS

In retrospect, there was so much muck on my mental windshield: the limiting belief that if I left the government, all the years I spent studying would now be "a waste." The irrational belief that I would have to "start over" in my career if I left the one I had. The fear that people would some- how pity me if I ended up at home again and unemployed. The judgment that I was being reckless in my career or ruining my resume by leaving.

It's no surprise we find ourselves stuck in careers we hate, relation- ships that rob us of our joy, or anything that isn't in alignment with our true nature. Part of human nature is seeing ourselves in the context of others' perceptions of us. My truth was that I was a happy person, a humorous person, someone who doesn't take life too seriously. So what was I doing working in counterterrorism? It wasn't in alignment with who I was, or my CORE SKILL SET. I was simply stuck in the deadly trap of "It's *a good job*."

THOUGHTS ON QUITTING

During my long walk over to the shooting range that morning after my Bearded Man takedown, I found myself still trying to put the night's kidnapping experience behind me, but I couldn't. The feeling of being overpowered by those men, the bag over my head, my throbbing headache from crying myself to sleep, and the bruises on my body from being thrown around like a war criminal were hard to ignore.

I wanted out but didn't know how I would even go about quitting. I'd devoted years of my education, and some lofty student loans, to studying the government, and I even had a master's degree in international relations. I'd learned foreign languages and told the whole world that this was my path. It was my shiny little plan that kept people from worrying about me. *Shit, it kept* me *from worrying about me.* How could I just up and quit?

I would discover that quitting isn't always for *losers*; it's actually sometimes reserved for *winners*. After all, it takes a certain level of courage to admit that something sucks and isn't working for you. In a world that values plans, the number of years listed on your resume, company loyalty—all of it—quitting is for badass human beings who are willing to face the truth of where they are and have reserved the courage to do something about it.

THOUGHTS ON DECISION-MAKING

Even when I knew it was no longer working for me, I was scared at the thought of *You Turn*-ing out of the Pentagon. I was even *more* terrified of the unknown. The devil you know is better than the devil you don't, right? Wrong. My pain was so great that I was forced to wake up. For the first time ever, I was willing to ditch my excuses and the stories that kept me stuck:

"I should just wait for my promotion."

"I'm so lucky to have gotten this job."

"I'll never get something this good again."

"I just need two years of this job on my resume."

"Work is supposed to be hard."

"I need to climb the ladder."

"My next boss might be worse."

"I worked my whole career to get here—it's a waste if I leave."

I brushed off my tears and stepped onto the firing range. My gaze fell on the entire scene for a moment before a series of unexpected words slipped out of me—just talking to myself quietly: "You don't *have* to quit; you *get* to quit." This distinction changed everything for me. Instead of feeling like a victim of my job, the one I was grateful for, I found myself empowered. I realized that being unhappy with my job doesn't mean being ungrateful. I felt more in touch with my freedom than I had in months. I realized that real freedom wasn't about the amount I saw in my bank account, it was about my willingness to commit to the truth of my heart, regardless of all other temptations. I wanted a life that was more than just "fine," even if it was at the price of feeling comfortable or fitting in. I cared about myself too much to stay miserable. Leaving that job felt like an honor that reminded me of my freedom in the world, the freedom to create my own career and be in charge of my own life.

As soon as I tasted the flavors of this newfound freedom, despair crept right back in: *What would everyone say if I suddenly came home? Would they think I'm a failure? Would they pity me for coming back to LA?* We talked about this duality earlier, but I am fascinated by how we are able to hold two completely opposing emotions inside our minds: freedom/despair, joy/heartbreak, gratitude/grief, etc. Looking back, this is often what happens when we try to make a *You Turn* in our lives: our old way of being, our ego, fights for dear life to keep its grip on us, trying to keep us in our comfort zones. We either grip it or rip it.

But magic doesn't live in the grip. Magic lives in that moment where you look your old way of being straight in the eye and, with confidence and trust in your heart, say, "Not this time. I'm not listening to you this time. Today, I choose the person I want to be." Magic lives in the rip.

After my tormented walk to the dreaded training facility, I found myself standing alongside the marine sergeant passing out handguns for our civilian trainees. I was there physically, but mentally I was a million miles away. Looking out into the woods behind the weapons range, I thought of the scary movie *The Hills Have Eyes*. There was a creepy stillness to the forest. I felt small and insignificant. I went from freedom, to despair, to no longer caring about anything.

Pop. Pop. Pop. Gunfire erupted around me and snapped me out of my emotional tornado. With each sound of the firing weapons, my body and mind reacted like I was in a war zone, suffering shell shock. In reality, I was indeed at war, a war with my thoughts, a war with my higher self, who knew it was time to go home.

Amidst all that gunfire, one of my students tapped me on the shoulder.

"Here," he said, "hold this. I have to pee."

Before I could reject his request, I slowly looked down to see a loaded .45 resting in my hands. It was warm from recently being fired, and it was heavy. Chills went down my spine. I realized it was the first time I'd ever held a gun. I decided it would also be the last.

What the fuck am I doing here? I thought. This sort of moment, the one when you know you are absolutely done, only comes when you haven't listened to yourself all along. Suddenly, the truth becomes so loud, you have no choice but to abruptly listen to it. I walked over to the sergeant, handed him the weapon, and walked away.

"Wait, where are you going?" I heard the sergeant say, but I didn't look back. The civilian who'd handed me his gun was walking toward me, but I didn't make eye contact.

I just kept walking. Alcoholics Anonymous has a well-known concept for this: breakdown-breakthrough. Others have called it the "great emptying." All of this means that, in order to fill yourself up for something new, you need to clear your life out. In doing so, you create space for a surge of new energy. Later, I would learn there is a dignity to hitting rock bottom. It's a sacred place where the most profound awareness of your life can permeate you—if you let it, that is. So, even in the hardest times, never rob yourself of the dignity of rock bottom. Sitting in the midst of a sacred rock-bottom moment, I was filled with fear.

You know, coworkers can betray you, significant others can betray you . . . but the worst betrayal of all is the betrayal of the self. I went to the barracks to pack up, and my supervisor walked in. "Ashley, you can't go," he said. "Fourteen ambassadors from the State Department nominated their countries to receive this training program. We want you to travel to South Sudan, the Philippines, all of it. We'll pay you more."

I thought about how those four words—"we'll pay you more"—are often ones that hold so many hostage. I remembered that goals are just something we chase because of how we think they'll make us feel when we reach them. In a way, we're just chasing the feelings that we think our goals will give us. I thought money would give me security, but I was exchanging it for my sanity. In that split second, I decided that my peace, and my destiny, were too much to give.

It felt like the universe was testing my commitment to myself, as it often does. But I knew there was no price to be paid that was too high for my own freedom—the freedom to be me, the freedom to find what I loved to do for work, the freedom to say fuck no. "This is my two weeks' notice," I said. "I'm going to hop on a flight to DC and find someone to replace me."

He liked me too much to be harsh, so he surrendered and said, "I understand."

After months of trying to quiet that little intuitive voice, the one telling me it was time to leave, my moment was finally here. While some might find themselves sad in a moment like this, I was inspired— tired, but inspired—because the thing that matters about life is how we unwrap moments like this one, how we relate to our experiences. *How you relate to the issue is the issue.*

THOUGHTS ON INTUITION AND
USING YOUR SECOND BRAIN

I picked up my phone to call my quirky aunt Gwenda: "Gwenda, I don't know how I'm going to tell anyone this, but I think I need to quit my job and move home."

"Congratulations!" she responded. "Time for your soul to stop dying. When are you coming home? We're going to throw a party!"

Next, I called my best friend from high school, Kara. "Shit," she said. "What are you going to do? How are you going to pay your bills? Are you sure you want to do this?"

I hung up on her, and for a flash, I questioned my own intuition. People have long connected the human gut (our small and large intestine) to the brain—we call it "gut instinct" for a reason. But recently, studies have begun to show just how deeply our two "brains" are connected. They call our gut the enteric nervous system (ENS), aka the second brain. Our gut is made up of 200 to 600 million nerve cells (the same size as a cat or dog's brain!), working alongside the complex ecosystem of microbes.[2] When things are going right, our gut communicates the good feeling to the ENS, which serves as the link to our actual brain. It's why we "feel" the right action in our stomachs, as well as our own "wrong" decisions. Ultimately, we must go where we are guided.

I was now facing the question of where I would go next. An incredible career starts with who you are and what your natural skills and gifts are, not what you love or think you love. In that moment, I did a self-audit: I was great at negotiating. Great at job hunting. Great at writing. Great at people. I was a hard worker.

Later, as a career coach, I'd discover that there are ten CORE SKILL SETS most employees fall under within the workforce, and every worker tends to have a primary CORE SKILL SET they lead with in the workplace. While your CORE NATURE is all about your energy and how people experience you in a room, your primary CORE SKILL SET reflects a natural skill you have, and the modality you work best in; this could be anything from writing to crunching numbers to building things. In short, your CORE NATURE is about the energy you bring, and your CORE SKILL SET is all about the skill you're best suited to use and lead with in the workplace. How do you know what your primary CORE SKILL SET is? It tends to be a skill that bleeds into your job no matter what your job responsibilities are, because you can't help but be you. As I said earlier in the chapter, my CORE SKILL SET is *words*. My ability to use words was an overarching skill I'd bring to any table and was foundational to my contribution in the workplace. No matter what sort of job I had, even when I was sixteen and working at a preschool front desk, I always found a way to make my job about *words*. I'd edit brochures, talk to parents who walked in, or write newsletters for the school's email list—even when they didn't ask me to write, I'd offer to do it. One time, I even hijacked the stage at the preschool's graduation and gave a speech about my feelings around growing up. The preschool director didn't know what to do with me, but there I was, shining in my CORE SKILL SET of *words*, giving an unplanned speech because it felt fun.

In the past, I'd overlooked all these natural talents and never thought I was that unique. I assumed words were just as easy for everyone else to access. They weren't. I didn't know it then, but I'd go on to become the first millennial career coach on the internet, creating millions of dollars in revenue via a top-selling online course that would help users land a new job they would love. My Job Offer Academy program was scaled into thirty-one countries around the world.

Of course, that was beyond my wildest dreams in that moment, as all good things are when you feel stuck. Society teaches us to "stay the course" and never give up, even if giving up means honoring the path we are truly meant for. Sadly, most people don't make a change until the misery they feel in their current situation outweighs their fear of the unknown. *Why* do we do that? Why do we wait to be miserable or hit rock bottom before we make a change? In my case, I waited until there was a bag over my head on a military base. What I needed to do to make a change, what we all need to do, is tap into our CORE SKILL SET and make a *You Turn*. Access the courage to connect to yourself so deeply that you're willing to step into the abyss of the unknown with an eye toward adventure.

YOU TURN #2:
DISCOVER YOUR *core skill set*

QUITTING

As a career expert, I'm often asked when it's time to quit. The answer: when you feel that you've exhausted all growth in your job, and you're no longer sharpening your CORE SKILL SET, the one you will carry with you throughout your career, or when you're in a bad mood at work beyond the point of no return, it's time to quit. When we don't quit, we end up burning out.

BURNOUT

As of 2009, the World Health Organization identified work burnout as "an occupational disorder," characterizing the disorder as "feelings of energy depletion or exhaustion; increased mental distance from one's job, or feelings of negativism or cynicism related to one's job; and reduced professional efficacy."[3]

Unfortunately, when we keep striving for something that just isn't working, we push and push until we discover that willpower doesn't work. For months I had been trying to make sense of my feelings of isolation. I didn't realize it then, but I was working in a way that wasn't optimizing my CORE SKILL SET. When you take a job that calls forward a skill set that isn't your CORE SKILL SET, you'll often end up in burnout.

The longer I stayed at it, the more I began to experience what the World Health Organization calls vital exhaustion. My body wasn't just tired; my entire psyche needed a break. Burnout has a handful of root causes, all of which take place over extended periods of time.

1. *Powerlessness*: This means you feel like you have no control over a situation, which often triggers a sense of hopelessness and eventual resignation, or numbness.
2. *Tiredness*: This could be a lack of sleep or simply a lack of rest.
3. *Loneliness*: This means you may not have a community that can support you, hear you, or love you.
4. *Lack of Purpose*: This means you feel disconnected from the reason *why* you're putting time into something, whether it's in your personal or professional life.
5. *Low Self-Esteem*: This means you don't believe in yourself to fulfill a mission, and as a result, you are constantly trying to feel worthy at work (or in life).

The longer we go without reviewing our belief systems, or changing course, the more burned out we become, staying stuck in the wrong job, relationship, or city. In short, burnout is one of the most emotionally expensive paths we can take. It is estimated that job stress and burnout cost US businesses $150 billion to $300 billion annually.[4] It's in these moments that we must learn to love ourselves.

SELF-LOVE

So why do we push through? Because we don't love ourselves. If you truly want to love yourself, you'll listen to your body, the only one you've been given through this lifetime. Once a friend of mine asked me: "If your body could talk, what would it say?" I wondered: *Would my body thank me for treating it well? Would it tell me that it trusts me?*

I don't trust you, were the immediate words I heard in my mind as a message from my body. Let's face it: if your physical body isn't working for you, if you're not feeling well, your mental and emotional capacity goes out the window. Everything starts with your body. So how do you love yourself?

The concept of self-love is confusing and elusive. We live in a world where self-love is often misunderstood as an escape from the world, or responsibility. We see magazine articles urging us to "love ourselves" through bubble baths, eating that extra slice of cake, or playing hooky from work in order to get a massage. But here's the deal: self-love is a journey, not a destination, and it's all about investing in who we really want to be in the world, our best selves.

Self-love begins when you get honest with yourself. And yes, that can look like celebrating life. But it also looks like creating an honest relationship with yourself, honestly admitting when some area of your life isn't working for you, and using that awareness to make a *You Turn*.

My self-love over the years has looked like taking a nap, buying myself flowers, or going to a delicious dinner solo on a Tuesday night. It's also looked like making a spreadsheet of my debts and a financial plan to pay them off, going to the gym sometimes when I'm not in the mood, and saying no to cheese plates because I know dairy gives me brain fog. It's also looked like giving myself the things that contribute to the highest version of who I want to be in the world. That means meditating in the morning because I know I always start the day off better if I do. That means spending an extra dollar on the organic apples I like because it's better for my body. That means saying no to social events that sound tiring, even though people think I "should" be there. A lot of the time, self-love looks like the word *no*, because becoming who you want to be starts with ditching all the things you're not.

LIMITING BELIEFS REVISITED

As renowned life coach Tony Robbins says, "Beliefs have the power to create and the power to destroy. Human beings have the awesome ability to take any experience of their lives and create a meaning that disempowers them or one that can literally save their lives."

So what meaning would I make of my time at the Pentagon? The disempowering meaning I made of it was that I was a failure. The other meaning that I made of it, the one that saved my life, was that my time at the Pentagon was no mistake, but rather it was meant to happen, and meant to help me find myself and where I was supposed to go in the world.

The Ten CORE SKILL SETS

I've determined that there are ten CORE SKILL SETS. And, like I said, the way to know what your CORE SKILL SET is comes from noticing the skill you tend to use, whether or not it's called for in the jobs you do. It's your natural way of being in the world and unique to you. The challenge with identifying your CORE SKILL SET is that it's often so obvious to you that you almost don't realize it's unnatural for others.

The ten CORE SKILL SETS are *words, innovation, building, technology, motion, service, beauty, coordination, analysis,* and *numbers.* I'll unpack these a bit now. As you know, mine is *words.* This means that I'm a born communicator, whether I want to apply it quite literally as a speaker or a writer, or as an editor, a content strategist, or anyone who uses *words* as a foundation for their career. I could be a talent agent, a real estate agent . . . just think *words.* In fact, I can't help but turn every job I'm in into an opportunity to use *words.*

Knowing whether you're an introvert or extrovert is key to each of the ten CORE SKILL SETS, as it influences the ways in which you use your skill. Another point to consider as you read through the CORE SKILL SETS is that you'll resonate with many of them. Know that everyone tends to have a primary CORE SKILL SET as well as a secondary one. Your work is to dig deep and discover what primary CORE SKILL SET you lead with, although knowing whether you have a secondary one is helpful!

Core Skill Set #1: Words

Let's say you're like me, and your CORE SKILL SET is *words.* You need to know whether you're an introvert or an extrovert in order to determine how your affinity for words can be expressed in the workforce. Do you get your energy from people? Or do you feel depleted by them? This is the biggest question for a *words* person to ask themselves, because the ones who are extroverts tend to be "good with people" versus the introverts, who are better off writing on their own, marinating in their own magical creativity without people.

> Possible Career Paths for *Words*: speaker, author, marketer, advertiser, blogger.

Core Skill Set #2: Innovation

Someone who is into *innovation* is typically the idea person in a company. If they've created the company, they're the entrepreneur. If they are an inspired and inventive person within the company, they're an intrapreneur. Intrapreneurs include anyone close to the founder who makes creative recommendations, or anyone within a company who manages their own book of business. One key distinction I've found between an innovator who's meant to go off on their own versus one who's meant to remain in the workforce: a hunger for freedom versus being satisfied with some basic flexibility.

Most innovators I know who are meant to be entrepreneurs will feel a great deal of pain if they're not granted full freedom. This means they're able to manage their own schedule, call the shots on what gets created or not, and work when they choose to do so. A lot of this also has to do with the conversation you have going on in your head about security. What kind of risk-taker are you? Do you feel deep pain if you're not given absolute freedom at work, or do you like taking direction and having structure? If you're pained without full freedom and you're comfortable with taking risks, you're likely an entrepreneur.

Innovators who are meant for the workforce, the intrapreneurs, are typically creative and cutting edge, simply needing flexibility, and not freedom. They don't feel a deep ache if they can't go away for three months, but they do want a culture that gives them space to come up with ideas, see them through, or create their own client relationships. Typically, an intrapreneur values the financial security of a company behind them, but also yearns for and appreciates the spaciousness of building their own book of business—they're essentially independent within an institution.

Ask yourself: Am I an innovator who absolutely needs freedom (entrepreneur), or flexibility (intrapreneur)? There's a big difference between needing to work on your terms fully, and simply needing the freedom to work from home at will or go to doctor's appointments without feeling like you need to make an ordeal out of getting a hall pass from your boss. Flexibility is an issue of corporate culture; freedom is an issue of the soul. Also ask yourself: What's my relationship and yearning for risk-taking and financial security? The innovators who are entrepreneurs are willing to risk it all because they love the game. They're willing to marinate in failure for the upside of reward. The innovators who are intrapreneurs would ideally want to pass on that.

> Possible Career Paths for *Innovation*: entrepreneur, investor, consultant, insurance agent, business developer, real estate agent, product manager . . . The sky is the limit.

Core Skill Set #3: Building

Then there are the builders. These are the awesome rebels who actually have the ability to bring an innovator's vision to life. They'll tend to think of something—and have the inspiration to go create it. Think of the construction worker who is physically building a home with their hands based on a blueprint of the home. Think of the architect who had a vision for the Apple stores (they, by the way, probably also have *numbers* as a primary or secondary skill set, since numbers are core to an architect's job—we'll get to that one). Builders somehow can see the whole picture, and either use their minds or their hands to execute it. They're mechanics, engineers, UX designers, construction workers, web designers, the person who can assemble furniture as if it's nothing, and more. They're fearless in their willingness to see their vision through. They're someone who is good with their hands, or perhaps has good hand-eye coordination. This isn't to be confused with someone whose CORE SKILL SET is *technology*. While some builders may use technology to build something, it's not the only *building* skill they'll use.

> Possible Career Paths for *Building*: architect, car mechanic, construction worker, UX designer.

Core Skill Set #4: Technology

The *technology* person can easily pull a computer apart and put it back together. They're who you'll find sitting up front at the Genius Bar, or on a team developing new artificial intelligence, likely in support of a visionary innovator. They love fixing or creating technologies or making sense of them, and they tend to have a particular thrill for the future of electronics. They do also sometimes happen to have *building* skills since they so innately understand technology, but builders don't just create technology—they create so much more. The *technology* group is all about fixing, using, making, or just working with technology in general.

> ❯   Possible Career Paths for *Technology*: coder, IT support team, artificial intelligence developer.

Core Skill Set #5: Motion

Then there's *motion*. People who love *motion* are the literal movers and shakers; they tend to be on their feet, whether it's physical trainers, athletes, or even tour guides. The nature of who they are and what they do is physical, and whatever they're doing, they tend to be the adventurers who love the outdoors, or the people who love moving.

When you combine someone whose CORE SKILL SET is *motion* with someone whose secondary skill set is *innovation*, for example, they'd have entrepreneurial tendencies, which means you may get a fitness influencer or something of the like. If you combine the CORE SKILL SET of *motion* with someone who has *building* tendencies, maybe you'll get a general contractor. If you combine *motion* with someone who has *technology* tendencies, perhaps you'll get an app developer who's focused on adventures or travel experiences.

> ❯   Possible Career Paths for *Motion*: personal trainer, physical therapist, tour guide, dancer, professional athlete, film crew.

Core Skill Set #6: Service

The sixth CORE SKILL SET is *service*, and wow, do we need these people. They're the nurturers, the natural supporters. This could be an assistant who runs someone's business or life, or it could be the customer service rep who fixes the relationship that someone else on the team almost burned, or the community manager who people appreciate so much for their follow-through, or just the person who loves to be of help in general. While writing *You Turn*, I had an editor on my team who was a *words* person as their CORE SKILL SET and a *service* person as their secondary CORE SKILL SET—and it was such a dream. The combination of being great with words and a natural desire to help me take work off my plate, for them to go above and beyond, was amazing.

This core skill set of *service* particularly reminds me of my mom's close friend Mayumi growing up. She always remembered to cut up orange slices and bring them to all of us little kids back when I had soccer practice. Mayumi was always two steps ahead, because being in a mindset of *service* was so natural for her. People who lead with *service* are ones who are pulled to give and think of ways to support that others tend not to. They see being helpful as an "easy" and natural thing to do. People who excel in *service* might work as supporters, customer service professionals, community managers, and assistants. And they often tend to be great gift givers, too!

> ❯ Possible Career Paths for *Service*: customer service representative, community manager, personal assistant, nurse.

Core Skill Set #7: Beauty

The seventh CORE SKILL SET is *beauty*. This is the person who can't help but notice and create beautiful aesthetics around them. This is not to be confused with builders. For example, a person who has *building* tendencies will build a shelf, but a person whose CORE SKILL SET is *beauty* will decide how it looks and where it goes in a room. Big difference.

> Possible Career Paths for *Beauty*: interior designer, ceramicist, editor in chief, illustrator, stage designer, graphic designer, jewelry designer.

Core Skill Set #8: Coordination

The eighth CORE SKILL SET is *coordination*, which is so far from my own talents. These people naturally think in details, love the little things, and get a thrill from bringing pieces together and seeing the final product. As great multitaskers, they don't mind logistics and take a lot of pride in their work. Take someone whose primary CORE SKILL SET is *coordination* and whose secondary skill set is *beauty*, and you may get a wedding planner.

> Possible Career Paths for *Coordination*: event planner, operations manager, logistics lead, project manager.

Core Skill Set #9: Analysis

The ninth CORE SKILL SET is *analysis*. These people are fueled by answering the question of "Why?" and get a high from finding the answers. They influence our world by finding answers to some of the world's biggest questions and often need to be at peace with being one small part of an otherwise large puzzle.

> Possible Career Paths for *Analysis*: researcher, therapist (though many may lead with *words* and have this as a secondary skill), intelligence professional, paralegal, data analyst, scientist, economist.

Core Skill Set #10: Numbers

Then there's the tenth CORE SKILL SET, *numbers*. This is everyone from the bookkeepers to the investment bankers, making sure we don't go as broke as I did after watching my first company nearly go under and lose $5 million in revenue. Math overwhelms me (although, fun fact: I used to be a math tutor in high school). We need these people to ensure our numbers are in rhythm. They are not to be confused with *service* professionals, like tellers or managers at banks. Tellers are more under the realm of *service* (helping customers), and managers are better with people, which means they're extroverts who are good at *words*.

> ❯ Possible Career Paths for *Numbers*: accountant, financial advisor, investment banker, chief financial officer (CFO), bookkeeper.

USE THIS NOW

Define your CORE SKILL SET

1. Which of these ten CORE SKILL SETS are you (words, innovation, building, technology, motion, service, beauty, coordination, analysis, numbers)?
2. Struggling to find out? Here are some questions to ask your four closest friends, colleagues, or family members if you want to know:
   a. When have you seen me at my best? (Then assess which of the ten CORE SKILL SETS you were using.)
   b. Where (or how) do you think I make the most impact in people's lives?
   c. What do you think is my best skill set?

Perhaps you have a secondary skill set, and that is useful to know! But everyone has one CORE SKILL SET they lead with in their career and their being.

As you can see here, the fast pass to finding your purpose in the world isn't about looking at your passions, throwing them into a hat, and picking one. Sadly, that's what most of us do in our careers and it gets us really stuck in a career that doesn't align with our CORE SKILL SET.

Evaluate Your Self-Love

1. If your body could talk, what would it say to you? Get quiet and ask it, in case you hear an answer . . . Would it thank you for treating it well? Would it tell you that it trusts you?
2. What are the ways you practice self-love? Do they help make you the best version of yourself?
3. Examine each area of your life and ask yourself: What is working, and what isn't working? Rate each category below from one to ten (one being awful, ten being incredible).
   a. Job/Career
   b. Romantic relationship
   c. Friendships
   d. Finances
   e. Health
   f. Wellness
4. What is one doable first step you can take toward improving each area in #3 above?

Evaluate Your Limiting Beliefs

1. What story are you telling yourself about your career or life?
2. Do you feel empowered, or small, based on the following circumstances in your life?
   a. Money
   b. Friendships
   c. Relationships
   d. Career

CONCLUSION

Having an incredible career is about owning your truth and raising your standards. That means knowing when to walk away from what isn't aligned with your CORE SKILL SET and knowing that you have greatness inside you. Everyone does. The evidence of subpar results in your career is simply feedback that it's time to make a *You Turn* and evaluate whether you're using both your primary and secondary CORE SKILL SETS. In a world where we seek advice and feedback on our careers, making a *You Turn* is about becoming your own friend and listening to that wisdom inside you. Choosing anything less is self-betrayal.

PART two
TURN SIGNALS

Intuition is knowing what you know, without knowing why you know it.

—You Turn Podcast
Episode 49: "How to Access Your Intuition"
with Noah Berman

Chapter Three

Grief and Greatness
Go Hand in Hand

MAY 29, 1997

Have you ever felt grief, sadness, or nostalgia for what *should* be a really positive time in your life? May 29, 1997, would prove to be one of those days that would shape the woman I was to become, whether I liked it or not.

Summer was approaching, and if you have ever spent any time in Southern California, you know the temperature is almost always perfect; this day was no different. Before I even opened my eyes that morning, I felt myself smiling, not because of the usual smell of bacon from Mom's kitchen, not because of the pretty new pajamas I was wearing, but because it was my tenth birthday. Opening my eyes, I expected to feel different, but I didn't. I remember thinking, *I should feel something, right?* I had no idea how much that day would shape my relationship with money.

Springing out of bed, I shot into the hallway and ran downstairs.

My aunt Janet laid eyes on me: "Double digits!" she cheered with her usual huge smile.

My eyes zoomed in on the giant pink gift bag in her arms, almost bigger than my entire ten-year-old body. After a ceremonial kiss on the head from my aunt, I ripped into the bag with intense focus. Inside, I found a little girl's dream: a one-hundred-pack of Crayola markers (including ones in shades of pink that only had lived inside my wildest dreams), a fifty-pack of crayons to replace the ones I drew to the nub since Christmas, a fifty-pack of glitter glue I'd use to deface the walls of my bedroom, a pack of puffy stickers I could put all over my face, fake tattoos that would soon cover my body, a brand-new diary for me to write all my secret ten-year-old thoughts in, and a sketchbook to draw all the images of how I saw the world.

I smiled with delight because art supplies were an ideal gift for a girl with an overactive mind. Just when I thought Aunt Janet's present had reached its final reveal, she said the art supplies were merely the "preamble." She often talked this way, using complicated words to help me expand my vocabulary. It made me feel smart, and I remember being proudly named the spelling bee champ of my class. Looking back on it now, Aunt Janet was one of the reasons I became a writer and lover of the arts. And there, at the bottom of the gift bag, was one of the most sacred gifts I have ever gotten in my entire life: a copy of Shel Silverstein's poetry book *Where the Sidewalk Ends*. I lit up.

That woman, my aunt, always seemed to know what was living inside my heart. There is something special about receiving a gift that matches who you are and what you're about; it makes you feel like the person gifting you understands you, and knows you. Do you have someone thoughtful like that in your life? Her gifts felt like an honoring of my CORE NATURE: communicative, wise, joyful, curious, bold, and funny. Plus, she could already tell at my young age that my CORE SKILL SET in life would include words, with some form of creative expression.

I realize that kids are naturally more connected to their self-expression, intuition, and freedom. They are less afraid to be who they are and more willing to follow what lights them up, seeing the world as a place of play. That's why I love asking clients what they gravitated toward when they were young. Even if a child faces adversity from a young age, their soul is always naturally pulled toward some sort of exploration. Our experiences as little kids give us a peek into our best inspiration, even if we evolve as adults. From this creative state, we can become true individuals, creators, and change-makers. Yet, when we leave this part of us behind, we tend to feel more jaded and lost, as if we're just another face in a world that seems to be getting more and more crowded with every passing day.

Looking back, I have always had a love for the arts: poetry, creative writing, painting, you name it . . . And like so many of us do, I got lost in my teenage years trying to fit in, and then became lost about who I was and thirsty for career clarity in my twenties. I thought I'd have to choose a career based on what would pay me well, and I got lost in my quest to be liked. I stopped listening to that sacred intuition I had, and I stopped paying attention to the signals I was getting from the universe about who I was.

By making career decisions out of fear, and by morphing myself to fit in with the people around me, I wouldn't thrive in the long run; I'd only survive in the short run. It took me all of my twenties to come home to myself, the young, creative girl inside me who was always meant to be a writer. In retrospect, I often laugh when I think about how much I've gone off course only to come back to what I've always known, yet rejected, about myself. It is all a matter of noticing what I now like to call TURN SIGNALS, signs that it's time to reevaluate your life; these include anxiety, panic, frustration, and so much more. If only I saw my pain as a TURN SIGNAL, as feedback from the universe that it was time for me to make a change, I'd have taken action on it.

THE POWER OF FEELING UNDERSTOOD AS A KID

I would later spend my birthday afternoon in our backyard hammock, reading through the entire collection of Silverstein's poems. I remember wishing I could be an artist or a writer like Shel. I'm thirty-three years old and still working to get there, but then again, isn't that what life is about—the journey to becoming?

After a giant hug to thank Aunt Janet, I couldn't stop my mind from racing: *If this is what Aunt Janet got me, I wonder what Dad's present will be?* To give you a little backstory, my father was a self-made man. He dropped out of UCLA and built a huge financial firm at a young age, so my earliest years were marked with extravagant birthday gifts. To give you an idea as to how extravagant, one year he got me a huge circus-sized carousel pony to ride *in my bedroom*. Another year, he got me a train I could sit on that ran around the house. Up until this point, my birthday presents had always been over the top. One belief I'd eventually adopt from this super fun gifting he did was that when you make a lot of money, you get *big* things.

On this birthday, however, we had just moved to a new, much smaller, home, and I loved it even more because we were all closer together. I wasn't aware that the reason we all just moved into this small home in the suburbs was because, after twenty-five years, my dad's business was declining and, as happens with so many people, he had to make the painful choice to close the doors of his company. In the wake of closing his business, we had to move, and I noticed some of his friendships changed, and I even overheard him fighting with my mom for the first time.

"All right!" my dad said, rubbing his hands together with excitement. "Present time! Asherbug, come on over!" As he stepped aside, I saw a giant box with Hello Kitty wrapping paper, on the floor behind him. Rushing over, I tore off the wrapping paper and my mind was filled with all sorts of possibilities: a puppy, a Malibu Barbie House, or maybe even a bicycle. Tearing open the box, I felt a wave of confusion as I saw a picture of a red, yellow, and blue luggage set. My mind raced: *Luggage?*

No . . . Maybe he wrapped the wrong box . . . Why would he give me luggage for my tenth birthday?

"Look! Luggage!" my dad said with a quiver of artificial excitement in his voice.

This moment left an imprint on my memory. All I thought was: *This is ugly. I don't travel, and I'm not using this.* Spoiled, I know. But I was only ten, and that was where I was. I started crying because, for whatever reason, the gift made me feel unimportant and confused, and the story I told myself at that moment was that my dad must not really even know me or understand what I really loved. This was also the first time I experienced what I now like to call "birthday trauma."

Do you have any birthday trauma or "gift trauma"? There is something about opening a gift in front of someone, and bracing for the discomfort of smiling and thanking them as if you're feeling connected, when, at the same time, you're feeling a disconnect between you and the gift, and therefore you and the person giving it. With tears in my eyes, I turned and asked where my *real gift* was, because this surely wasn't it. When he didn't answer, I knew this wasn't a mistake . . . He got me carry-on luggage for my tenth birthday.

I felt as though his gift was no reflection of who I was, my CORE NATURE. After a long, silent pause passed between us, I did what most bratty ten-year-olds would do in a situation like this: I threw a loud, unforgiving tantrum right there on the living room floor. With my gangly legs and arms flailing about, I closed my eyes and screamed.

Through my own self-imposed chaos, I faintly heard my dad's kind voice quiver as he said: *"Daddy is doing the best he can. He can't afford something big this year, honey. Money's tight."*

MAKING MEANING OF MONEY— FOR THE FIRST TIME

I wondered if his words, and tone of voice, meant maybe we wouldn't always have money, or maybe the fun days were over. I stopped as he spoke and reflected on what money must be: something painful, a struggle, or something you could easily lose. Looking back, I hardly noticed that this house was a lot smaller than our last one. If anything, I preferred the new, smaller home because my room was a lot closer to my parents' room, as well as my little brother Josh's room. Who, by the way, quickly joined in the conversation with, "I'll take it . . . I think it's cool."

Normally, Josh was the perfect little brother, low maintenance and always optimistic, but his cheerful attitude toward my *disappointing* birthday present made my fit of rage surge. Turning, I grabbed the suitcase and threw it at him like a total psycho before running down the hall to my bedroom. With every word I write about this now, I am forgiving myself for acting like such a spoiled little kid. I know that if I knew better, I'd do better . . . *We all would.*

When the tears finally stopped, I couldn't help but feel slightly ashamed of my behavior about the birthday present. In retrospect, my sadness came from making my dad's gift mean that he must not really see or understand me for who I was. And yes, at ten years old, I simply wanted to get a cool gift, too. So there I was, sitting in my room, hoping someone would come in to see if I was okay. As kids, sometimes we create chaos in order to get attention from our caretakers, and ensure we're loved. We also tend to carry this with us into our relationships as adults. It's not a great strategy, obviously, but it worked at the time: my sweet mom eventually came into my room and started rubbing my back with compassion.

She explained what was going on. "Asherbug, Daddy just closed his business after many, many years and he is sad about it right now." The room became silent as she continued. "I know it's your birthday and one day we'll make it up to you, but today I need you to be as big of a girl as you can and go hug your dad and thank him for his gift. He worked so hard because he loves you and wanted to give you something useful."

My mom has always been compassionate, loving, and patient. She left the room to go comfort my dad.

I knew what I had to do. I needed to apologize to my dad. Filled with a heavy dose of embarrassment and a little shame, I walked down the hallway to his room. Peering in the crack of his bedroom door, I saw that he was on the edge of his bed . . . in tears. My heart sank. I would love to say that my sweet dad and I had a good cry together, or share how we both experienced some sort of cathartic lesson about life, but I can't. What really happened that day was this: my father had a panic attack. I'd never seen one before, and I could tell it even caught him by surprise; it was heartbreaking. His breathing was erratic, and his chest was heaving in and out like he was hyperventilating. Have you ever seen a parent sick, or in pain? I felt powerless.

"Mom, Dad needs you!" I screamed down the hall. "Something's wrong!"

When I turned back, my dad grabbed my hand. He had this strange look on his face. He was scared. I had never seen him like this. Then, he said six words that changed my mindset and inner MONEY BLUE-PRINT forever: "This is going to kill me."

I didn't understand what he meant, so I asked, "What is, Dad? What's going to kill you?"

With his face white as a ghost, breathing erratically, he looked right at me and said, "Money." In that moment, I believed him. I believed my dad was about to die because of money.

Before I went to bed the night of my dad's panic attack, I made a pact with myself: I'm going to make a lot of money so that life is easy and I can save my dad from dying.

Overdramatic and heavy for a ten-year-old? Of course, but let me tell you something—I believed I could fix things for my dad so strongly, and with so much passion, that it in fact became a key element of my subconscious money mindset that would end up running my career for years . . . What did you make money mean for you when you were a kid?

Our young mindsets are so malleable. And this influenced the form mine took. I heard my thoughts race: Money is hard to make, harder to keep, and easy to lose . . . I want nothing to do with it, I thought, *because it is going to ruin my family.* And then my next thought came in, nearly opposite the last, and ingrained itself into me for years of my adult life: *I'd better make a lot of money to fix all this, save him and my family.*

From that day onward, the world felt like a heavy place for me when it came to money. Nonetheless, my dad was resilient, and after years of working hard, he rebuilt his success just like all resourceful entrepreneurs do. He worked really hard so that he was able to buy me my first car at age sixteen, and he even paid off my college loans. While I can now see my tenth birthday as a completely transient blip in time, it's easy to get stuck in memories and beliefs from the past. I adored my dad so deeply, and to see him suffer like he did left a mark on me and my belief system.

Here's the truth of the matter: money is neutral, but how we emotionally relate to it is not. That's why we're now going to examine your money mindset, and your opportunities to heal. What childhood memories do you hold about money? What meaning do you create for yourself when you do make money, and when you don't?

THOUGHTS ON THE MONEY MINDSET

My dad's pain wasn't just about his choice to close the doors on his business; it was more so about the identity he had to release with it. He spent *years* building that company. He identified with his success in some way, like so many of us do. In those moments of solace after closing the doors, he would sit on his own and have to fill that newfound space with a new identity. Who would he be in the world without that company he put so much of his time into over the years?

What are some things you identify with, or hide behind? Who are you without those? Success, I've found, is one of the warmest places you can go hide. It's a place that can keep you from being vulnerable, because it looks shiny and desirable to the world. My dad, a loving and funny man, hid well behind his. Without it, I don't know if he felt worthy of love, though in my eyes, he was worthy all along, regardless of his success.

YOUR TRAUMATIC MONEY MEMORIES FORM YOUR LIMITING BELIEFS ABOUT IT

Do you have any memories from your childhood about money that were painful? What meaning did you make of those memories? How do these beliefs now show up as behaviors in your life? Whether I liked it or not, my dad's experiences with money (both good and bad) would influence mine. With these experiences, I would create my own blueprint with limitations for how I would see and operate in the world. I would buy into two competing beliefs: (1) that making a lot of money is a burden or some kind of heavy responsibility, and (2) that saving everyone financially was a burden I should bear. I say that because, as a little girl, I saw how much money it cost my father for me to even exist. He was so loving toward me, and he worked so hard to give me all he could. From my tenth birthday forward, I always felt stressed when I needed to ask for something, whether it was a backpack for school or a new outfit. Did you ever feel like a burden on your parents because they had to spend money to support you?

This led me to believe all sorts of interesting things that were unique to my own mindset or inner blueprint of how I related to money. Competing thoughts floated through my mind, like rain clouds in a threatening sky: *If I make a lot of money one day, will I lose it? Am I a failure if I don't make a lot of money? Will my family have less fun if we don't have money? Can I be the one to stop all this stress my dad has?*

STEP #1: NOTICE YOUR SUBCONSCIOUS PROGRAMMING

As someone who has facilitated countless clients in shifting their own mindset on money, I know that my mindset was just that, a trap of negative stories I told myself, most of which were fear-based. That's often how the mind works: our conversations and experiences, especially the ones we have with our caretakers up until age twelve, settle upon us like dust, which forms many of our subconscious, deep-seated beliefs about the world. While fear is a necessary and natural inner alarm system, it's a learned mindset and we tend to take it too far as life throws us curveballs. In fact, we watch our caretakers get hit with curveballs or challenges in their careers, or perhaps we grow up around kids who aren't always kind to each other, and eventually, we make it mean something—about us, about the world, or about other people. These learned thoughts often become our adopted beliefs, and they tend to become ingrained without us noticing.

This is also referred to as our subconscious programming, the part of us that is operating on autopilot as a result of the thoughts we've collected throughout our upbringing. We hear our parents say things like: *Life is hard. It's hard to make money. You have to work hard and get a lot of experience in order to xyz.* And, eventually, no matter how wonderful our parents are as humans, we buy into their limited thinking. The meaning we make about life contributes to our mindset about what's possible for us. These limiting beliefs influence our choices and behaviors in the world, and they stay with us until we become aware of them and challenge them.

YOUR LIMITING BELIEFS HAVE VETO POWER OVER YOUR CONSCIOUS DESIRES

You tend to manifest the stories you tell yourself about what's possible, which are often rooted in your limiting beliefs. These inner beliefs have veto power over your conscious mind, which is why you don't always get what you say you want, but rather what your beliefs *tell you that you deserve.* Have you ever said you're ready to find a wonderful life partner, only to choose someone who doesn't value you? Have you ever said you deserve a big promotion, only to cower when an opportunity presents itself? This sort of incongruence is feedback that you're up against one of your limiting beliefs. Ask yourself: What thought was I buying into that kept me from fully pursuing what I really wanted in that moment?

Welcome to self-sabotage. You see, we all have an image we hold for ourselves, and a belief system that we're committed to about what's possible for us in life. If your outer reality (job, relationship, health) isn't matching your inner reality (your limiting beliefs and subconscious programming), you'll find a way to sabotage your beautiful results so they align with who you think you are, or what you think you deserve.

Personal development is the art of aligning what you want to happen with the mindset it takes to actually execute on it. The process looks like a lot of healing, which looks like becoming aware of your blueprint that holds all your subconscious, automatic beliefs, questioning that blueprint, and taking deliberate direction toward your desired action. This is also the work we need to do with our trauma. Our beliefs become habits; we spend so much time hearing them or thinking them that they develop a hold on how we see the world and what is or isn't possible. As Warren Buffett says, "The chains of habit are too light to be felt until they are too strong to be broken." What result do you really want to create in your career? What are you believing about yourself, or the world, that is keeping you from having it?

These questions give us the freedom that was always available for us.

SUBCONSCIOUS PROGRAMMING VERSUS TRAUMA

One of the biggest misunderstandings about trauma, defined as a deeply distressing or disturbing experience, is that it *only* represents a *big, terrible* event. Psychologists argue that trauma actually takes on two forms: "small t trauma"—like when a friend you aren't even that close to forgets to invite you to their birthday party—and "big T trauma," which could include what society typically sees as trauma: sexual abuse, neglect, or domestic violence, to name a few. According to research by the Centers for Disease Control,[1] more than 61 percent of adults in the United States have experienced at least one "big T trauma" before age seventeen. However, it's the small traumas that I'm most fascinated by, because without your realizing it, they can have a *big* impact on the mindset you carry with you throughout your life. Trauma is about how one emotionally relates to an experience, or reflects back upon it. Maybe a moment was small, but the meaning you made of it was *big*. Perhaps you made up a story about yourself as a result of that birthday party you didn't get the invite for: that you're *boring, not a good friend, forgettable*, any of it. In a sense, a forgotten invite from someone you're not that close to is no big deal, but if you think about it in a way that really damages how you see yourself, and, as a result, your thoughts have morphed a simple experience into a trauma as a result . . . that most definitely shifts your subconscious programming. Never underestimate the damage your self-esteem or mindset can take on from a "small t trauma."

Witnessing my dad's panic attack at age ten was probably a "small t trauma." After all, everyone's probably seen a parent have some form of a meltdown at one moment or another. That said, the way I emotionally held this small moment, what I made it mean—that *money stress can kill my dad, and one day me*—influenced my career for years. It wasn't until later in life, when I was creating results I didn't like in my bank account, that I would work on myself and uncover this memory that deeply influenced my mindset about money.

Trauma stays with you until you notice it, become more aware of it, and process it. That's why the processes we uncover throughout *You Turn* are about how you can harness your pain into incredible growth and healing.

THOUGHTS ON YOUR BELIEFS AND RESULTS

My mindset about money and, thus, my behavior in the outside world was stunted for the next two decades. My limitations around money would run my career and catapult me alternately into both success and self-sabotage. That's why another shortcut to discovering your subconscious programming, or inner MONEY BLUEPRINT, is to simply look at your results in the world. Take me, for example. I made a lot of money and then lost it all. How this happened, from a mindset perspective, is as follows: just like my father, I actually have no fear around creating money as an entrepreneur. In fact, my dad has gone on to create some pretty great things in the world. At a young age, I followed in his footsteps, creating a company that quickly generated millions of dollars in revenue, but because I didn't trust myself to be able to keep that money, I hired expensive lawyers out of my programmed fear of "losing it all," thinking they could perhaps assess any gaps or liabilities in my business to make sure I was safe. And guess what: they found every gray zone they could in my business because that's what they're hired to do, and I listened to and implemented every light suggestion they made to the point that my business actually stopped working. I spent an exorbitant amount on legal fees, and ironically, I became the reason that contributed to the demise of my business. It's wonderful to be driven to put safety measures into place, but when those measures are rooted in fear, as mine were—this is how self-fulfilling prophecies work. I became so afraid I'd lose all my money that I changed the way I operated, and as a result, brought my deepest fear to fruition. It's as simple as that.

Looking back, I amassed a great amount of wealth in a very short amount of time, and I did not know how to manage it, much like a lottery winner. In fact, did you know that lottery winners are more likely to declare bankruptcy within three to five years of their gains, compared to the average American?[2] How is this possible? Well, like mine, their money mindset probably wasn't ready to acquire that massive amount of wealth. Everyone has an inner set point of how much they think they deserve. When their set point is exceeded, they tend to unconsciously engage in self-sabotage so that they can go back to their comfort zone. This is vital when it comes to negotiating salaries. In my

Job Offer Academy course, I have walked many clients through how to ask for what they deserve, and a lot of this work means releasing limiting beliefs.

THOUGHTS ON PLAYING SMALL

The question now is how do we become aware of these subconscious beliefs so that we can face them, heal them, rewire them, and finally get on with the adventure we always wanted to have? Becoming aware of your mindset and belief system starts with simply looking at the results you're creating in your life right now. So think about it: What are your outer results right now when it comes to money?

Are you sick and tired of applying for jobs and never hearing back? Maybe you're telling friends that you're qualified and ready for that next big leap, when, deep down, in your subconscious, you actually believe you're not qualified or deserving of the jobs you're applying for? Or perhaps you're just applying for one job at a time, telling yourself you'll "wait to hear back" before continuing on your job hunt—this is a form of self-sabotage. Your subconscious programming, which hosts those limiting beliefs, will always win until you question thoughts like:

I don't have enough experience to provide value.

I'll be found out if they hire me for that.

Something's wrong with me.

I will probably get fired.

Your ego (full of limiting beliefs) is hardwired for your survival in the world, and that means it's always on watch, fearfully looking for reasons you won't survive. This is a good-hearted and yet self-protective act, as the intention of looking out for reasons you'd fail is to prevent you from failing or being hurt. The problem is that the ego tends to take this need for survival too far, because along the way, out of fear, people tend to stop trying or putting themselves out there at all. In fact, they choose to buy into all sorts of limitations to keep themselves small.

Welcome to your comfort zone, a place where your limitations will fight to keep you stuck where you are. I've had clients tell me their massive debt somehow motivates them to make money. Or that they don't want to make too much because it'll feel lonely or alienating. Or that it'll ruin their marriage if they really become the financially successful boss-babe they're meant to be. In a way, some people feel a sense of ease (or comfort) in their mental chaos, because the thought of breaking free, of being more, or of doing more is beyond their limiting beliefs or comfort zone. Being optimistic or hopeful after you've been hurt is the ultimate act of vulnerability. Being optimistic and hopeful if you have not been hurt can also be a trap because you may not know what you have to lose, or what could go wrong. Your career is a place where you must find the balance between optimism and practicality.

STEP #2: BECOME YOUR OWN STALKER

My transformational shift began the minute I became my own observer, or, if I really want to be frank, my own stalker. What do I mean by that? I started paying attention and noticing how I was operating in the world. I took note of my triggers, or the moments when I felt frustrated, angry, upset in any way, or shut down. And I paid attention to the thoughts I was having in those moments. Then I traced back in time to when I first felt like that, so I could identify the root of my trigger. These thoughts, in my moments of upset, created less-than-ideal behavior patterns. This awareness exercise helped me notice how my emotions, behaviors, and results were ultimately responses to my deep-rooted fears about money. Some of my negative behavior patterns were: One, when I was crushing it at work, I would purposely slow down or dim my light in front of my bosses, subconsciously fearing success. Two, I turned down a promotion that would have doubled my salary, in fear I didn't have what it took to deliver or that the pursuit of extra money would rob me of my livelihood. Three, I quickly hired a financial planner without paying enough attention to the quality of the service provider I hired, and the financial planner ended up losing me a lot of money.

All of these negative behavior patterns were reflections of my own fear. While some of them looked like healthy steps on the surface, each one of them was rooted in a different fear. My dimming at work represented my fear of success. My declining the promotion represented my fear that making a lot of money would create stress that would kill me. The desperate speed with which I hired the financial planner represented my fear of losing all my money. All of these were rooted in a lack of trust in myself. On a conscious level, I wanted to do well, but on a subconscious level, I wanted to stay "safe," which created detrimental results in my life. So many of us have a relationship with money that links to safety, and the desire for safety fuels many decisions. But is that where you want to choose from?

THOUGHTS ON SELF-FULFILLING PROPHECIES

Unfortunately, our limiting beliefs tend to be so loud that they influence the way we behave in the outside world, and become self-fulfilling prophecies. Did you notice how my fear of losing all my money motivated me to act in a certain way that resulted in me somehow manifesting the loss I was trying to avoid? By being immersed in my fear of losing all my money, I hired people too quickly and made bad choices. I was literally blinded by fear. Once I lost it all, I, too, experienced a type of panic, like what my dad experienced in his panic attack, that felt as though the stress was going to kill me.

But it didn't.

This was when I started questioning my fears, and realizing that most of them are totally made up. From there, I started challenging them and replacing them with new, more empowering beliefs and decisions around money. What limitations are you subconsciously buying into in your life? Do you choose to keep buying into the belief that it has to be hard in love, money, or your career growth? Pay attention to where you're creating results you're not thrilled with. And ask yourself: What belief am I buying into that keeps me in the same result I'm creating?

STEP #3: CREATE A NEW BELIEF SYSTEM

The good news about childhood trauma is that the residual cracks that are left behind are entry points to shed light on ways to heal. That's the beauty of being human, and that's what we're here for: to grow. Remember, Albert Einstein once said, "You can't solve problems with the same level of thinking that created them." In a sense, with every new belief you buy into about the world, an old part of you—an old way of being in the world, an old way of seeing the world—is dying. As you step into a new mindset, you leave the old version of you—and much of what came with that persona—behind. What emerges is often a new, wiser version of yourself, one that got tired of shrinking into limitations that didn't align with who you truly are or who you truly want to be.

While your metamorphosis is beautiful, and often for your highest good, the transition can be painful, sad, or difficult. Remember to hold these negative feelings lightly throughout the process of change. Don't make the pain mean that you should descend back into a version of yourself that wasn't working in the first place. This often holds true in happy times. Think of the new father who has a beautiful baby, and deep down feels grief and nostalgia for losing some part of his partner's attention. Think of the beautiful bride on her wedding day who's suddenly missing all her girls' nights out. These exciting changes can come with conflicting feelings such as guilt and shame. However, this confusing grief is usually just a part of your ascension and growth, of your human experience, and of making a change.

The minute I started making real money, some part of me missed being in the struggle. I know it sounds weird, but I felt lonely being as successful as I was, and I couldn't fully relate to my friends who were still in the struggle. While I knew their stress all too well from my own experience, I was in a new chapter now. If I was showing up at my old five-dollar happy hour with the girls, I felt silly because, deep down, I knew I could finally, after years of hustling, afford going to a nicer place, and yet if I went to a nicer place for drinks, I felt like an imposter who didn't actually belong there, either. My transition into success put me completely out of my comfort zone, and this feeling is usually what triggers thoughts and behaviors that unconsciously begin to sabotage success.

THE GOAL LINE VERSUS THE SOUL LINE

So many of us are operating on what the University of Santa Monica calls the *goal line* in life. We aspire for more results in our outer lives . . . more money, more fame, more beauty, bigger titles, more weight lost, more, more, and more. Stuck inside this yearning, we often miss the polar opposite, which my graduate coursework in spiritual psychology calls the *soul line*.[3] The soul line is where your growth, purpose, and expansion reside. This means picking goals that truly light you up or inspire you. What's missing in your career is often the choice to walk on what I like to call the GOUL line—pronounced like "goal line," but aligned both with goals and the soul. The GOUL line is a blend of concrete goals that help you exist in today's physical world, teamed with what lights up your soul. A lot of people are buying into the belief that they cannot have both, and it's simply not true.

What's driving your goals right now? The goal line can be a fun place to pursue your dreams, but know that true happiness exists in merging the soul line—your growth and what lights you up—with the goal line. Know that your soul wants and needs transformation, no matter how much it can hurt.

THE HARD TRUTH:
REACHING A GOAL WON'T MAKE YOU HAPPY

Far too often, we think about a goal we want to reach without considering the time we will spend on our way to that goal, and all the time that we have to fill after we reach it. Reaching a goal is fleeting. It's the time you spend, the journey, that counts. Know that in order to pick a goal, it's important to check in with your soul and make sure it's willing to go on the journey that comes with it. That time, my friend, is your quality of life.

THE FIVE STEPS TO PROGRESS (AND HAPPINESS)

Healing comes when you are ready and willing to take five key steps:

1. *Find* the beliefs hiding inside your subconscious mind by examining the conversations that influenced you as a kid and discovering your subconscious programming. Become your own stalker, and notice the way you're operating in the world now. What beliefs are inspiring these results you're not thrilled about?

2. *Feel* the beliefs that break your heart. See moments when you're feeling disconnected or "upset because" or you "can't get to where you want to be because" as an invitation to get curious. Examine the beliefs and question whether you can even know for sure that they're true.

3. *Forgive* yourself for buying into this limited interpretation of reality . . . and upgrade your thoughts with something new, helpful, and also true. That could sound like, *I forgive myself for buying into the belief that I will lose all my money. The truth is, I can learn how to manage money, so it will be easy to keep and make more.* Thank you, University of Santa Monica, for teaching me this self-forgiveness tool.

4. *Form a new narrative*. We started doing this in #3 by updating our limiting beliefs with a new, more empowered version of the truth. Explore a new, more empowering truth or story that you can use as a replacement for the outdated belief that isn't serving you. Every situation has many lenses through which you look at it. Instead of looking through your lens of limitation, choose a belief that works for you and restate it every time you feel the old belief coming through.

5. *Fulfill* your new narrative. No matter how small the step toward your new narrative, take one. Your mindset is malleable, and it can change at any moment, but when you choose to take action, to simply do something different than your usual limiting narrative would tell you to do, you're in charge. This could look like applying for that job you typically wouldn't have, because your new narrative is telling you that you *can* get it. It could look like sending a cold email to that person in your network that you used to tell yourself isn't accessible, because your new narrative is that you could reach out to anybody.

Happiness comes not from reaching goals, but from making progress toward our GOULS. When your goal is in line with your soul, then the process can be more enjoyable. When you're operating from your GOULS, and stay focused on them, there is a deep satisfaction in what you achieve and who you become. The key with a GOUL, however, is to understand that it requires your willingness to be experimental and course-correct along the way. One of the biggest mistakes people make in their career is to stay so narrowly focused on a goal that they forget to check in with who they are becoming in the process. Who you are changes throughout your process of pursuit. Don't stay so committed to one goal that you lose yourself on the sidelines to the point where it becomes out of alignment with who you are, or who you want to be.

This happens to celebrities all the time. They chase the dream to become famous, based on the belief that getting "there" will feel a certain way, only to have a breakdown when they arrive. Why? Because success didn't feel like what they thought it would. Perhaps they are no longer completely the same person who chose that goal in the first place, or perhaps they feel like the same person but their goal came with new responsibilities and realities they weren't aware of—and possibly didn't want. This is why we must take a self-audit along the way and make adjustments as necessary. This is what GOULS are all about and why a great career is a process, and not a destination. It takes an alchemist to continually honor their GOULS, because GOULS are not stagnant. They're moving. They're a living, growing organism, just like you are. When you simply set and follow goals without questioning or shifting them along the way, success can sometimes feel as unsettling and empty as failure.

FEAR VERSUS INSPIRATION

The final question to ask yourself today is this: Are you being fueled in your career from a place of fear or inspiration? For years, I set big goals based on the belief that achieving them would make me more important. My deepest fear was that I didn't matter. Many of us live in the illusion that the fear of not mattering can be eradicated by achieving something in the world. That doesn't silence that inner voice of unworthiness, and it is a very slippery slope to go down. Why? Because if you happen to have a hard year, or lose your job, or even lose your fortune, your worthiness goes out the door with it. This is not sustainable, and yet, it's a trap that so many people fall into.

If you're interested in a sustainable career, my friend, I highly recommend the path of inspiration. Choose from what lights you up. That is sustainable. That pulls you forward in the day. Remember that who you are moves. As you change, so will what lights you up . . . your inspiration. Honor that and change with your inspiration. This doesn't have to mean that you need to ditch that side hustle, company, or career you've been building for years; it could just mean your inspiration is pointing you to making some small tweaks and course corrections on your vision or project, ones that will have a lasting impact on your being. That is the nature of GOULS.

Operating out of the fear you won't matter, fear of failure, or any sort of limiting beliefs that you adopted in your childhood can keep you in the realm of "fine" or lukewarm. It's a place where you might chase goals that perhaps aren't even meant for you. You don't have to live there anymore. This is the new you, the one that has decided on making a *You Turn*. Not tomorrow. Not next week. Today. So let's get going.

YOU TURN #3
UNLOCK YOUR *money blueprint*

Our belief systems are formed in many ways: by attachment to our parents, how our family or culture operates, our experiences with school at a young age, experiences with friends, and more. They're also influenced by our genetic makeup: how fast our brain or mind works, how we learn, how much anxiety exists in our lineage, how volatile our emotions are, and how we process information—to name a few. If we tend to have a more positive lens through which we view our experiences, life feels a bit friendlier. That being said, our negative experiences and challenges can strengthen us, and are often necessary for our growth. However, an overabundance of negative experiences can inevitably lead to a limited mindset on what's possible for you, and damaged self-esteem. This is when perhaps it helps to seek support from a professional.

Some information on your attachment to your parents: there are four different types of attachment, according to Amir Levine and Rachel S. F. Heller in their book *Attached: The New Science of Adult Attachment and How It Can Help You Find—and Keep—Love.*[4] The research that Levine and Heller used to solidify these types included a study evaluating how babies respond to their mother when she walks away. Babies' early experiences with their parents are the foundation for the attachment styles they develop later in their romantic relationships, and life as a whole. I'll provide a brief overview on these, and note, I'm writing about how these attachments show up in romantic relationships because those relationships are specific places where, as humans, we feel more vulnerable, and as a result, more reactive, but these attachment styles are in play in all our relationships, including those at work.

> **Anxious** (roughly 20 percent of the population): The baby cried when the mom left and punitively cried when the mom returned. The baby is both happy to see their mom but also punitive with their anger.

  - This attachment style tends to come as a result of inconsistent parenting, where parents may have been nurturing at times but insensitive or emotionally unavailable at others. This inconsistency in behavior led children to feel confusion and insecurity in relationships that later permeates into adulthood.

  - In an adult, this sort of attachment looks like someone who craves connection or intimacy and yet is on high alert for any threats to their security. This translates into them often becoming more easily anxious or worried and feeling as though others are reluctant to get as close as they would like.

  - In romantic relationships, for example, they tend to be more preoccupied about where the relationship is going, or whether they're wanted. Their anxious tendencies only recede when in contact with their partner, and while apart, they may fall into the trap of ruminating over issues or needing excessive contact to ensure their relationship is okay.

> **Avoidant** (roughly 25 percent of the population): The baby didn't cry when the mom walked away, and looked unaffected when the mom returned. Yet inside, the baby is neither calm nor collected. In fact, this baby's brain activity appears much like that of the anxious one. This means that while their external

demeanor appears uninterested in intimacy, their internal brain waves reflect distress.

- This attachment style tends to come as a result of avoidant parenting, where the child's emotions (happy or sad) were not welcomed when outwardly expressed, but rather were viewed as shameful or weak. Unrealistic expectations may have been upheld at a young age to keep emotions in check and maintain a level of independence. While some of their needs were met (e.g., food and shelter), others went unattended (e.g., being held). Parents may have been distracted by work or only interacted to impart pressure to improve in school or extracurricular activities.

- Adults demonstrating this sort of attachment style tend to have a deeper fear of intimacy, and keep people at an arm's-length distance. They may come across as cold, detached, and disengaged.

- In romantic relationships, this tends to look like the "emotionally unavailable" partner who runs when you get closer. This can be based on the avoidant interpretation that intimacy means a loss of freedom.

> **Anxious-avoidant** (roughly 3 to 5 percent of the population): The baby was, you guessed it, unpredictable. At one moment, the baby looked fine, and the next, they were crying. The baby craved comfort yet wanted to push the mom away as punishment for leaving.

- This attachment style is often the result of negligent childhoods where parents didn't respond appropriately to their children's needs. In some instances, the children's needs were met, followed by an inconsistency of follow-through. For instance, one day a child may have cried at night out of fear and received comfort from their parents; this would then be followed by nights on end of crying with no support provided.

- In an adult, this could look like a power struggle, a stable instability of sorts. They often can have emotional turmoil in many areas of their lives.
- In romantic relationships, people might hold a fear of intimacy and yet feel unstable and anxious when in a relationship. They may unpredictably lash out or, on the flip side, shut down emotionally.

> **Secure** (roughly 50 percent of the population): When the mom walked away, the baby cried. When the mom returned, the baby was happy, because their needs were once again met.

- This attachment style is often the result of a childhood where children's needs were often met, and the children also received ample love and affection. Their parents were responsive to their needs and instilled a sense of strength to safely venture out into the world.
- Adults with this attachment style are more resilient, and emotionally stable overall. They are comfortable with being close and are often more skilled at communication, and less defensive.
- In romantic relationships, they hold a sense of ease with intimacy and treat their partner well. Forgiveness comes easily to them.

When your attachment to your parents is secure, it can help you to properly develop your nervous system and how you respond to the world around you. This often translates into a more graceful response to challenges in life. These healthy attachments support you in better weathering trauma and becoming resilient. But when parental relationships and attachments are unstable or insecure, it becomes more likely that you'll hold insecurity within yourself, and project that onto the people or situations around you in life. An anxious environment, for example, becomes a comfort zone. It becomes your normal, and from there, you choose things within your comfort zone and develop compensatory behaviors. This could look like many things. For example, choosing unstable relationships or jobs, reaching for smaller stars, or pursuing goals we may not even want. Getting stuck in a job or situation we don't like, continually achieving sub-par results. These are all signals for a *You Turn*. In my home, I was brought up with the entrepreneurial spirit, which can come with tremendous success, but also a constant undercurrent of anxiety. This resulted in my creative spirit, always willing to take risks and try new things, combined with generalized anxiety and an ongoing fear of failure, or losing it all.

WHAT I KNOW NOW

Our thoughts are like clouds, floating across the landscape of our minds—and yet the moment we buy into them, the moment they've repeated themselves just one too many times in our psyche, is the moment they become our automatic beliefs. Good or bad, these become our mental habits and how we define ourselves. On a conscious level, I did believe that life could be easy and happy *without* a lot of money. But on a subconscious level, I didn't believe that to be true—not by a long shot. I wanted a carousel for my tenth birthday, not a suitcase.

It's time to wake up to what's possible for you with regard to money. What are your automatic, or subconscious, beliefs? Here are some possibilities:

I'm not going to get a raise.

They're going to find out I don't know what I'm doing.

I don't actually deserve a better paycheck.

I'm not a great hire.

I'm too lazy to hire.

I don't even want that job I'm going for.

That job is going to be a bummer.

I don't feel like dealing with a new boss.

It feels tiring to work with a whole new schedule.

My all-time favorite author, Stephen Chbosky, might have said it best in his book (a true work of art) *The Perks of Being a Wallflower*: "*We accept the love we think we deserve.*"[5] It's a statement that Oprah says all the time. Unless you're paying close attention, you can sabotage a great opportunity in life because you think you don't deserve it, or because you don't think you have what it takes to even apply. (Think, for example, of your ideal job opportunity.)

USE THIS NOW

PART I: MONEY MINDSET OVERVIEW

1. Fill in the blanks below with whatever words come to mind first.
   a. Money is _____.
   b. Rich people are _____.
   c. The reason I cannot create the financial results I want is because _____.
   d. If I create a lot of financial success, I'm afraid I'll lose _____.
   e. If I create a lot of financial success, I will gain _____.
   f. The worst thing about money is _____.
   g. The best thing about money is _____.
   h. If I don't have money, I'm _____.
   i. If I do have a lot of money, I'm _____.

2. How much money feels like too much for you to make?

3. How much money would you have to make to feel like you make enough? Notice if you accepted the approach of your caretaker or perhaps even chose the opposite, to repel their approach.

4. What was the conversation like in your house about money or success?

5. How did your parents treat money? (Were they strict or spenders?)

6. Was money discussed openly or were your parents private about it?

7. When did you realize that money influences what you have in your home? Do you remember?

PART II: MONEY MINDSET QUIZ

We all have beliefs around money. Some positive and empowering, others negative and limiting. To find out where your money mindset might be holding you back, let's assess your beliefs in this two-part quiz!

Step 1: Rate each thought below from one to five. One means you completely disagree, five means you completely agree.

1. Money is always there for me.   1 2 3 4 5
2. I am grateful for the comforts and joys money brings me.   1 2 3 4 5
3. There are unlimited ways for me to earn a living.   1 2 3 4 5
4. More money for me doesn't mean there's less for someone else.   1 2 3 4 5
5. I always have more than enough money for my expenses.   1 2 3 4 5
6. I always find a way to pay for what's important to me.   1 2 3 4 5
7. Making money is fun.   1 2 3 4 5
8. Wealth is possible for me.   1 2 3 4 5
9. Wealth enables people to give generously to causes they care about.   1 2 3 4 5
10. By positively using money, I can help change the world.   1 2 3 4 5
11. Money isn't intrinsically "bad"; it does whatever humans decide for it to do.   1 2 3 4 5
12. I am open to the opportunities all around me for making money.   1 2 3 4 5
13. I can make great money doing what I love.   1 2 3 4 5
14. I am worthy of being happy, healthy, and wealthy.   1 2 3 4 5
15. I am worthy of having money to fund my dreams.   1 2 3 4 5

16. I'm happy to invest money in myself and
    my dreams.   1 2 3 4 5
17. I am comfortable with leveraging credit and
    some financial risk.   1 2 3 4 5
18. I am great at managing money.   1 2 3 4 5
19. I am comfortable asking for money for
    my services.   1 2 3 4 5
20. I give myself permission to invest in experiences
    I enjoy.   1 2 3 4 5
21. I don't let other people's judgments dictate my
    financial choices.   1 2 3 4 5
22. I forgive myself for my money mistakes. I am
    always learning.   1 2 3 4 5
23. I attract more money through positive thinking. 1 2 3 4 5
24. With more money, I can hire more support to
    help achieve my goals.   1 2 3 4 5
25. Enjoying money does not make you greedy
    or materialistic.   1 2 3 4 5
26. Many beautiful things have happened in the
    world thanks to money.   1 2 3 4 5
27. Money buys choices, and choice is freedom.   1 2 3 4 5
28. I am available to make as much money as it takes
    to live my best life.   1 2 3 4 5
29. I can be financially successful *and* have a fulfilling
    family life.   1 2 3 4 5
30. There is no limit to the amount of money I'm
    capable of earning.   1 2 3 4 5

Now get out your calculator and add up your total for Step 1. Then read the instructions for Step 3.

TOTAL STEP 1: _____

Step 2: Now this time, rate each thought from zero to two. Zero means you disagree, one means you're on the fence, and two means you agree. Check in with your gut and be honest about how you feel deep down, not what you think, so that you can release these limitations and fears for good.

1. Money is the root of all evil. 0 1 2
2. Money doesn't matter. 0 1 2
3. Money ruins relationships. 0 1 2
4. Most wealthy people did something dishonest to create their fortunes. 0 1 2
5. Wealthy people either come from wealthy families or they just got lucky. 0 1 2
6. Wealth makes you less spiritual. 0 1 2
7. It's hard to make money. 0 1 2
8. It takes money to make money. 0 1 2
9. I should never take on debt. 0 1 2
10. It's essential to stretch every dollar. 0 1 2
11. I'm afraid of losing or wasting money. 0 1 2
12. I don't deserve wealth. 0 1 2
13. I'll never be rich. 0 1 2
14. I'm not smart enough to get rich. 0 1 2
15. I'm too old or too young to build wealth now. 0 1 2
16. I'm not good with money. 0 1 2
17. My passions aren't profitable or marketable. 0 1 2
18. My dreams are too expensive. 0 1 2
19. Asking for money makes me feel icky. 0 1 2
20. If I'm rich, my friendships won't be as connected or authentic. 0 1 2
21. If I'm rich, people won't like me. 0 1 2
22. If I'm rich, I'll become greedy and always want more. 0 1 2
23. If I'm rich, people will use me for my wealth. 0 1 2

24. In order to make money, I will have to sacrifice
    other aspects of my life.   0   1   2
25. I'm not good enough to make money doing
    what I love.   0   1   2
26. More money, more problems.   0   1   2
27. Making a lot of money is too much responsibility.   0   1   2
28. This just isn't the best time for me to
    pursue wealth.   0   1   2
29. I have enough. No need to make more money.   0   1   2
30. The only reason to work is to make money.   0   1   2

Now get out your calculator and add up your total for Step 3. Then read the instructions for Step 5.

TOTAL STEP 2: _____

Now subtract Step 2 from Step 1 to get your final score.

   Step 1: _____

     minus

   Step 2: _____

MY SCORE: _____

Learn more about yourself based on your score!

Sidenote:

Money beliefs run deep. Rest assured that a lower score is perfectly normal as you're starting your healing journey. See this as your opportunity to assess your mindset and create an even more powerful one. In Step 1, you assessed your empowered money beliefs, so you'll want to revisit any beliefs where you put a four or less. What's it going to take for you to believe them? Do you have any evidence in your life right now that what you wrote is not actually true?

  Step 2 shows you the limiting beliefs you're still possibly subscribing to. Take a look at how these affect your choices. Notice when these come up, and choose a more empowered money belief. Bringing up these beliefs with your therapist or mentor could change your perspective so that you start creating a more empowering mindset.

After a period of time, consider taking the quiz again. You could be ready for your next money mindset upgrade!

Money Mindset Quiz Results

130–150: You're Financially Empowered

Amazing! You have a positive, empowered mindset around money, and that is rare. Consider that only 29 percent of Americans are considered financially healthy according to the US Financial Health Pulse, and a 2017 Gallup Poll reports 85 percent of people hate their jobs. It's not common to be so at peace with your financial prospects, and you are crushing it in that category. But unless your score was perfect, you may still be holding yourself back from creating wealth in the way you desire. Ask yourself: What action would you take if your belief system rated all fives in Step 1 and zeros in Step 2? It's time.

> **Book Recommendation:** *Secrets of the Millionaire Mind* by T. Harv Eker[6]
> **Podcast Recommendation:** *You Turn Podcast*, Episode 100, "MINDSET: "How to Have a Millionaire Mindset with Leisa Peterson"[7]

100–130: You Have a Pretty Clean Money Mindset

This is a solid place to be. You're probably financially stable and generally positive about your prospects. You've also probably done some work on your beliefs, or received some empowered messages around money growing up. As positive as you are and as far as you've come, you still have a few thoughts that limit you. This is your chance to remove those blocks and get even stronger. As bestselling author Napoleon Hill says, "If you do not see great riches in your imagination, you will never see them in your bank balance."

> **Book Recommendation:** *Think and Grow Rich* by Napoleon Hill[8]

> **Podcast Recommendation:** *You Turn Podcast*, Episode 39, "MINDSET: How to Uplevel Your Money Mindset with Chris Harder"[9]

70–100: You've Got Money Woes on the Mind
Doesn't everyone? According to the 2020 Mind over Money Survey from the Decision Lab, 52 percent of Americans said they have difficulty controlling their money-related worries. If that's you, your transformation starts now with uprooting your limiting beliefs. Get organized, and start making plans to hit your savings and career goals while you upgrade your mindset.

> **Podcast Recommendation:** *You Turn Podcast*, Episode 61, "MINDSET: 6 Steps to Upgrade Your Relationship with Money with Morgana Rae"[10]

40–70: Your Money Beliefs Are Seriously Limiting You
"Life reflects your own thoughts back to you," wrote bestselling author Napoleon Hill. And indeed, financial stress has a measurable impact. In the Decision Lab's 2020 Mind over Money Survey, 40 percent of Americans reported spending more money than they make, 43 percent said their financial stress caused fatigue, and 25 percent said it was affecting their relationships. Consolidating any debt you have with a trustworthy company like SoFi, who helps you get your money right, could also be the move to get you feeling empowered and secure. If your life is financially stressful, it's not money that can't be trusted. It's your beliefs about money secretly running the show. Changing your money mindset should be a top-priority focus as you continue on your *You Turn*.

> **Book Recommendation:** *The Soul of Money* by Lynne Twist[11]

> **Podcast Recommendation:** *You Turn Podcast*, Episode 58, "MINDSET: How to Get Out of Debt with Ashley Feinstein Gerstley"[12]

40 or Less: Your Money Beliefs Need Deep Healing

I feel for you, my friend. This stuff is hard. We get so many mixed messages about work and money growing up and they seem so painfully real. Fortunately, now you've noticed and can take action. For you, healing your money mindset should be your top priority. Rest assured, it doesn't need to take a long time.

> › **Book Recommendation**: *Overcoming Undearning* by Barbara Stanny[13]
> › **Podcast Recommendation**: All of the above!

1. Star which of the negative beliefs in Step 3 of the money quiz feel the most true for you . . . and pick the three that hurt the most deeply.
2. Forgive yourself out loud for each of your top three negative beliefs, and update them with a new version of the truth. *Example: "I forgive myself for buying into the belief that _____."* *(Insert painful belief in Step 3—money is the root of all evil.) "The truth is _____." (Insert a new truth—e.g., money makes a lot of good things happen in the world, like people who donate to nonprofit causes.)*
3. For each of these three negative beliefs, upgrade it by finding a concrete example that it is not true.
   Example:
   Belief: If I am rich, people won't like me.
   Upgraded story: My best friend is incredibly wealthy and I not only like her, I love her.

CONCLUSION

What do you want to believe about your career, or the world around you? Do you want to believe that your career can be fun and lucrative? Do you want to believe that you're worthy of greatness in your career? Do you want to believe that money is easy to make, grow, and keep? The truth of the matter is that your limiting beliefs from the past will keep winning until you choose new beliefs for your future. That means you must look at your current results and examine what belief is keeping you stuck. With that often comes grief: for your old self, your old habits, and your old way of being. Let the grief be okay. Don't make it mean you're off course. Worthiness is your birthright. Live according to what's possible, instead of being confined by your past. Don't forget the five steps to progress: *find* the beliefs that are holding you back, *feel* the beliefs that cause you pain, *forgive* yourself for buying into the limiting beliefs, *form* a new and more empowering narrative, and take action to *fulfill* your dreams.

Chapter Four

Stay in Your Own Time Zone

MAY 24, 2012

I was so proud of myself when I bit the bullet (pun intended) and left Washington, DC. I'll never forget the plane ride back to LA, which reeked of burnt coffee and political banter. Sitting on the plane felt great. Great in that I had finally listened to the ping of my soul, one that had been nudging me for years, almost pushing me into a new direction. Great in that I was sitting in an aisle seat. Great in the feeling I would soon be surrounded by friends and family at a "Welcome Home" party as if I were coming back from war.

In the midst of all the proud feelings came a wave of grief, a sadness for the fact that my dream to work in counterterrorism wasn't all I thought it would be, a sadness that a version of me, the girl who had a dream of working in national security, didn't exist so much anymore. Then I thought about how so many friends confided in me about their grief during such positive times in their lives: the new mothers who loved their babies, and yet grieved their freedom; the newlyweds who were happy in their marriages and yet grieved that dopamine rush that comes with dating someone new. Over time, I would eventually see grief as a moving target, knowing that even with good change can come extraordinary sadness.

While I was in DC, I'd totally lost sight of who I was and of my CORE VALUES, the foundational principles I wanted to live my life by, ones I held close to my heart. I felt comfort in telling myself that nostalgia is a very human feeling, and I decided to see it as feedback that I was just in the process of releasing my past, not that I'd made a poor decision for myself. After all, not everything is all bad or all good. That old life that wasn't working for me in DC came with some joys. Yet, many of those little joys wouldn't fit into my new life. As Nobel Prize winner André Gide writes, "Man cannot discover new oceans unless he has the courage to lose sight of the shore." You have to be willing to leave your old self behind, to lose sight of your old shores throughout your *You Turns*, as they are just layovers on the quest home to your heart.

During takeoff, I adjusted nervously in my seat and put my earphones in to drown out the two little boys next to me playing video games. As I nodded off, lost in my thoughts of what would come next with my life, I was roused by the sound of a slap. The two boys next to me were now fighting.

As their mother apologized, the sound of the slap brought me back to 2008. It was my junior year of college and the moment I first decided to work in counterterrorism. I was a foreign exchange student living in Nantes, France, and it was one of those gray, rainy days that felt as though the sky would never stop crying. As the raindrops pelted my umbrella, I heard the unmistakable sound of an open palm slapping a face echoing in the alleyway next to me. I quickly turned my head toward the sound of a man yelling at his wife in a language I didn't know. As I stepped closer, the woman turned and locked eyes with me through her pink veil, drenched from the rain. She held a baby in her arms and sobbed as he kept punching her body and face. The air in my lungs evacuated; I couldn't believe what I was seeing. I quickly looked around, hoping I would catch a police officer nearby, and my heart sank as I realized the streets were empty.

In the cold, gray downpour, for a moment we locked eyes, human to human, as if my panicked gaze could say to her, "I'm sorry." This woman's pain was palpable and her silence made me want to give her a voice. It didn't matter what she had done or even said to her husband; nobody deserved to be treated this way. This moment brought me into the rawness of what it is to be human. It didn't matter that we were from two different countries, spoke different languages, or had different skin colors . . . I wanted to love her. I wanted to save her. I wanted to spare her. Instead, I made a career decision because of her.

DISCOVERING YOUR CORE VALUES

Looking back, I realized the man was violating one of my CORE VALUES: connection. Our CORE VALUES, principles that sit within the core of our being, are the north stars of our career path. Of the hundreds of people I've coached, I've learned that the majority deeply hold no more than four or five CORE VALUES. Mine are *freedom, inspiration, learning, humor*, and *connection*. Without so much as one of those words, I'm not being me in the world. They're nonnegotiable parts of me.

I had a client named Jessie who dreaded the fact that she felt like she "had" to hire me. She said she'd tried everything—hired other career coaches, talked to all her smart friends—and she felt like she was at rock bottom. She didn't know what she was going to do in her career. She'd spent three years in law school and taken on massive debt only to hate her job at a big law firm. Did it pay well? Yep. But she found herself in tears every Sunday night, dreading Monday morning. "I don't want to *start over*," she said to me.

"Start over?" I asked. I told her there was no such thing.

I believe we can pull skills and experiences in our career from the thread of the past, no matter what our role was, and make sense of our past for our career's future. Regardless of where you go next, there's *always* a way you can communicate about your past experiences that positions you as an asset for your next step. No skills are a waste of time. No experiences are useless. After looking at Jessie's CORE NATURE and CORE SKILL SET, I was confused. All signs affirmed that being a lawyer was feasible for her, along with a couple of other career paths she found interesting.

The gold was in discovering her CORE VALUES. She looked at my Core Values Guide and replied with words that resonated for her.

"I value peace," she said solemnly.

"Really?" I asked. "Because you don't strike me as the most peaceful. I mean, you're a lot of things, but you don't feel like peace. I hate to be this honest, but I want to serve you and help you really grow here."

She laughed and admitted that I was right. She was far from peaceful. I explained to her that one of the biggest mistakes I see people making in their careers is in choosing aspirational CORE VALUES, meaning words they *wish* they embodied, versus picking words that actually reflect who they *are*.

We got focused again, and she listed them off: *achievement, discipline, financial security, leadership,* and *balance.* I stopped breathing for a second when I heard her say *balance.* But first, I wanted to find out what each word meant to her. Just the week prior, I had two clients who had chosen the word *adventure* as their core value. "What's *adventure* mean to you?" I'd asked. One client, a young woman, told me it meant trying new restaurants by her apartment in Miami; another client, an older technology executive, told me it meant going skydiving . . . Needless to say, we hold our CORE VALUES differently.

Jessie explained each word, and when she got to the word *balance,* she smirked and said, "Balance for me means having time to myself when I need it."

During the following few months of my coaching with Jessie, I discovered that she was just a few millimeters off from her ideal career fit, as we all often are. Far too often, we buy into the belief that because we don't like where we are, we're far off from where we should be. I've found this tends to be untrue. We're usually much closer to where we're supposed to be and want to be than we know. It was this exercise that helped us with her next steps in her career. She had chosen being a lawyer in mergers and acquisitions, and if you know someone who does that, you'll know that's the sort of law that prevents you from even sleeping during the period when a business deal is being done. Essentially, that sort of law was violating her CORE VALUE of balance. So what did she do next? She transitioned into family law, and worked on specializing with that focus. She ended up loving her work, and had all the balance she needed.

ANXIETY IS A MESSENGER, AND YOUR CORE VALUES ARE A FILTER

"Why are you so anxious?" my mom asked over the phone when I told her I was leaving DC. Perhaps she noticed my heavy breathing, my conversations about my insomnia, or my constant worry about what would be next for me if I actually gave up my hard-earned national security career, and she was right on the money.

I was wrought with anxiety, even when I didn't want to face it. Back then, I didn't know why I was so anxious. If I had been reading this book at that moment, I would have noticed my anxiety and panic were just friendly indicators that the path I was on wasn't meant for me, that I wasn't making myself available to listen to the truth of what my heart wanted. I would have noticed that I was choosing the wrong plan out of fear that I'd otherwise have no plan at all.

What happens when we start making decisions from this place of fear and scarcity? The same thing that happens when we're driving on cruise control: disconnection from the self and our truest purpose in life. We lose sight of our CORE VALUES. We just move, without questioning it, without getting curious about ourselves, and without awareness. The next thing we know, we find ourselves at the end of the road, stuck somewhere we don't want to be, and totally out of gas. Empty.

Disconnection can look like Jessie, who had that Sunday night sickness, a nagging feeling that sets in knowing Monday is coming. For others, disconnection looks like aimlessly walking around the cubicle at work, counting down the minutes until 5 PM. For others, it looks like a divorce, a new sports car, or perhaps insurmountable credit card debt. In my case, it looked like moving to Washington, DC, working for the Pentagon, quitting suddenly, and falling into an identity crisis over flashbacks while on an airplane next to two boys fighting over a video game.

If you're too disconnected to hear life's truth, it will come get you anyway. When I saw the woman getting slapped in the face in the alleyway, I did what so many people accidentally do in their career path: I made a career decision without considering my CORE VALUES. Working in politics, specifically in counterterrorism, would throw me into an arena of cultural clashes, war, and, of course, disconnection . . . the exact opposite of my CORE VALUE *connection*. Had I used my CORE VALUES as a filter to evaluate each of my career options, I'd have made totally different choices. After all, my CORE VALUES of *freedom, inspiration, learning, humor,* and *connection* are sacred. They're me. And when they're violated by my job in some way or my job doesn't have space for them anymore, I feel off.

As I sank deeper and deeper into my seat, I felt the flight attendant tap me on the shoulder. Startled, I quickly wiped away my tears, avoided eye contact, and hoped she wouldn't see my despair, but she did. Leaning down, she smiled and asked, "Would you like a drink?" I smiled and said, "Sure . . . do you have whiskey?"

Now, I don't know what she thought of the request, but from the odd look on her face, I assumed she wasn't expecting my quick reply for a whiskey. I mean, it was seven forty-five in the morning. Most people were ordering coffee or juice. As she handed me a cup of ice and a travel bottle of Jack Daniel's, I leaned in to admit that I'd never actually had whiskey before, let alone any alcohol at this ungodly hour. Seeing the tears in my eyes, she smiled and said, "First time for everything, right?"

She laughed. I cried.

Pouring the whiskey, I felt a wave of heaviness wash over me. It was like someone was standing on my chest, because I couldn't breathe or shake an overwhelming feeling of groundlessness. I was in unfamiliar territory. Until this moment, I'd always had a plan for my life. I always knew what I wanted to do or where I wanted to steer next. But, as you can probably imagine, my hands were no longer on the wheel. I had no direction. No purpose. It felt like I was floating aimlessly, without a home, plan, or clear vision for my life.

Have you ever felt like that? Lost? Confused? Frustrated? Like someone had pulled the rug out from under you? To make matters worse, I was the one pulling the rug. Here's the thing about this kind of accountability . . . it's confrontational. There's no place to hide when you're the instrument of your own destruction. Or was it my resurrection? Was I simply throwing myself into the fire so I could rise, stronger, on the other side of the flames?

THE DIVINE UNKNOWN

My grandma Lorraine once referred to this feeling as the Divine Unknown, a sacred place where magic is always brewing if you're willing to get still and allow it. To me, there was nothing divine about leaving DC and feeling clueless about what career move to make next. Honestly, to me, the "Divine Unknown" felt like some kind of secret code for hell.

Sitting in the aisle seat, I suddenly remembered some insight Grandma Lorraine gave me when I was ten years old. I was trying to land the lead role in my first school play and dealing with all the torment that comes with trying out for a play. I would constantly ask my grandma to drive me to the school theater, because I wanted to see if they'd posted the cast list yet. So as she pulled into the parking lot for the fifth time that week, she told me something that has always stayed with me: "Dearest Ashley, you know, your happiness in life is directly tied to your ability to sit in the Divine Unknown."

Looking back on it now, it was a profound comment. Unbeknownst to me, Grandma Lorraine was dying of cancer at that time. She didn't tell me how dire it was, and later it really put things into perspective. That was my grandma Lorraine, a loving woman who didn't say much, but when she did choose to give me advice, it emblazoned on my heart.

The advice didn't end there. She continued: "Are you going to buy into the chaos by grabbing on to a plan for the sake of having one, or are you going to sit in the silence, and trust that you'll hear the right answers when it's time for you to hear them? You know, it's just like time zones. People in New York are eating dinner right now because it's their dinnertime . . . But, Ashley, it's not our dinnertime right now, because we're in Los Angeles and it's a few hours back. Listen, we all have our own timing in life. Trust yours. Don't be mad that everyone in New York City is feasting right now—know this: your dinnertime is always coming."

I remember I looked up at her, processing her words, sort of like how that rainbow spinny thing appears on my MacBook screen when there are too many files open on my computer.

Get answers when it's time to hear them? I immediately thought to myself. *Lady, I've got to find answers and I've got to find them now.*

During times like these, battling the chaos of the mind, it's only natural to feel a sense of groundlessness, to feel as though you're floating, to feel as though your life has completely unraveled. We desperately try to grasp for grounding, and one way we do that is by searching for plans. Plans make us feel safe. Plans manage our anxiety about the unknown. Plans offer us an illusion of control, and yet, that's just our ego, our inner safety mechanisms, grasping to gain control of an otherwise uncontrollable situation.

Once I finished my audition for the play, the casting decisions were out of my hands. There were no guarantees. The only thing we can do is show up, be our best, and rest in the sense of trust. When we resort to worry, doubt, and fear, we catapult ourselves out of the Divine Unknown and into control.

This takes us out of sync with life.

With all these realizations moving through me, and after another sip of my whiskey on the plane, I thought of the boyfriends I had held on to in my past, simply because I was afraid I wouldn't find someone else. I thought of the "best friend" I was afraid to let go of when I was in elementary school, despite the fact that she would always put me down in front of my peers in the cafeteria. And, of course, I thought of my time at the Pentagon, and all the plans I made for myself in my alleged national security career. I realized yet again that the truth of who I really am or what I really wanted was inescapable, that it would always bubble up and scream for me to face it, like a kettle with too hot of a flame.

Our intuition will always chime in.

Sitting there with tears running down my face, my back pressed into my seat, and my chin lifted just slightly, I felt the truth of who I truly was starting to shine through the chaos of my mind. *I am bigger than my missteps. Who I am today doesn't have to mean anything about who I get to be tomorrow.*

So here's the reality: when you feel groundless, you are actually closer to the reality of life, because all your plans are just that—plans. Life will inevitably interfere. The highest level of love you can give yourself during times of groundlessness is to foster a willingness to get comfortable with it and know that it's transient. So like a shaken-up snow globe with little flurries of snow floating around, thoughts flew through the winds of my mind, and I stopped trying to figure it all out. Instead, I decided to just pause, sit quietly on the plane, and let my thoughts settle like snow onto the ground, where they eventually would land and melt away. In that stillness, I hoped answers would come to me, as they always do. Thanks to Grandma Lorraine, I started to make friends with the Divine Unknown. For whatever reason, I started to see life, or I *chose* to see life, as a playground of possibility.

As the plane descended into the sprawling lights of Los Angeles, I leaned into the powerful feeling that had been welling up inside my soul. It was a sense of confidence that I knew I had, because, after all, I had just walked away from a secure job with benefits, with no real action plan to follow. Who does that? I do. And no, I don't necessarily recommend it. In my case, I was ready to step into a new life.

NEW LEVEL, NEW DEVIL

What I would learn as I committed to the truth of who I wanted to become was that being who you truly are feels so good, and so liberating, that the other parts of your life that aren't working, other inconvenient truths, will start to loudly appear everywhere. It's this phenomenon—the truth creating more momentum for more truth—that keeps people from choosing to awaken to what's actually possible for them. Let's face it: the truth can unravel your life. But what people don't realize is that it creates a new, pure foundation upon which to create a much more fulfilling life. And such is our human experience, a process of letting go and shedding old versions of yourself that no longer fit. And with that, adopting new ways of seeing the world.

Never again would I be the girl who wanted to move to DC. That felt intimidating. In fact, so did life. I realized in that moment that being alive in and of itself is such an achievement. I mean, think about it. In order to participate in society, you have to go to school, do well enough to graduate, get a job, and then show up every day. That in and of itself is work. It takes showing up, full participation, and a true commitment to yourself and who you are to become. You know what's easier, at least in the short term? Pretending you don't have to do any of the showing-up part. That's the big thing: to actually show up, especially when you're not in the mood.

I exited the plane wondering what happened to the beautiful woman I came across in that rainy alleyway in France. I wondered what her life would look like if she chose to make a *You Turn* and leave that man who was abusing her. I wondered who her little baby would become, too. In the midst of my stupor, I hailed a taxi curbside, and reminded myself that I am so much more than the results I've created thus far.

And so are you.

YOU TURN #4:
DETERMINE YOUR *core values*

It hurts to watch so many people take their greatness and shrink it into one job title for their career. Here's what I've seen: those who love their careers have three key bases covered. Their CORE NATURE aligns with the nature of their job; they are actively using their CORE SKILL SET; and their CORE VALUES have served as a filter for their choice of whether to accept the job they're in. I've heard it all too often:

I'm good at writing, so I think I'll be an editor.

I'm good at arguing, so I think I'll be a lawyer.

I'm good at math, so I think I'll be an investment banker.

I like science, so I think I'll be a doctor.

Once you clarify your CORE NATURE (how people experience your energy), and your CORE SKILL SET (what you're best at), you will probably generate some job titles, based on what you know about the world and the people who are out there, doing work that aligns with what you think you're into. Stopping right there is the mistake most people make in their careers.

Creating a beautiful career is about being who you are. That means defining your top five CORE VALUES and using them as a filter for your potential career options. I want to show you how to tap into your CORE VALUES, as they are the ultimate filter for the job titles and paths you're considering in your career.

If you're not clear enough on what those jobs actually involve, remember: clarity comes from engagement, not thought. Engagement could look like many things: taking a class, talking to someone who is in the position you think you want, reading a book, attending networking events, or even taking a job in and of itself. After all, your career is an experiment, and part of your success rides on you loosening up so you can actually try on the career ideas you have, like clothes you may or may not want to buy.

WHAT I KNOW NOW

One of the biggest missteps people make in determining their CORE VALUES is in picking words, or principles, that feel aspirational for them. Let's not forget my client Jessie, who picked the word *peace* and slowly admitted that this word couldn't be further from the truth of her CORE VALUES. Picking aspirational words shows us what we want more of in our lives. Take note of that. Look at these aspirational words that we wish we held as CORE VALUES and come up with plans to bring them into your life, based on the question: What can I do in my life right now to create more of that word? Sure, it's not your CORE VALUE, but it's something you're hungry for. Honor it.

Now back to your actual CORE VALUES. As mentioned, my personal CORE VALUES include *freedom, inspiration, learning, humor,* and *connection*. I know these are true to me because if any one of them is taken away from me or violated, I experience a visceral reaction. When a CORE VALUE is missing in your job, you'll tend to feel like "something" is missing. When your job, on the other hand, is violating a CORE VALUE, that's when you tend to have a visceral reaction or unhappiness in your work. For example, if I don't have time for the books I read and podcasts I love (learning), I get irritable. If my career starts taking up so much time that I lose my balance and feel like a slave to work, I start to hate my work (freedom issue). I'm going to have you go through a list of CORE VALUES, so that you can read through it and pick yours.

Let's also remember that how you express your CORE VALUE, and what it means to you, could look totally different for someone else. Remember the dissonance between my two clients over the concept of "adventure"? One person saw it as trying new restaurants; another saw it as skydiving. Big difference, huh? This gap, I'd argue, is also where people miss the mark in love. They focus more on whether they have the same CORE VALUES as someone, and forget to actually ask their partner how those CORE VALUES look to them in their lives.

Needless to say, you're a total snowflake and that's why your CORE VALUES are so unique to who you are in the world—it's all the more reason to take the words further and explore how they actually look as principles in your life. From there, they become the ultimate career filter. Look at each path or job title on your list of possible careers and ask yourself: Does this align with *all* five of my top CORE VALUES? And just as importantly, does it violate any of them?

USE THIS NOW

1. Write down your CORE NATURE, and come up with a career list of jobs that align with it.
2. Write your CORE SKILL SET, and use it as a filter to cross job titles off your career list that you generated as a result of unlocking your CORE NATURE.
3. Choose your CORE VALUES from the following list. Start by circling the top ten words that are most innate to who you really are *at your core*. This means you're not being you in the world if that word isn't happening in your life. Focus on who you are—not who you want to be, but who you are.

Core Values List

Abundance	Fun	Loyalty
Authenticity	Generosity	Openness
Balance	Genuineness	Peace
Caring	Giving	Peace of mind
Commitment	Grace	Perseverance
Community	Gratitude	Presence
Compassion	Growth	Promises
Concern for others	Happiness	Prosperity
Courage	Harmony	Respect
Creativity	Health	Responsibility
Devotion	Helping	Self-actualization
Discipline	Honesty	Self-expression
Doing my best	Honoring myself	Sense of accomplishment
Empathy	Humor	Serenity
Excellence	Inspiration	Service
Faith	Integrity	Sharing
Family	Joy	Sharing my gifts
Family	Kindness	Strength
Freedom	Learning	Trust
Friendship	Loving	Willingness

4. Write down the top three CORE VALUES you wish you embodied more fully, meaning that they're aspirational words you want more of in your life.

    a. Write down what activities you do in your life that give you the feeling each word does. The great news is you can embody what you want to feel more of when you're intentional about creating that feeling in your life.

5. Define each of the ten CORE VALUES you chose. Ask yourself: What does each of those ten words mean to you? How do you embody that word in your life?

6. Pick the top five CORE VALUES that you can't live without. It's hard, but we must narrow it down!

*Note that words such as excellence or mastery may sound similar, but mean something different to you or how you live your life when you personally define them.

7. Look at your job title list and filter each job title through your top five CORE VALUES. Which jobs meet or violate your CORE VALUES?

8. Write down the top five people who inspire you most in their career. It can be anyone from your mom to Jesus to Barack Obama. Ask yourself, what is it about them that you find inspiring? What do you see in them that you want to develop more of in you?

CONCLUSION

There are so many factors that go into creating a career that aligns with who you are. Notice when you're feeling a sense of anxiety or disconnect in your life, and ask yourself: What is that pain trying to tell me? Usually, it's simple feedback that you're not in alignment. If you look carefully enough, you'll likely find a disconnect between your work and your CORE VALUES. Treasure your top five nonnegotiables and see them as the compass your career always needed. They've definitely been my career's north star, and they very well could be yours as well.

Chapter Five

Either Fear or Inspiration

SEPTEMBER 6, 2012

A month after returning home to Los Angeles, I contacted a therapist I found on Yelp, Alyssa Nobriga. A magical woman, she would go on over the course of several years to help hundreds of clients, from celebrities to business leaders, on their journey to find and feel worthiness.

A part of me hoped she'd join me on my ongoing quest into denial, pretending everything was fine. After all, the devil you know is better than the devil you don't, right? I wanted to change, but I was scared of how changing my life would look . . . and how much work it might be. Would I have to break up with my boyfriend? Leave another job? Change and growth can often be scary and look like chaos . . . and I was tired.

I gripped my phone nervously as it rang, without knowing what I was in for. Alyssa's voice was pure and warm, inspiring me to open up more than I ever planned for on our initial consultation. "Tell me what's going on," she said. I responded in word vomit.

"I don't know what I'm doing with my life, and I hate my job. Oh, *and*, I don't know if I'm dating the right guy. We haven't had sex in what feels like forever, and when I was just talking to my friend's mom about it the other day, she told me that's just how it is with long-term relationships. But something inside of me kind of wonders if that's really true."

I stopped for a few seconds, letting my words settle into the air, and nervously continued: "What about you? Are you married? Is that shit true? Does sex just go out the window?"

She laughed in a sweet way and said, "The biggest challenge I'm hearing here is not what's going on; it's the anxiety in your voice. Come into my office next week and let's see what we can do."

I told her I'd be happy to work on my anxiety, but what I really needed was a career plan. She laughed, and we hung up the phone. I was just seeking plans as a way to ease my anxiety, and give me a sense of control.

After I got off the phone, a wave of grief hit me. I missed the old me, the one who felt like she had it together, the one who thought the Pentagon was *it*, and the one who used to think her boyfriend was *the one*. Seeing things differently, and choosing to grow right now, felt like an inconvenience. I thought of how caterpillars turn into butterflies, how snakes shed their skin, and how seeds burst when plants start to grow out of them. Each of their transitions looks like total destruction. *That's me*, I thought. But there was no guarantee that it would work out for me as it did for the butterfly, the snake, or the plant. Maybe I would just sit in destruction, the Divine Unknown hell I was getting used to.

I walked into Alyssa's office, nervous and excited about what was about to come out of our conversations.

"Let's call in the light," she said. I nodded in agreement, even though I had no idea what "call in the light" even meant. She smiled and said, "Close your eyes." From there, she continued into a guided meditation.

I had never meditated before, but I trusted her for some reason, because there was something soothing, magical, and healing about her presence.

As soon as the meditation ended, I tensed up again because the productive worker in me wanted to shift into getting things done. It was time to figure out my career right then and there. If it could be accomplished in the hour we had together, that would be great. I almost felt my life's clock ticking beside me as I sat there in the room.

"Thanks for that," I said. "So about my career . . . Any ideas on how I can figure this thing out? My resume is literally starting to look like a graveyard of my trials and errors. I've tried so many different types of jobs and internships and it *still* feels like something is missing."

At the time I started seeing Alyssa, shortly after my move home from DC, I had also just started a new job at a political risk consultancy in downtown Los Angeles, managing a team of intelligence analysts tracking security threats for a corporate client with staff working in unstable regions across the globe. She started asking questions about my job history, so I told her about how my first job after graduate school was as an underpaid administrative assistant at an advertising agency, and how I took the job thinking I had to "take what I could get" because *no one* replied to my job applications. I then went on about how I quit my admin job out of nowhere and moved to DC, where I'd landed my job offer working for the Pentagon. I told her about how the process of learning how to job-hunt and create options for myself changed my life.

I told her about how the week I decided I'd leave my Pentagon job in DC, I got a job offer here at home in LA to do what I was doing now, all because my job-hunting skills were continuing to pay off. I networked so hard, in fact, that job offers from my networking conversations in DC trickled over to me consistently throughout the course of an entire year. I started sharing stories of terrorists we were studying in the office throughout the day, and how it made me feel to mentally hold so much intelligence that was critical for people's safety.

Alyssa raised her eyebrows and nodded: "Sounds like you have a lot of responsibility on your plate at work."

I do, I thought, as a variety of terror attacks flashed through my mind. That week alone, I sat with my North Africa analyst to assess a video of people running away from a bomb in a small farmers' market, in hopes we could analyze the attacker. That shit sticks with you, you know? I thought about how I came into work that morning for a training class with an FBI agent, who was trying to make light of the heaviness: "What's today's problem of the day, my friends?" he said. "Are we workin' with footage of extremists this morning? White supremacists? Lone wolves with a gun issue? You tell me."

I refocused my energy back into the room with Alyssa. "Oddly, my job itself isn't even really why I feel heavy. To me, it's everything . . . *else*."

"Okay," she continued. "What counts as *everything else*?"

"Well, for one, the feeling that I'll never really figure this out, that I'll never really know what I'm meant to do with my life. Feeling like my time on this planet is meaningless, like I don't even matter. Feeling like my new normal in life will look like being in a cubicle or sitting on a financial carousel collecting one paycheck after another, with a 3 percent raise each year, if I'm lucky. There's a hopelessness to it all, you know? So that's one thing—my career, and really wanting it to matter. The other stuff, I don't know."

She sat there, almost waiting to see if there was anything else pending from my life download. I felt my chest tighten at the thought of the *other stuff*. I inhaled, looking for a breath of air, feeling like I was beginning to suffocate from it all. Then she asked if I was okay. I felt like I was opening Pandora's fucked-up box of worms. Except, it was more like a box of baby piranhas. I told her I felt like I was suffocating in my chest, like I was cornered.

She asked me: "If you could give the suffocation in your chest a color or consistency, what would it be?"

Weird question, I thought to myself, *but fuck it, I'm here; may as well go along with it.* I went on about how it felt like dark blacks and grays, like a thick, slow suffocation gas seeping into my lungs and heart. I was smiling, uncomfortable, and surprised at my own answer.

She sat there for a moment before giving her reply: "When's the first time in your life that you remember that feeling, the dark black and gray suffocation gas seeping in?"

Reaching into my memory bank felt like I was reaching into a black void. All I saw was nothingness. And then I didn't. Suddenly, I remembered something that I don't talk about often: being molested when I was young.

"I remembered something weird," I admitted. "I was seven years old or so, just waking up from a nap in my canopy bed at the house I grew up in . . . I opened my eyes to a boy I had known my whole life, who was visiting the house that day. He was standing over me, naked, asking me to touch him. I had no idea what he was talking about, and it was *really* scary to me . . . I was so young, I hadn't learned about sex yet."

Alyssa sat in silence, and I noticed her eyes moisten.

"Look," I said, "I could go on about this, but I already saw a shrink in college to talk about it, and I feel like I have *totally* let it go. *And* it only happened once."

She interrupted me: "Once is enough."

"What's any of this have to do with my career?" I asked defensively, abdicating all hope that we'd get anything done that day.

"A lot," she said with unshakable certainty. "I hear that you've talked through what happened to you, but have you felt it? I ask this because some people just *talk and talk and talk* about painful things as a way to act like they're processing something, when really they're just speaking from their mind as a way to avoid actually feeling what is happening in their heart."

PUT A LADDER DOWN FROM YOUR
HEAD INTO YOUR HEART

I thought about all the breakups and losses I'd been through in my life, about how I'd rationalize them and talk about them to no end, only to face random nights of tears and heartbreak alone in the dark. I thought about how once at a juice shop I saw a juice the color of the shirt the boy who molested me wore and started crying in line. This is how trauma can work: an emotional reaction can be triggered from seemingly out of nowhere.

The mind is a place we often like to go to justify our pain and to feel it less. After all, our mind is wired to protect our survival in the world, and part of what it likes to do is protect you from really feeling the breaks of your heart. But that pain you collect throughout your life—from those who passed away, breakups, or rejections—its residue often remains, waiting for your permission to let it surface (and heal). I realize now that people often go to desperate lengths not to feel their feelings, because let's face it: pain is intimidating. It can wipe you out for a day, hurt your performance at work, and more.

As a coach now, I can see that Alyssa helped me notice two ways people operate when their life feels painful or overwhelming: *resistance* or *indulgence*.

Everyone seems to have their own personal preference, and in my case with Alyssa, it was resistance. Resistance often looks like not talking about something at all, or it can even look like talking on and on about whatever the issue is, as a way to avoid just sitting with it and truly *feeling* it. I know that sounds counterintuitive, but talking can look like just sharing information from a mental level, without really feeling its weight on your heart. But, as Carl Jung once said, "What you resist, persists." That's why it's in meeting the feeling, really getting curious about it and being with it, that you are able to release it.

So there I was, with Alyssa, in *resistance.* I was talking as a way to appear as though I was processing something, without actually having to bear the weight of feeling it. Have you ever done that in your life?

Talk, and talk, and talk, sharing your story of pain with everyone and their mom, in hopes they'll say something magical that makes the pain go away. Where do you notice yourself doing this? These moments are actually ones where we need to just lie there with the covers over our heads, allowing the pain to flow into our bodies like a rising ocean tide.

If you're not in *resistance* to feeling your feelings, perhaps you're in *indulgence*, the other side of the spectrum. As a coach, I've noticed this is when you're so emotional about something, so overwhelmed by it, that you choose to marinate in the drama of it. Being in the drama of something is often just another way to avoid feeling the breaks of your heart. As spiritual leader Eckhart Tolle wisely says, "When you live in complete acceptance of what is, that is the end of all drama in your life."

Alyssa outlined this concept of *resistance* versus *indulgence* for me, and it never left my mind. I thought about all those creepy times at the Pentagon where I caught myself crying in the bathroom mirror, feeling the drama of the moment, inspiring me to cry more. I smirked and thought: *Alyssa's interesting; I better keep coming in to see her.* It was as though she was my mother in a past life, and this meeting was somehow our reunion.

GIVING YOUR FEAR A VOICE

Alyssa asked if I was open to her asking me more about the memory with the little boy, and I nodded, settling into the beige velour couch like the typical scene of someone in therapy during a romantic comedy. For whatever reason, I trusted that she knew who I was on the other side of this anxiety I'd carried with me since that day with the little boy, and she somehow helped me feel like I was bigger than whatever was making me anxious.

"So, tell me, when the boy was on top of you, how did you feel?"

"Scared, shocked, confused . . . I don't know," I said, still feeling a small wall come up around me. Next, she asked me a question that would forever influence my work as a coach.

"And if your fear in that moment could talk, what would it say?" Alyssa asked.

I imagined a thick gray gas seeping into my chest.

"My fear would have said to him: 'Get off of me; why are you doing this? *I'm not safe anymore*, not even in my home.'"

"What do you think you made this experience mean about you?" she asked.

"That I'm disgusting, that I don't matter, that I'm powerless in my life."

I was stunned by my words, as they abrasively cut through the air between us. We often have two experiences: the first one is what happens as a fact, and the second one is what we make it mean—about ourselves, about the other person, about the world. This meaning, especially in traumatic situations, often shifts our wiring and belief system, and these limiting beliefs, if they emerge, can stay with us for *years* on repeat, until we notice them. It was so profound to see how much confidence I carried with me into my career, and yet how anxious I was because of an event, rooted in an experience that appeared totally unrelated to my career. What events in your life have triggered a deep emotional reaction? Do you carry them with you today?

Alyssa reflected on my comment about feeling powerless and replied: "Does that feel true, that you're powerless, or disgusting?" she asked.

I replied, "Not right now, but in that moment, it did. And when I think about it too much, it does."

In this moment, I realized who I am is so much bigger than the meaning I make of myself. I wasn't disgusting; I was human. I sat there, feeling so human and so compassionate toward myself. I thought about all the times I didn't feel safe in the Pentagon and all the times I felt alone, my feelings rooted in this one traumatic experience of being molested by someone I knew and trusted.

"Does that feeling of not mattering come up for you in your career, that if you don't figure out what you want to do with your life, you don't matter? Or that you're powerless to actually figure it out?"

I nodded yes and awaited her insight like a dog desperate for kibble.

"What would it be like if you didn't believe that your career had anything to do with how important you were? What would it feel like if your career didn't even matter?" she asked inquisitively.

"It would feel like *freedom*," I admitted. "But it does matter. And I want to do something that counts."

She reminded me that I could do anything I wanted with my life and then gave me an insight I still think about today—that we're all like cars, driving around the world, choosing to fuel up with one of two different types of gas: either fear or inspiration.

Up until this point, I'd been driving my car around life with a gas tank full of anxiety and a fear of failure. The great news about fear is that it can often motivate you to get where you want to go. The bad news is that the entire journey can suck. And that journey, those sucky years, can become your life.

Alyssa looked at me. "I'm interested in seeing you have fun in your career and life. So, you tell me, what fills you up with inspiration?"

This was the first time I thought about the concept of a *You Turn*, the idea of coming home to myself, and best of all, to my inspiration.

"I don't know," I admitted, feeling defeated. "I guess I don't know myself."

THE PERSONAL DEVELOPMENT POWER TOOL: COMPASSIONATE SELF-FORGIVENESS

As the session was coming to an end, Alyssa looked at me and said, "Let's have you forgive yourself for the judgments you bought into that day you were molested. Your judgments about him, yourself, and the world as a whole. I'm going to show you a tool that I learned at the University of Santa Monica's spiritual psychology program. It's called compassionate self-forgiveness. Put your hand over your heart and repeat after me: *I forgive myself for buying into the belief that . . .* Now say what you believed about yourself during what happened with the little boy," she directed me.

I awkwardly put my hand over my heart, trusting her with so much vulnerability, and repeated, "I forgive myself for buying into the belief that I'm disgusting."

"Well done," she encouraged. "Now, what's the truth? Start with, 'The truth is . . .'"

The truth is, I thought to myself, *I was just seven years old, and I didn't do anything wrong.* Sitting there, I felt my body shaking, and I said those words aloud to her, caught in that moment we all tend to feel before we start to cry and our bodies know it.

"Okay," she said warmly. "Next, let's have you forgive yourself for buying into the belief that you're powerless. Make sure to update it with the truth."

I looked at her, vulnerably trusting her with every word, and showed her my fragile heart in a way that I'd never shown it to anyone before. I sat in stillness, and words started flowing out of my mouth:

"I forgive myself for buying into the belief that I'm powerless in my life. The truth is that I'm powerful. The truth is that some things are out of my control. The truth is that surrendering is actually quite a powerful thing to do. The truth is that my experiences don't all define me, that I'm more than any of them."

I sat in the poetry of what I discovered: powerlessness is actually quite powerful, because it's in our powerlessness that we get to surrender and commit to trusting the universe to have our back, to be a net and catch us in the air as we leap. I put my hand over my heart, quivered, and continued silently in my mind:

I forgive myself for buying into the belief that my career is what makes me matter.

The truth is that I matter, and that I have a positive impact on the world with or without my career.

I forgive myself for buying into the belief that my value is tied to how much money I make.

The truth is that I can provide value regardless of how much money I have, and the best things in my life have nothing to do with money.

I forgive myself for buying into the belief that I'm not safe.
The truth is that I have my own back and I'll take care of me.

Those last words felt like air coming back into my lungs, or *really*, like black and gray smoke leaving my body.

"See you next week," Alyssa said. "In the meantime, will you do two assignments before you come back?"

I nodded. This woman, her spirituality and loving nature, was so mesmerizing that I'd probably jump off a cliff if she told me to.

The first assignment she requested of me was a joy journal, where I'd write down the one moment that lit me up the most each day at work for the next thirty days. From there, she suggested we take a look and see what patterns existed in my joy. The second assignment was to sit with the question: What is the payoff of my anxiety?

None, I thought. *What a crazy fucking question.* I rolled my eyes. "Okay, Alyssa, I've had enough of this vulnerability today." She laughed, and I walked out a different woman.

Walking to my car, I kept thinking about Alyssa's question, and grabbed my phone to call my best friend, Nicole Nowparvar, who is also a psychotherapist with clients around the world. *Interesting*, I thought as the phone rang. *I am surrounded by therapists. What does this mean about me?*

She answered the phone hungry to hear about my session with Alyssa, and I mentioned this question she asked me to sit with, where I'd explore what the benefits were or the payoff was of keeping my anxiety intact. As always, Nicole asked me great questions: "Well, when you get anxious, Ash, what do you do? Who do you become?"

I replied with the ultimate example of Alyssa's resistance concept: "I don't know. I freak out, and I call you and I talk and talk and talk."

She laughed and interrupted me with words that blew my mind. "Sounds like a full-time job, Ash."

She didn't realize it then, but I did: *that* was the payoff for me. When life became too much to handle, instead of facing it, and sitting with it, I'd go somewhere familiar: my anxiety. My anxiety gave me permission to totally check out of any situation and jump into an encapsulating hurricane with myself. It helped me avoid life when it became too much. Like an addict who turns to their drug of choice when life feels like too much, I'd turn my focus to anxiety.

Anxiety, just like a lot of other emotional states (such as anger or depression), was my frenemy. It was the friend I'd hang out with when I was too much of a mess for other people to sit with. In a way, anxiety would absorb me and excuse me from dealing with whatever was in front of me.

I thought about how this one guy I knew was irritated all the time. I thought about how he seemingly used his anger like a miserable vacation spot he'd go to visit when life was too much to handle. The payoff? He didn't have to be with whatever situation sparked the anger; he didn't have to take responsibility or feel the feelings that actually came up from a situation. His anger was an opportunity to run away from facing his pain in any given scenario. In the same way I chose anxiety as a way to check out and avoid responsibility, he chose anger so that he could just escape and marinate in that comfortable—though miserable—feeling. Anger was his drug; anxiety was mine. People also can get so overstimulated by these feelings that they form a habit of emotionally checking out as a defense mechanism, or they could go in the complete opposite direction, where instead of checking out, they activate and try to control others so that situational outcomes are in their favor, soothing their anxiety or frustration. This is the shadow side of "empaths"; while they tend to "feel others' feelings" and compassionately want to help, sometimes they simply want to fix others' problems so that they themselves can feel better, versus properly helping the other person. All of this can be very damaging to relationships.

THOUGHTS ON COPING MECHANISMS

What "frenemy" do you hang out with when life starts to feel like too much? What emotional drug of choice do you tend to turn to when you feel overstimulated by a situation? Is it anger? Indecision? Shame? Blame? Anxiety?

In retrospect, I learned that these painful feelings are messengers more than anything else. It's okay that we resort to them. In fact, these feelings are not negotiable. They're here whether you want them to be or not, but what you do with them is in your control. You don't have to let these feelings hijack your peace, but rather you can choose to see them as powerful messengers, perhaps shining light on issues and showing you something in your life that needs handling. My anxiety was just an indicator that I was out of alignment and avoiding something I needed to handle: *the truth*. Looking back, my anxiety let me know when it was time to end romantic relationships that weren't working, or quit jobs that I hated. *Anxiety is friendly in that way,* I thought.

When you feel these challenging feelings, see them as an alarm that your peace is about to be hijacked, and realize you have an opportunity in that moment to choose your response. This is growth. When the gravitational pull of the universe wants to keep you in your old self, growth is about choosing to be who you want to be. All of this said, sometimes you don't notice when your peace has been hijacked. The way to work with this is to start taking note of how you behave when you do notice you're not in alignment. In my case, I tend to speak quickly, and almost talk like I'm spinning out in circles, and I start needing to catch my breath. When are you off-kilter, and how do you behave? Knowing this, you can make a *You Turn* back into your sanity.

Looking back, there were so many moments in my life when I decided to step out of anxiety and into the truth:

The day I confided in my mom that I was molested.

The day I broke up with my high school boyfriend after five years together.

The day I let go of that "best friend" who always put me down.

I realized that the truth can be painful, but more often than not, there's no anxiety in the truth. Often, the truth is simply a painful gift packaged in calm, raw honesty. In a way, the truth doesn't tend to feel anxiety-ridden (that's what avoiding it feels like); it just feels sad, inconvenient, or whatever else. Everything else—the anger, depression, sadness—is just a coping response we've adopted over the years of our lives.

TRACKING WHAT LIGHTS YOU UP EACH DAY

As prescribed, I kept a daily "joy journal" for the next seven days.

Day One: My joy journal entry was, ironically, helping one of my intelligence analysts with her resume. I was surprised at how much I enjoyed helping her find a new job, and she was surprised at how good I was at resumes. She was leaving her job not because she hated the work, but because she wanted a change of scenery. Since she was one of my top-performing analysts, I appreciated her mastery, and I always told her that, one day, if she wanted to make a move, I would support her.

Day Two: The highlight of my Tuesday, and my joy journal entry, was when my friend called asking for advice on whether she should break up with her boyfriend. I went on about how she was avoiding the truth, and that's why she felt anxiety, which resonated for her. *Takes one to know one*, I thought.

Days Three, Four, and Five: On Wednesday, Thursday, and Friday, my joy journal entries were about how the best part of my day was editing an intelligence report, somehow making me feel like I had an ability with words.

Day Six: On Saturday, the highlight was reading a personal development book, called *A New Earth* by Eckhart Tolle. It's still one of my favorites.

Day Seven: On Sunday, the highlight of my day was meeting friends for coffee and talking about how to land more job interviews, something I had come to master.

YOU'RE EXACTLY WHERE
YOU'RE SUPPOSED TO BE

The following day, I parked my car down the street from Alyssa's building and noticed that it was rush hour. A girl sauntered down the sidewalk in front of me, her eyes glued to her phone, walking eerily close to the edge of the curb, where drivers were flying by and abruptly switching lanes. I started approaching her more closely as she seemed more distracted with every step she took. As I closed in, she stumbled and was about to fall into the stream of whizzing cars. Reaching out, I grabbed her backpack, pulled her from the curb, and we both fell to the sidewalk. Hard.

She screamed at the commotion, almost as if she was about to yell, "Watch where you're going," yet quickly realized that I had just stopped her from facing what could have been her last moment on this planet. She looked over at me and said in shock, "Wow. Thank you."

"You're welcome." I continued, "Please, be more careful."

After we helped each other to our feet, I turned around to walk away and heard her voice faintly amid the noise of cars humming by, asking what my name was. I yelled "Ashley" into the wind, and she replied, telling me that she thought I may have saved her life.

I turned and looked her in the eye for a quick moment. It was one of those odd moments where your lips open to say something totally unexpected. "You must be meant for something really big, avoiding an accident like that."

I guess now I know why I was five minutes early to my appointment, I thought to myself, unexpectedly trusting that life is always unfolding in its own perfect way, even when it doesn't seem like it.

What's gotten into me? I wondered as I walked into Alyssa's office. Setting my bag down, I sat on her couch and handed her my joy journal. I was curious as to what she'd have to say about my entries. By this point, she'd started to feel superhuman to me, like a force of femininity and truth that I'd never encountered before. Opening the journal, she looked at the first page in silence. She sat there for a solid two minutes before finally looking up at me.

"You seem to love helping people in their job hunt," she told me, with a curious tone in her voice.

I smiled, because it was true. I did love helping others get job offers, or even figure out the best career path for them . . . and I was great at it. Alyssa smiled back at me and asked if I'd ever thought about becoming a career coach.

"What's a career coach? Like a hockey coach?" I laughed. "Like, sitting on the sidelines of people's career, cheering them on?"

"No," she said softly. "You would simply show them how to land job offers the same way you were able to."

I thought about what she said for a minute before offering my assessment of the idea. "The term 'career coach' sounds like code for broke and unemployed."

She responded with a compassionate smirk, as if she had some master plan in store for the woman I was meant to be. "We'll see about that," she said, laughing just slightly.

YOU ARE HERE FOR SO MUCH MORE THAN YOUR CAREER

Toward the end of our session, I told her about what happened before our session, with the woman on the street. She listened intently and asked me only one question:

"What if the sole reason for you being on this planet was to save that girl from getting hit by a car today? Would you feel like that was enough to give meaning to your life? Is it enough to know that, because of your presence, another human being is alive?"

"Maybe?" I said, in a tone that sounded as though I was asking a question.

She responded with a reassuring smile, telling me how interesting she found it that I had discovered a lot of meaning in my life, meaning that was unrelated to my career.

I surrendered to a thought rushing to the surface of my mind: *I guess I matter . . . with or without my career.* I simply smiled over at Alyssa as she said, "Worthiness is your birthright. You are born with worthiness, and you don't have to hustle to earn it."

As I walked back to my car, I thought about the principle of oneness. No matter the circumstance or appearance of things, we are all connected. I remember having read somewhere about the butterfly effect: how when a butterfly flaps its wings near the North Pole, its wings collectively influence the winds in South America. This idea falls under the chaos theory, where small changes initially can lead to drastic, unpredictable changes over time.[1] I thought about how I was able to help that girl get out of harm's way just because I was on the right side of the street that day, standing behind her at the right moment. I thought about how her family would have had to attend her funeral if she fell into that traffic, and I felt an inexplicable sense of trust that we are exactly where we are meant to be . . . moment by moment.

Later that night, I cozied myself onto the couch with a freshly poured coconut chai latte and googled the job title "career coach." At first, I saw a few purple websites, ones with images of rainbows and waterfalls, and even saw one for a stripper-turned-life-coach. I had seen enough. I closed my Mac and sat there for a few minutes, sipping my warm latte.

Then my curiosity started to spike. I opened my Mac back up and kept searching. I found a couple of websites with more polished career coaches who looked interesting. I remembered my first meeting with my career counselor, and thought to myself, *Man, I could have used a person like this in my life.* I remember walking into my career counselor's office, with her looking at me, as I asked: Do you have any guidance on how I can pick a major?

PASSION DOES NOT MEAN SUCCESS

She gave me every boring platitude you could think of: "Do what you love and the money will follow." I rolled my eyes, thinking I could've read that in any self-help book . . . The conversation was as useful as my own appendix, honestly.

I looked at her and asked, "What if I don't *know* what I love? What if I don't *know* what careers are out there? What if *nothing* is a fit for me?"

I walked out wondering if liking something or being passionate about something guaranteed your success in it, and my instinct was no, passion does not mean success.

I caught myself lost in this memory, and then started typing on my Mac again. I narrowed my search and googled:

"Career coach for millennial women."

"How to get a job offer."

"How to figure out your purpose."

"How to find your best career fit."

I immediately noticed how little was showing up in direct results as it related to career coaches. I kept googling and googling and googling until I found myself in what felt like an internet black hole. There were no career coaches to help young women like me. I realized that maybe, just maybe, Alyssa was right. Maybe I had found my niche.

In a world telling me it had the answers, I finally realized that all the answers I really wanted were inside me. I turned inward and finally listened to that wise voice in my head, paying attention to the things that brought me joy on a daily basis. This guided me to finally make a *You Turn.*

And for the first time in my life, Grandma Lorraine's Divine Unknown felt inspiring.

YOU TURN #5:

LEARN HOW TO
befriend your blocks

Your career is a playground, and this chapter is here to remind you that while it's a vehicle for your own self-expression, your career is not a prerequisite for your worthiness. You are worthy *without* a career, and your life is meaningful *without* a career. All of this said, a career is simply a vehicle for you to play with and use as a way to add more self-expression and purpose into your life if you so choose.

This chapter is also about understanding what emotional experiences have created trauma that holds you back in life, and in your career. Needless to say, I never thought being molested would catapult me into anxiety, and that I would bring it with me into my career—until I healed it. We all have painful memories that can create trauma, and each of our traumas translates differently. The moment I was molested, my brain froze and went into a "What do I do?" mode, and that same response (and anxiety) is what I carried with me into anything in life when I didn't know what to do or felt overstimulated—just freeze, panic, or shut down. After realizing that I was doing this, I went in the opposite direction and started spinning out, which looked like talking very quickly, or trying to get a sense of control by quickly handling or fixing something. These two responses—freezing or spinning out—are very common. For some people, painful memories have generated a common life experience of anger; for others, it's anxiety, victimhood, powerlessness, sadness, or grief. One thing is true: these experiences are woven into the fabric of your life until you understand the root and decide to heal. That's what we're going to do in this section.

WHAT I KNOW NOW

For a long time, I would motivate myself through negativity and fear of failure, and I would have to work through my automatic response of freezing or spinning out. I'd look in the mirror and hear the words *You're fat*. Those would motivate me to go to the gym. I'd be writing my resume and hear, *You went to a mediocre college*, and that would motivate me to build a network or job-hunt even harder. Our negative aspects have a payoff.

My anxiety was also a motivator. That mean-girl voice in my head calling me fat when I looked in the mirror is what motivated me to work out; that anxious voice I heard in my head as I wrote my resume inspired me to hustle and network. But eventually, our fear, anxiety, freezing, and spinning out gets exhausting, and we all wonder if there is perhaps another way. The truth of the matter is that you can achieve very big dreams from a place of fear. It's just that the journey is a lot more tiring.

What holds us back? Negative thoughts. Challenging memories. Trauma. Our personal pain, and the meaning we make of it. All of this forms some aspect of us. Which one do you carry? According to research, more than 50 percent of US citizens will experience major trauma at one point in life; in fact, I've read research that indicates that this number is as high as 80 percent. Major trauma literally alters the chemical reactions and development taking place in your brain, so it's no wonder that so many people experience stress, anxiety, and depression.[2] While trauma may take place in a moment of time, it's the cascading pain and beliefs you buy into that imprint the trauma on your nervous system and mindset. This is where the real damage is.

In fact, if you look at Dr. Masaru Emoto's study on the molecular composition of water, you'll see that these thought patterns occur not only on an emotional level, but also on a physical, molecular level. Dr. Emoto examined the impact of one's thoughts on the molecular composition of water by performing a split test: one audience was to look at the water and think positive thoughts, and a separate audience was to look at the water and think negative ones. Upon examining the difference in the water based on the thoughts of the audience, Dr. Emoto discovered that negative thoughts actually impacted the molecular bond between hydrogen and oxygen in the water.[3] Given that we're 70 percent made of water, it is key to understand that every single thought creates form on some level, and it is completely in your control to decide how it will inform your life.

Trauma also appears in our physical expression, which is often sneaky and hard to notice. For me, in Alyssa's office, it looked like sleepiness. She'd comment on how I'd come in energized, and when we started talking about different experiences from my career or life, ones that stored some level of trauma, my eyes would glaze over, I'd start yawning, and I'd become incredibly sleepy. This sort of physical response, chronic fatigue, is incredibly common among those who have experienced trauma, and six times more likely to occur when working through childhood or sexual trauma.[4] Unfortunately, the effects don't stop there; memory takes a toll and either you over-remember the event or dissociate to some degree and bury the memory within yourself.[5] Both paths are difficult to carry but represent your body's way of fighting to protect itself.

There are two ways you can build your life: on quicksand or on a rock. Quicksand looks like a pendulum. You're happy or sad. You're winning or losing. A rock looks like an unwavering sense of inner joy and gratitude, regardless of what happens outside of you. That sort of life requires a lot of awareness healing, which you'll do in the exercise below. Much of your reactivity is rooted in past memories. In fact, usually when you're feeling negative, it's because your mind has come up with a story about the situation you're in, and if you tune in to that memory, you'll find that story will somehow remind you of your past. Take a moment when you're feeling negative or your peace is disturbed. Choose to search briefly in your memory for a time that felt similar in the past. The memory you find represents the root of the limiting belief you face today. If you can work through it, you become freer.

USE THIS NOW

1. How do you tend to emotionally respond to challenging situations? Is it sadness? Fear? Panic? Guilt? Shame? Anger? Anxiety? Indecision? Mentally checking out?

   List your coping emotion of choice. This emotion is an aspect of you that probably traces back into your life and memories and often can serve as a block in your career, confidence, and relationships.

2. Get curious about when you felt that emotion first in a memory.

3. Ground yourself in the memory. What were you wearing? What time of day was it? Who was there? What disturbed you?

4. Tune in to what was happening for you on a mental level.

   a. What thoughts were you having about yourself in this moment?

   b. What judgments or thoughts did you have about the other person or people (if one or many were involved)?

   c. What judgments did you make about the world as a whole in the moment that your memory took place?

   d. What did you make the situation mean about life?

5. If that emotion had to be a color, what color would it be in your mind? If it had a consistency, what consistency would it be? Thick, knotted, airy? If you had to give this part of you a name, what would it be?

6. Fill in the blank with a few answers. "I'm the one who _____."

   Example: I'm the one who people like, has good fashion sense, and loves rap music, or *I'm the one who gets in the way.*

   a. Ask yourself: Where did this identity come from? Is it working for you or holding you hostage to a career or life that isn't actually working for you, or aligned?

CONCLUSION

There is no force stronger within yourself than the part of you that wants to have an identity. It creates a sense of safety to decide on who we are, and it gives us a framework to make decisions. That being said, you can outgrow your identity or be highly limited by it. Our trauma and experiences influence the identity we hold of ourselves, and how we operate in the world. However, when we heal trauma, our identity shifts in a big way. This loss of our old identity can cause a natural grief that can feel confusing, but know that grief like this can come when you're simply onto something greater.

All of this said, sometimes trauma or pain requires more than the exercises in this book, or a conversation with a friend who loves you. If you're struggling, know that there are resources out there for you, and the decision to seek the support of a professional therapist or psychiatrist is courageous. As well-known actor Jim Carrey once said, "I think if we all acted the way we really felt, four out of eight people at a dinner table would be sitting there sobbing." I've always believed that everyone needs a therapist. Your pain is a part of your human experience, and you deserve the life you can create as a result of your healing. Resources I love include PsychologyToday.com's "find a therapist" function, or websites offering more affordable virtual therapy, such as BetterHelp.com or TalkSpace.com. Know that finding the right support can be a process, and it's simply part of your investing in your transformation. If the first person you work with isn't a match, stay the course. You deserve the transformation available for you on the other side.

Chapter Six

A Passion Is an Interest Set on Fire

SEPTEMBER 9, 2009

I squinted into the city lights as my airplane descended into London. Just weeks ago I'd graduated from college, but it felt eons away after having spent the summer doing a political science course in Washington, DC. I walked off the tarmac at Heathrow Airport and went through customs in a fog. I felt nervous, wondering what my first day would be like as a grad student, having only a few days to move in and meet my internship advisor before classes started.

As I exited the Russell Square tube station, I realized the area looked familiar. I reached into my memory and suddenly remembered this square was the exact image I saw on Wikipedia when I googled "2005 London Bombings" for one of my final college research papers just months before. That paper marked the first time I ever noticed a little whisper inside of me, perhaps my intuition, wondering if I was even meant for a career in government. Foreign affairs was just one of many

CORE INTERESTS I had, and I'd eventually learn that there's a big difference between a CORE INTEREST and a passion. It's similar, in fact, to the difference between excitement and passion. Here's the deal: excitement tends to run out; passion doesn't. CORE INTERESTS vary; passions live deep in your heart.

My thoughts were interrupted by a young man's voice. "Can I help you with your bags?" he asked with warm energy, toting a King's College London bag. I looked at him curiously, and he continued: "I'm Barry Griffin . . . I'm guessing you're moving into the King's Halls, too?" He reached out his hand to grab my oversized duffel, and I noticed that he had a political polish that I rarely see in people. Behind his perfect white smile and nautical half-zip sweater, he looked like a leader, reminding me of DC in an oddly comforting way.

"Ashley," I said, extending my hand, excited to meet my first friend in the city. "Are you a new grad student here, too?"

"Yep. I'm going into the international law cohort; after that, I plan to go back to the Bahamas and eventually run for political office." He spoke about his dreams as if they were a fact, a plan already in motion, which totally inspired me. I noticed he had Jay-Z playing on his iPod. *Cool*, I thought. *We like the same kind of music . . .* I didn't know it then, but in the months ahead, Barry would become a best friend—family, really. Years later, he'd also make good on his word to become a political leader in the Bahamas. Looking back, he's one of those people who really makes things happen in the world for himself, and a lot of that had to do with the way he related to his dreams. He never spoke about them like they were a fantasy; he spoke about them like they were happening, with micro goals along the way and timelines he'd set. How do you talk about your dreams? Do you relate to them like they're some wish, out there, far away from you, or do you talk about them like they're plans?

My internship didn't start for a few weeks, and I was relieved by the opportunity to settle into my dorm room and get into a flow with my new class schedule. On the third day of class, I realized I would never fit into my London life. I remember that day with a freshness most memory lacks. It was a brisk fall morning, and I bundled up in layers for a day of lectures. The lecture hall wasn't heated, so I shivered in my chair as if I were stuck in an igloo. The topic of the day was US foreign policy in Israel, so I knew the room would be tense. In fact, the students in my lecture halls were so international that I felt as if I were standing somewhere between an inspiring cultural rainbow and a massive culture clash.

I sat down next to my classmate Yasin, a seemingly carefree guy who I'd met in the previous session of this class, and asked how his week was. He talked about how different life was in London, given that he just moved here from Iraq. I was so curious about his life there that I was asking lots of questions, and then I found myself unexpectedly nervous when he asked where I was from. In a lecture hall of passionate foreign affairs students from around the world, there were a lot of opinions about the United States' decision to send so many troops to Baghdad. I am proud to be from the United States, but I didn't want to be judged by my nationality.

"I'm from . . . Los Angeles," I said in a cold, neutral tone.

"American," he retorted, with irritation in his voice. "Interesting."

INTUITION VERSUS FEAR

My intuition piped up as it did when I saw the square from the London bombings photo on Wikipedia. It said, *Ash, this career path isn't for you. You're too sensitive for it.* What I know now is that there are two forces that often influence our decisions in life: intuition and fear. *Fear* is emotional and often charged with beliefs that we form as a result of panic or trauma from past experiences. *Intuition*, on the other hand, is unemotional; it is absolute and the helpful feedback that guides us through life and our challenges. It sounds clear and neutral, like: *This is good for you; this is not good for you.* That intuitive voice is your soul's compass.

For years, I would silence those messages and allow my fears to control my decisions. My inner fear was in a constant state of survival and panic. I was in denial. As a result, I wasn't able to see the truth of my life and my current situation.

Your intuition is often clear, based on how connected you are to your body and your second brain, the gut. Needless to say, I wasn't willing to honor any of it at this time.

As the lecture began, I felt Yasin restlessly shift in his chair when Professor Frost started talking about US diplomacy in Israel.

"What about Israel?" a girl asked, standing up in the middle of a lecture on extremism. "What's their strategy?"

I heard Yasin whisper under his breath next to me: "*Who cares? . . . We should just blow Israel off the map.*"

I trembled in my seat, looked back at him, and felt an ache swell up in my heart. The CORE VALUE I hold closest to my heart is *connection*. How did I manage to overlook this sensitivity, and end up choosing a career that was so . . . *disconnected*? As you know, when a CORE VALUE is violated through your career choices, it's a heartbreaker. Are any CORE VALUES being violated by your career right now?

At the end of class—because God knows I needed a glass of vino—I rushed out of my seat for happy hour with a few friends from the lecture. I noticed they couldn't stop talking about politics. My friend Mcclina went on about US foreign policy objectives in the Middle East, asking each of us what we thought.

Joe interjected: "What do you think of Obama sending eight thousand more troops to Afghanistan? Do you think he'll really pull them out in July 2011 like he says he will? Sounds like a bloodbath to me . . ."

I rolled my eyes so far back into my head that I thought they'd get stuck. I cared *a lot* about world affairs, but I needed a break from it after a long day in class. I looked at my friends. "Can we talk about something else?"

"What else is there to talk about?" they all asked me back, as if I were taking a drug away from them.

"Shit, I don't know," I said. "Anything . . . Life. Fashion. Love. The weather. The fact that Michael Jackson died." They looked at me as if I was in their way.

INTEREST VERSUS PASSION
(KNOW THE DIFFERENCE)

I missed a fundamental distinction that I'd realize later in my career: *interest* versus *passion*. Think about it: I was interested in world affairs, but I was also interested in a *million* other things: fashion, travel, movies, to name a few. So what's the difference between an interest and a passion? An *interest* lives among many curiosities you hold in your mind, whereas a passion lives in your heart. A passion is an amplified, deeper interest that represents a part of who you are. While a passion will light you up or lend itself to a colorful conversation, it's just not enough to get you through the workday. Plus, there's more in play than passion when it comes to building a successful career. According to research, young professionals in the workforce report job security and community as top priorities in having a fulfilling career.[1]

What's on your career wish list? Remember, neither your CORE INTERESTS nor your passions are useful in your career unless they're backed by a natural ability or CORE SKILL SET. If you aren't careful, passion creates a fixed mindset that can narrow your focus and close you off to other opportunities. This is why experts suggest that passion can even backfire in your career.[2] And who you truly are as a person is rooted in your natural abilities, the skills that come so easily to you that they feel like they should be obvious to others. Except they're not, because they're just easy for *you*.

So what happened to so many of my "passionate" friends I went to college with? Like many people who "follow their passion," they totally missed the mark. Some followed one of many interests, versus a passion, and others didn't ensure that they worked in an area that allowed them to use their passion *along with* their CORE SKILL SET or CORE VALUES. Have you ever led with passion in your career, without aligning it to your CORE SKILL SET or CORE VALUES? That's just a TURN SIGNAL, letting you know it's time to consider a *You Turn*.

As for my friends, many had enough passion in their hearts to commit to a career in government, and they carried that obsession with them as they descended upon Washington, DC, where they would join the hopeful change-makers of our time, landing jobs in the State Department, the Defense Intelligence Agency (DIA), and the American Red Cross. Most people would look at my friends and think: *They made it; they were working in a field they were passionate about.* But the truth is, many of them were unhappy. What about you? Do you love your job or does it feel like something's missing?

Passion may point you toward an industry you're inspired by—something you like to talk about—and that's great if you end up standing in a building that inspires you, surrounded by people having conversations that fascinate you.

Passion matters. But what matters even more is knowing who you are—your CORE SKILL SET, your CORE NATURE, and your CORE VALUES—being able to identify your natural, God-given talents, as well as being able to recognize the skills you have honed throughout your life. Your CORE SKILL SET points to how you should use your energy throughout the workday.

RECAPPING YOUR CORE SKILL SET

I've been a career coach for years now with clients in thirty countries. I can tell you that the biggest career disasters I've seen are in clients who "follow their passion" without first taking the time to consider who they truly are and what CORE SKILL SET they hold as sacred in their career. Are you aligning your interests and passions with your CORE SKILL SET?

The industry you're in perhaps represents a *passion* or CORE INTEREST, but your CORE SKILL SET is linked to what you do, the daily tasks and responsibilities you take on at work; it's a part of who you are as a person. And how you expend your energy, the tasks you take on during the day, is priority number one. Focusing your career on an industry you love, without first considering who you are and your CORE SKILL SET, is like becoming a janitor at your favorite five-star hotel. What's the point of spending all day in your favorite place if you don't like how you're spending it?

That's where I come in, helping you explore your passions, but more importantly, first supporting you in making the most important *You Turn*: figuring out who you truly are and when you stopped tuning in to your truest self. This means anchoring into your CORE SKILL SET.

When I went to London to get my master's in international relations, I opted to treat an interest like a passion without giving it sufficient thought. I've had far too many clients get themselves in trouble doing the exact same thing.

INDUSTRIES ARE LIKE PIES

As a career coach now, I see the industries that exist within the workforce as if they were pies, each one having many different slices within it. For example, industries like government, fashion, or finance each represent one pie, and each of these pies encompasses various slices, or CORE SKILL SETS, which is why it's so key to know yours.

Here's where it gets tricky. Far too often, people who end up miserable in their job make the mistake of thinking they're in the wrong industry, and they decide to throw away the entire career pie and pivot into a new industry. Usually the case in these scenarios is that they're actually just a couple of millimeters off. When something's not clicking, instead of thinking, *Shoot, I don't belong in government* (or wherever you are), the real issue is often that you're eating the wrong slice of the pie, meaning you're not primarily using your CORE SKILL SET. If that's not the issue, perhaps it's just that your job is infringing on a top-five CORE VALUE you hold close, or lacking a key CORE VALUE altogether. Both of these indicate that you shouldn't look at an industry and think, *Well, I'm done,* but rather ask yourself: *How do I try another slice of this industry pie, one more aligned with my CORE SKILL SET or CORE VALUES?* As an emotional eater myself, I know we must never throw away a pie without questioning it—am I right?

So what does one do when hitting a wall? *You Turn* around. *You Turn* toward your true self. You notice your TURN SIGNALS you may have been avoiding the entire journey. In short, you make a *You Turn*. And what did I do? I chose to carry on with this career path, and silence that intuitive voice piping up inside me. My body was telling me answers my mind wasn't ready for. It was inconvenient to make a change, and I was so disconnected from my soul that I didn't even know what interests of mine were actually passions. I didn't want to believe that I had to make a *You Turn* after years of college, learning foreign languages, and more.

DON'T FALL VICTIM TO HOPE ADDICTION

I did what too many people do: I held on to the belief that maybe, just maybe, I was wrong. I operated out of hope, *hoping* that things would change, *hoping* that I would become someone else. Never create a career path where you're betting against your natural being in the world. It's the ultimate trap disguised in optimism.

Where are you going against the grain of who you are in your career? I used optimism, determination, and hope addiction to cloud my intuition, the ultimate TURN SIGNAL, while part of me, my intuition, was saying, *This is not right.* Where are you using hope as a tool to silence your intuition in your career? That year of grad school in London flew by, and I was excited to get home to Los Angeles and job-hunt. I thought to myself, maybe it was the school that I didn't like, or the students, or maybe it was the cold, rainy London days that left me feeling incomplete. It's convenient to blame everything else as a way to avoid the truth, right? Where are you dodging the bullet of the truth?

YOU TURN #6:
BE SURE TO
assess your core interests

When you avoid key TURN SIGNALS in your career—your CORE INTERESTS, your intuition, and your *passions*—you end up giving an unwarranted amount of focus to one of many interests that you have, turning into a career path you don't actually want. This is not sustainable. As the hours go by at work, eventually you'll notice that you're not that interested in the subject you're swimming in. The good news is, usually you just need to eat a different slice of an industry pie, meaning you need to use a different CORE SKILL SET within the same industry or even within the same company. That means you're probably due to connect to yourself, your joy, and your actual passions.

How do we get so disconnected? Well, we're born with so much love, inspiration, and curiosity. That's how we come into the world. In fact, think about the last time you watched a kid at play—totally in their curiosity and joy, following their flow . . . and yet, somewhere along the way, we're taught to fear. It starts off with our parents telling us to look both ways when we cross the street, for fear a car will hit us. They tell us not to touch a hot stove, in fear we'll get burned. It evolves into our parents telling us—rightfully so—not to trust strangers, because they could hurt us. The intentions of our parents were good, and I'm sure yours loved you the best they knew how.

But suddenly we wake up and notice that there's a wall around our heart, one we must have built up over time. The upside? When you dodge the vulnerability of doing what you actually want to do with your life, you tend to subject yourself to less criticism. The downside? Nothing can get out of your wall. You're stuck in your own limitations, and you struggle to attune to the wisdom of your heart. Your fears become so loud, and so sneaky, that you lose the ability to hear yourself think, to hear your intuition, to honor yourself, and to truly express yourself or your passions . . . to taste all the flavors of life that are meant to be uniquely yours.

WHAT I KNOW NOW

Throughout my years of career coaching, I've had tons of clients who worked in government. There's one named Jenna who I'll never forget. She was an intelligence analyst focused on North Africa. She was glum, but when we looked at her skills, it was clear that being an analyst was a great role for her. What was the issue, then? Turns out she was eating the wrong slice of the government industry pie. Most of the time, this would mean she was in a role asking her to use the wrong CORE SKILL SET, but in this case, her government work was focused on the wrong country. When we got clarity that she may better fit in a role doing analysis on a country in Europe, versus North Africa, she lit up.

She is now happier than ever, all because she was moved to being an intelligence analyst for a country in the EU. As Friedrich Nietzsche once said, "God is in the details"—and it's so true. Often, we're just a couple of millimeters off when it comes to our career fit. Be open to the fact that you're possibly just a couple of millimeters off, *even when your job feels completely off*. Instead of throwing away the entire pie, ask yourself if you're simply nibbling on the wrong slice of that pie, whether that means using the wrong CORE SKILL SET in an industry you otherwise love, or simply working under a toxic manager.

USE THIS NOW

1. List up to ten of your interests here without stopping or overthinking (e.g., fashion, politics, travel, writing, movies, feminism, etc.).

2. Star two to three interests that feel like topics you could read about or talk about all day long.

3. Evaluate the intersection between your CORE SKILL SET, CORE NATURE, and CORE INTERESTS. What job titles (slices of the pie) resonate? What industries align?

4. Write one question or concern you're having about your career right now, and write two or three possible solutions you could choose from, or decisions you can make about your concern. Check in with your "second brain" (your intuition) by tuning in to how your body feels when it looks at each possible solution. Is it expanding or contracting at different answers? Which paths is your body saying *yes* to? Which paths is your body saying *no* to?

5. Start *soul writing* every morning for seven days! That means every morning, write at the top of the page: *What do you want me to know?* Free-form write from your soul, not your mind. That means tuning in to the intuitive voice inside you that whispers, letting you know what feels good for you, what feels off for you, and what feels inspiring. You may be surprised if you just let your hand write every morning with little messages to you that you didn't see coming.

CONCLUSION

The biggest mistake you could make in your career is in being so reactive about a job that isn't working for you that you don't ask yourself these questions: Am I using the wrong CORE SKILL SET, or is it this entire industry that isn't working for me? What small tweak could make a big difference for me?

PART *three*
REROUTING

We forget that our subconscious is overriding our conscious behavior. It's not our fault that so many factors have impacted this, but it is our responsibility to make a change.

—You Turn Podcast
Episode 84: "5 Steps to Love Your Body"
with Sarah Anne Stewart

Chapter Seven

Never Underestimate Who You're Talking To

MAY 16, 2009

I know it can be hard to imagine, but more often than not, the best jobs don't really go to the best candidates. Instead, they go to the best job seeker, and the best job seekers may not have much "relevant experience" for their dream job, but instead are captivating communicators who never underestimate who they're talking to.

Just weeks before my big move to London, I sauntered down K Street in Washington, DC, comparing my small liberal arts college degree to the sea of people walking past me, likely with polished Harvard degrees, Stanford credentials, and Oxford resumes. I don't know if I was more scared or inspired by the challenge of standing out. After all, the person with the big career isn't always the one who got by on their resume, that tiny little sheet of paper that seems to determine one's value in the workforce. I thought of influential leaders who didn't have their college degree—John Mackey (CEO of Whole Foods), Ellen DeGeneres, Anna

Wintour (editor in chief at *Vogue*)—and still rose up. *If I don't have the best college degree or grades*, I thought, *I'd better learn how to make friends with everyone*. So how would I do that?

APPLICANT TRACKING HELL

Guess what? Even graduates from top schools need to join us normal humans in permeating the most hellish of software algorithms, known as Applicant Tracking Systems (ATS). These systems will sift through thousands of applicants for any one single job, and rumor on the street is that up to 90 percent of all Fortune 500 companies use some type of resume-screening software.[1] Bombarded with hundreds and sometimes thousands of resumes for a single job post, the ATS software is an invaluable tool for HR directors. The very nanosecond your resume is received online, HR computers run it through a parser, a computer program that removes all your resume's fancy formatting and breaks down its text into recognized strings of characters before analyzing keywords and phrases. Then, the ATS gives your resume a score, and spits out the "best" resumes to the HR director. This means, more often than not, when you apply for jobs online, your resume is getting declined without a human being even seeing it. And, seriously, all this is done faster than the time it took you to read this sentence.

More than 80 percent of available jobs aren't getting posted online.[2] Why? When a job opening comes up in an office, hiring is a pain. In fact, finding really good talent is a pain, and those who can notice good candidates are talented in and of themselves for being able to see their skill and talent. That's why recruiters ask everyone and their mom for referrals, and even go so far as to generously bonus colleagues who recommend someone who's a good match for the vacancy. All this often happens before the recruiter even considers posting the job online, which is a tedious administrative task in and of itself. That's why if you're applying for jobs online right now, you're accessing the bottom 20 percent of what's actually available in the market. You deserve more than tapping into that little 20 percent pool. You deserve options. Giving yourself options, creating abundance in your opportunities, that's straight up self-love right there. Have you been stuck on the application wheel, never hearing back? I feel you. During those few weeks in DC, prior to my London move, I learned that options start with learning how to talk about yourself in a way that turns more conversations into job interviews. That's the *You Turn* you're about to learn right now, friend.

LIFE IS A NUMBERS GAME

As you know, I wasn't down for the battle against the ATS bots, and I knew my road into counterterrorism would be anything but traditional. I decided to approach life as a numbers game, knowing that if you knock on enough doors, one will open. If you're not getting results, it's quite simple: you're not knocking on enough doors. This applies to your career, your love life, and your relationship with yourself. Are you feeling stuck right now? Where can you create more options for yourself, or what doors can you start knocking on?

The journey began on a muggy afternoon in Washington, DC. The year was 2009. After spending all morning unpacking my bags, I had just settled into my new row house on Constitution Avenue, feeling anxious for what lay ahead. I was close to graduation and moving to be a grad student in London. Tomorrow would be the first day of the Government Pathways Program I signed up for, which would give me the final three credits I needed to graduate with my bachelor's degree. The class was offered by the University of Redlands Government Department as an opportunity for students to experientially learn more about career paths in DC, which meant every day we'd be sitting in lectures from different political leaders throughout the city. Hearing from diplomats, lobbyists, senators, researchers, and foreign policy officers would be life-changing, but the skills I'd learn along the way would open more doors for me than I'd ever realize in that moment.

Unpacking my things, I overheard a group of fellow students playing beer pong downstairs. All I could do was roll my eyes. I was here to figure out what I was going to do with the rest of my life and my career, and it seemed like everyone else just wanted to party. *What a waste of time*, I thought to myself as I started organizing my clothing drawers. To drown out the noise, I blasted Ja Rule on Napster and opened the only window of the tiny room. The streets were buzzing with activity, and everywhere I looked, it seemed like people were walking with a sense of undeniable direction. It was like everyone had somewhere indisputably important to be.

I put my head out the little window and peered down Constitution Avenue, where I recognized a couple of senators engaged in hushed, private conversations, while staffers hurried behind them like a gaggle of minions, struggling to keep their pace. Following close behind the minions and jockeying for position were journalists begging for insights and answers about the political dilemmas of the day. I remember thinking to myself about how much I wanted to be just like these people—someone important, *someone who mattered*. Do you ever feel that in your career, a desire to stand out in secret hopes it'll make you more important? For the first time in my college career, I felt like I belonged, like I was going places. I'll never forget how much I felt at one with the universe, bathing in this grace I'd never felt before.

REJECTION IS THE PATH TO YOUR FREEDOM

Turning away from the window with a satisfied smile on my face, I cranked up Ja Rule and danced around the room as I got ready. I put on Audrey Hepburn–esque pearls and loaded my book bag. When everything was set, I realized that I was, in fact, ready. Ready to take the next step in life and create opportunities for myself here in DC. Perhaps a job offer was waiting after I completed my one-year master's degree in London. There was no looking back. This inspired me to research networking events online so that I could make myself busy every single night when I was in DC. The thought of walking into a sea of strangers every night gave me anxiety, but I wondered if it could almost be like rejection therapy: getting rejected so much that eventually it would set me free, and I wouldn't care anymore. In fact, rejection actually activates the same areas of the brain that experience physical pain,[3] so much so that taking acetaminophen (like Tylenol) can actually reduce your brain's sensitivity to rejection.[4] Like feeling the initial soreness and aches from hitting the gym to build muscle, if I could train myself with being rejected, it wouldn't hurt anymore. In fact, I started to see it as an experiment: thirty days only. I promised myself I'd just see what happened. Sometimes in life you have to make your own opportunities. If I didn't like what it did for my career, I told myself, I'd ditch the networking and give in to a future of applicant-tracking hell for job applications after grad school. What I didn't realize then was that this whole networking thing would be totally aligned with my CORE NATURE, the human in me who wanted to connect with people and grow.

I walked out of my brick-red row house, and even though I was flying solo to a networking event, I noticed a spring in my step. I felt powerful, motivated, and ready for anything. I was dressed to kill wearing a cobalt-blue dress and carrying a Kate Spade bag that meant business. After the long walk to Capitol South Metro Station, my smile connected with a toothless homeless man nearby. He held a cup that said *Hungry Vietnam Vet . . . Please Help*. I reached into my bag and handed him an apple and granola bar I had left over from my day of classes. Reaching out his hand, he looked up at me and smiled warmly. "Girl, you lookin' like a young Audrey Hepburn today."

Bingo! But was it *that* obvious? Was I trying too hard? Pushing back the momentary insecure thoughts, I looked back and said, "That's *exactly* what I was going for. With a little splash of Michelle Obama, maybe?"

I laughed and told him this was officially my first time on the Metro, so he helped guide me on purchasing my first Metro card.

He looked up and asked, "Where you headed?"

I felt a warmth wash over me and wondered why this sweet, tooth-less man would feel so comforting to me. I could tell that his CORE NATURE was kind, joyful, helpful, and communicative. I could see that he had a CORE VALUE of connection and perhaps service or gen-erosity. I assumed his CORE SKILL SET was *words*, because, wow, was he easy to connect with. I felt inexplicable love and understanding toward him. And then it hit me. For some reason, he reminded me of my big sister. She was insightful, an incredible writer, and funny as hell. She was also a drug addict for most of my life, and eventually became homeless because of it. When I look back, my sister was the ultimate heartbreak. For years, we'd house her, shuttle her in and out of rehab, pay her bills, and beg her to apply for jobs. In fact, we begged her to participate in society. She was an unexpected, yet still pleasant blend of depression and humor, like this guy. Eventually, she started to enjoy her homelessness in a way, or she seemed like she did, telling me proudly that she was the most competent person living in the park. She even called herself "the prom queen of the park." No matter what her cir-cumstances, she'd crack me up, like this guy here in the Metro. While I didn't assume he enjoyed his homelessness, my sister made me open to the possibility that he had a similar joy in his heart.

My heart ached as we spoke. I was missing my sister, remembering sleepovers we had and fun nights out before her life came undone. I won-dered where in the world she was in that moment, and who was talking to her. I wondered how she felt. This sort of wondering came in waves; it was a grief of sorts. I then got sadder, missing my family back home in LA, knowing I'd be off to London for grad school, right after this course completed and I graduated from University of Redlands. I quickly pushed the feelings aside and stayed present in our conversation. I didn't have time to be homesick. I was on a mission and laser-focused on what I was here to do, so I answered him through an engaging smile: "There's a networking event at US Institute for Peace, so I thought I'd go."

Matching my smile, past his missing teeth, he leaned back to say, "Well, look at you." He held my smile for a long beat before he continued: "When you get there, find my boy Benny. He's a cabbie in the line out front. He looks like me, but he always wears a paperboy sort of hat. You'll notice it. Just find him. Tell him Johnny from Cap South Station sent you. He's good people."

I thanked Johnny and took the escalator down to the train platform. I had to laugh because here I was, in DC, heading to my first networking event, and my first contact would be . . . *Benny the cabdriver?*

Stepping onto the train platform, I took in my surroundings. There were people from all walks of life: executives, staffers, families, waiters, and janitors. As my train pulled in, I stepped on with an emotional backpack full of thoughts: wondering how the event would go, worrying if my elevator pitch (my answer to "tell me about yourself") was as tight as it could be. I noticed a sassy woman with braids in her hair, standing in the center of the train car, grooving to the music from her iPod. She was in her midfifties, and the music coming from her earbuds had a musical beat I faintly recognized: the Black Eyed Peas. I thought to myself, *This woman has it going on.* I couldn't help but be inspired by how confident she was. She wasn't worried about how everyone on the train was noticing her dance in the crowd. Truly, she appeared as if she didn't have a care in the world. Now that's what I call spiritual freedom. That is, until she looked up and shot me a confronting glare as if to ask: *What the hell you lookin' at?*

For a brief second, I was like a deer caught in her high beams. After what felt like a full minute, I finally looked away. Thank God I did, because I would've missed the man sitting directly across from me— Michael Hayden, former director of the Central Intelligence Agency. I was immediately starstruck, seeing him just sitting there, riding the Metro, in an intense conversation with a marine in a full-dress uniform. I was surprised by the giddy feelings rushing through me, because I grew up in Los Angeles and had seen my fair share of celebrities. I was never one to be starstruck, and I always saw celebrities as everyday regular humans who just so happened to get extra attention, but this was different somehow. Right then and there, I fell in love with traveling on the Metro. I saw it as the ultimate equalizer for human interaction—an amalgamation of races, cultures, and mindsets. Regardless of social status, income, or appearance, we all sat together on the train.

I was gazing at Hayden and the marine like somewhat of a creep, and the marine started smiling right at me. As the train slowed into the next station, I flashed him a nervous departing smile before realizing he and I were getting off at the same stop.

"Where you headed?" he asked in a voice that every husky marine should have. He was about six-foot-five, and while this might sound like a cliché, he was a hunk of a man with beautiful broad shoulders, looking like he practically came straight out of *Saving Private Ryan*. Looking up, I quickly answered, "A networking event at the USIP."

Completely out of character, I felt the following words slip out of my mouth: "You should come." Surprised, he looked down at me, smiled, put his hand out, and said, "I'm Collin." I tried to calm my fangirl nerves because here I was, talking not only to a handsome man in uniform, but someone who spent the entire train ride talking with *the* Michael Hayden. I remember thinking, *This guy must be important if he was talking to the former head of the CIA.* I was still operating from the belief that one's career is what makes them worthy or valuable in the world. Do you have someone whose career inspires you? While it's important not to put them on a pedestal, take note of what it is about them that you're moved by. Usually, they're embodying something that you would like to step into.

As the sun began setting, we walked past the throngs of people rushing home throughout the golden streets, like little ants dispersing past the White House. Throughout our twenty-minute walk to the event, Collin talked about his life, his family in Georgia, and how, even though he'd been on three tours to Iraq and Afghanistan, he was eager for his next deployment. Like a perfect gentleman, Collin held the event door open for me and said, "We're here! We might lose each other, you know? It's a lot of people . . . So, um, you'll have to let me know your mailing address."

I smiled, took his arm as we entered, and retorted, "Why? Are you trying to stalk me, or are you just craving a pen pal?" As he rushed over to the bar, he smiled back at me and said, "Naw, I'm leaving for a tour in the Middle East next month, and I want to make sure my family invites you to my funeral."

NEVER UNDERESTIMATE WHO YOU'RE TALKING TO

At first, I thought he was joking, but seeing the look on his face, I could tell he meant what he said. *Good-looking and crazy*, I thought to myself. *I can sure pick 'em.* Although it was alarming to hear someone say something so dark and flippant, I brushed it off and scanned the room for opportunities. *I'm leaving this city with an internship if it's the last thing I do*, I thought to myself. *All I need is someone's help, just one person in this crowded room.* Upon finishing my initial survey of the room, I saw a man who looked a little like Johnny from the Capitol South Station. He was holding a paperboy hat in his hands, standing on the periphery of the event. This had to be Benny the cabdriver, I thought to myself, walking over.

"Hello," I said, with bright eyes. "Are you Benny?"

With an inquisitive smile, he asked, "Is it that obvious?"

We shared a quick laugh, and I told him how his friend Johnny at Capitol South Station was my first friend here in DC. Benny smiled and offered his hand. "Ah, girl, well . . . Welcome to the district," he said warmly.

As we were about to start talking, Collin walked back over and introduced himself to Benny. He pulled me aside, and the minute he started talking, I noticed from his voice that he was already buzzed, with a handful of cheese cubes in his hand from the appetizer station.

"Ashley, networking with a cabdriver isn't the route to landing an internship when you're back from London," he whispered, irritated on my behalf.

I walked back over to Benny, apologized for the interruption, threw my hands up, and said, "Time for me to work the room and meet some institutional folks who might help me land an internship." As I turned to walk away, Benny softly grabbed my hand and said, "You know, I drive for the Clintons sometimes. Let me know if I could help you get a meeting with someone over in the White House." He handed me his card and walked away. Benny the cabdriver just became my fairy god-father of the networking event. Dumbfounded, I grabbed the card in a stupor and said, "Thanks, Benny."

I thought about how Dorothy Parker, the author, once brilliantly said, "I hate writing. I love having written." This started to feel like how networking was to me. I didn't like what happened to my nervous system when I put myself out there, but I loved what happened because of it.

For the next hour, Collin introduced me to everyone he knew in the room, but I could tell the introductions weren't bearing the kind of fruit I was looking for. Collin took one last look around the room, turned to me, and asked curiously, "Hungry?"

"Yeah, but I'm broke as fuck. Where can we go for all the snacks at a price of approximately zero dollars?" I asked.

He laughed and said, "Who cares? I'll take you somewhere cool."

BUT, REALLY, NEVER UNDERESTIMATE WHO YOU'RE TALKING TO

We walked up to Marvin, a bar in the U Street Corridor of DC, where I couldn't help but notice that I looked like all the women, decked out in my best Audrey Hepburn gear, looking ready for either *Breakfast at Tiffany's* or a meeting with the president. As Collin headed for the bar again, I noticed a friendly-looking man in his forties sitting alone at the bar. His meal had just arrived and he was about to cut his juicy hamburger in half.

"May as well," I said to myself as I walked through the crowd and sat down right next to him. As I looked confidently in his eyes, he stalled and sensed I had an agenda, which I did. I was hungry. Looking down at his burger, I smiled and asked politely, "What are you going to do with the other half of that?"

He laughed, and to my surprise, he placed my half of his burger on a small plate and slid it over. As we ate, he asked me tons of questions about my goals and why I chose to come to DC now, when I lived in Los Angeles and was headed to London for grad school in just a few short weeks. The conversation was comfortable, probably because I wasn't trying to give an elevator pitch or verbally unload my credentials or resume. It was just two people talking over a burger.

"So tell me," I asked, "what are you up to here in the district?" His answer was the last thing I thought I would hear.

"I'm running for mayor," he said with a politician's sparkling, mysterious smile.

My mind immediately started to race: *Umm, I'm sorry, what? This is officially what I'd like to call a snaccident . . . snacking and creating chaos, all in one.* I started to laugh and cringe at the same time, which is why I quickly excused myself and told him I'd be right back. I walked into the dimly lit bathroom stall, where I'd breathe in and out to collect myself. I didn't know if I should feel amused or ashamed.

IF YOU WANT MORE MAGIC, HAVE MORE CONVERSATIONS

I thought about how interesting it was that Benny the cabdriver could help me just as much as this guy could, how we lived in a world of titles, fancy outfits, and elevator pitches that intimidate and somehow motivate us. I realized that we're all so connected, and just a couple of degrees separate us from just about anyone, even the head of the CIA or a guy running for mayor. Best of all, I realized that, even if I sometimes make a fool of myself, if I wanted to make art of my life, I'd just have to keep having conversations. If you ever wake up one day underwhelmed with the results you're creating and you want to shake things up, just ask yourself: Where can you go to have more conversations? Know that coffee shop lines are just as valuable as networking events. Conversations are where magic happens, and they have the power to turn the universe into a flow chart of opportunity.

BE A GOOSE

My friend's grandma once told me that when it comes to dating, "Don't ever chase men. Simply be like a white goose in a field, running slowly, letting them catch you." I always thought she was insane for saying that, but I realized that's kind of like how it is when you're building your career. It's not about saying, "What do I want to do with my life?" but rather, asking yourself, "What circumstance or what environment do I need to be in to get inspired by life, or for life to catch me? How can I become like these little white geese, allowing myself to just so happen to be caught in the beautiful junctions of life and opportunity?" Choosing to go to bars like Marvin, or choosing to go to networking events, created a magical alchemy of opportunity in my life, and I realized I just needed to keep being that white goose in the crowd, ready to be caught in the lines of opportunity.

As I walked out of the bathroom, I thought of the questions I would ask the man running for mayor, *or really, the same old dude I'd coaxed into giving me half his burger.* Questions like "What should I do with my life?" or "How do I get where I want to go?" used to paralyze me. As a result, I would do nothing because the fear of failing was too much for my ego to bear. It wasn't until now that I was able to see how much I was wearing perfectionism as a mask to keep me from feeling my extreme fear of failure.

When I finally returned to the bar, the man running for mayor was paying his bill, or should I say *our* bill? He gave me his email address, thanked me for *literally* sharing his dinner, and suggested we stay in touch. I couldn't help but think what a saint this man was. For the past two hours, I had talked about myself and ate half his dinner, only for him to ask that we keep in touch? In fact, I just outright asked him, "Why would you want to keep in touch with me? I just ate your dinner and talked your ear off!" He said something I'll never forget: "Because you're real, and this town needs you." My eyes moistened as he walked off. The whole thing was surreal and amazing at the same time. The way Johnny introduced me to Benny the cabdriver, the train ride, seeing one of my all-time heroes from the CIA, Collin, and now meeting a man running for mayor who was saying we should keep in touch?

CLARITY COMES FROM ENGAGEMENT, NOT THOUGHT

I learned so much that evening: about how many opportunities exist in life, and about how to talk to people organically. In this moment, I remembered a truth that I still hold sacred in my career: success (and clarity) comes from engagement, not thought. If you want clarity on what career path is for you, you must be willing to step into an experimental calibration with the universe. Engagement could be as simple as reading books or taking a course; or it could be as complicated as actually leaping into a job you think you might like. The willingness to work for your clarity, to engage, will move you forward. After all, there's nothing powerful about being in limbo. Instead, show up, make a commitment, and see what feedback the universe gives you. Remember, you can always course-correct along the way.

From that day onward, I saw my career as an experiment that could meet me where I was at any given moment, not a destination. I felt life's ubiquitous magic and opportunity . . . and I stopped worrying so much about my future. If anything, for that evening alone, I knew I was like the little white goose, ready to be caught by opportunity and on a quest to become the most interesting person I knew . . . *not for anyone other than myself.*

YOU TURN #7:

LEARN HOW TO

turn conversations into opportunities

Just recently, when I was the keynote speaker for a women's empowerment conference at MGM Grand Resorts, a woman stood up and asked a question I've heard all too often: *Why aren't I getting paid what I'm worth?*

If you've ever wondered this, I get it. And I want to help you overcome it right here and now. First of all, let's question your wording: "paid what I'm worth." You are, and always will be, worth so much more than a number, so make sure you check in with your worthiness while you're navigating the whole salary negotiation and job-hunt game. *Seriously.* Second of all, in my opinion, this woman's real issue wasn't that she's not getting "paid what she's worth," but rather that she hasn't created enough options for herself.

WHAT I KNOW NOW

Know this: if you're not getting the results you want in your job hunt or in your career, it's directly tied to a lack of options. Have you ever seen someone who's walking around with a bunch of options in their career? They look excited, they have a little pep in their step, and they seem so abundant. It's because they're someone who has committed to the art of creating options. And do you know how to create options? You have more conversations, ones where you're committed to living in your CORE NATURE. In fact, whenever I have moments in my business where I'm bored, I think to myself: *Hmm, it's time to create more magic.* And then my immediate next thought is: *Conversations create magic, so where can I go have them? Or, who is the person I want to have more conversations with?*

And believe me when I tell you that you don't have to overthink this. Just like Benny the cabdriver or Johnny in the Metro, magic is available everywhere. That's the trick when it comes to abundance. And it doesn't mean you need to be "on" and having conversations all the time; it just means you need to make yourself available—to the person looking next to you in the peanut butter aisle in the grocery store, to the person behind you in the bathroom line, to your postman . . . you name it. Magic is everywhere, and we tend to buy into the belief that there's a certain person, perhaps more seasoned, that we should be talking to. Does targeting who you have conversations with help? Sure. But, believe me, I've made some serious magic happen in my career through just going to the grocery store, or walking my dog, Jupiter, around the block, with one intention: connection.

USE THIS NOW

1. Where do you feel the most alive and in your CORE NATURE? List experiences, people, or places!
2. Star two to three of those options you feel most inspired to go to in the coming weeks.
3. After doing one of the activities or going to one of the places that put you in your CORE NATURE, free-form write any thoughts or ideas in your mind, within an hour of getting home. This means grabbing a pen, putting it to paper, and letting your hand write without knowing what it's going to write. See what inspiration comes through to you after you've gone out and stepped into your most natural self.
4. While I don't like exercising, I love having exercised. I also don't usually like networking, but I love having networked. What is one action you don't enjoy in the moment, but you always love afterward? How can you bring more of it into your life?
5. Go on meetup.com, and do some online research. What networking opportunities or events exist in your area? Start a list with dates and

times, and come up with a realistic number of events you'd be willing to go to each month or year.

CONCLUSION

I know it's uncomfortable, but here's the truth: you don't realize how much self-love you actually have until life is calling you forward to practice it. For me, loving myself in my career means putting my girl power pants on, and creating more options for myself. There's nothing inspiring about waiting for one employer to decide whether you're worthy of a raise. Why not see job hunting and conversations as a way of life? That way, you're just a conversation away from more options, and your life becomes more alive.

And let's just have a quick note here on being real. Truthful communication not only helps build stronger trust and a deeper relationship; it also helps keep you healthy. According to new research, headaches, sore throats, and anxiety are all symptoms of lying.[5] Keep this at bay and be authentic in your communication. *Who you are always wins.* Your true self always comes out, so you may as well be yourself now!

Chapter Eight

All You Need Is One "Yes"

MAY 20, 2009

Just a week into my month in DC, I felt possibility running through my veins. While I gained more confidence every day, I also started getting curious to learn what DC could offer me. In fact, I walked into class a few minutes early on a Monday morning, only to notice a few classmates in the front of the room, talking to the speaker of the day, a friendly colonel and lobbyist named John Garrett. I chickened out on introducing myself and just eavesdropped on the conversation while the room filled up.

BE AN EARLY BIRD

Then I realized something I'd take with me forever in my career: whenever you go to an event, especially one with fewer than a hundred people, make sure to get there earlier than everyone else does, because it gives you an opportunity to personally engage with the speaker, who also tends to arrive early. I've also learned to score a front seat at events, because usually the speaker looks to those of us in the front while he or she is speaking, and that creates a bond you can follow up on after their talk.

Colonel Garrett turned and confidently introduced himself to the rest of the classroom, which was now at capacity. He had a kind face, with an indisputable history impressed upon it. During his self-introduction, I began to wonder about all the places he had been for the government, and all the things he had done in the name of national security. He spoke about his personal values, about being a soldier in Vietnam, his experience of war, and the importance of making an impact wherever you go. He was inspiring to me. I can see now that his career was in full alignment with his CORE VALUES: service, discipline, adventure, and community—to name a few. It was admirable how the colonel was able to channel his CORE NATURE so seamlessly into a career with longevity, which is something we all look for in life.

TRAIN YOUR EAR TO KNOW THE INVITATION FOR AN ELEVATOR PITCH

When class was over, everyone got in line to personally speak with the colonel. As I stood and waited my turn, I pulled out a notepad and started writing down all the advice he gave to my classmates, and yet, I couldn't help but notice that all the students would struggle to talk about themselves. It went like this: a student would say hello and ask him their question, and then he'd respond by asking some version of the prompt, "Tell me about yourself," which is a clear invitation into an elevator pitch. The conversational cue could also sound something like, *What got you interested in government?* It could also sound like, *What are your goals right now?* All of these questions pointed to the same need: a short, concise, and well-rehearsed elevator pitch. Have you given much thought to how you talk about yourself? If not, it might be time to start.

When asked, 76 percent of hiring managers think "being interesting" is a top trait for a candidate to possess,[1] so how you talk about yourself and what you choose to share matters. It is only the most-asked question both in networking conversations and job interviews.

This question—or some version of it—I observed, was *the* question I heard most often when I was at another networking event with my classmates the night prior. I watched as some students had it together and sounded polished in their replies, while others seemed as though they were entering a conversational twilight zone as their eyes glazed over with panic. It seemed as though the best conversationalists first had their ear trained and prepared for that moment that would become an invitation to give their well-practiced, intentional elevator pitch. While waiting for my turn, I couldn't help but think about how ironic it was that so many people struggled to talk about themselves when they literally spend more time with themselves than anyone else. This got me inspired to start writing down bullets on how I could intentionally craft my own elevator pitch.

FOUR STEPS FOR THE PERFECT ELEVATOR PITCH

After paying attention to what elevator pitches seemed to inspire Colonel Garrett, I pulled out my journal and wrote down four words that seemed to sum it up: story, cuff, skill, and goal.

THOUGHTS ON "STORY"

"What got you into taking this course?" the colonel asked Rachel, one of the top students in the class. She replied: "I grew up with a dad who was an immigrant that moved to this country for the American Dream, and I'm the first college graduate in my family. I watched my father face a lot of discrimination when I was growing up, and those moments really solidified my passion to work in civil rights."

Wow, I thought to myself. She was invited into an elevator pitch, and she answered with a powerful story from her upbringing that somehow tied into her career. She took her current career desire and rooted it into years from her past, giving her answer a sanctity and power that most people don't communicate with. I was moved listening to her, as I could tell that she was sharing from her heart. The colonel leaned into her story more than he did with anyone else. He, too, was captivated.

University of California, Berkeley, recently shared findings that people exposed to an awe-inspiring experience or speech were more willing to change their beliefs.[2] For this reason, if you want to be memorable in your work relationships, or any relationships for that matter, you must instill a sense of awe. Not love. Not belonging, but awe. Do you know how to be captivating or create a sense of awe when you're talking to people? There is something fascinating about everyone, and it's key to know what that thing is about you. The most influential speeches of history, like those of Martin Luther King Jr. or Steve Jobs, have been based on capturing an audience with a compelling story that sparks inspiration from what is, to the dream of what could be.[3] The way Rachel started off that day, with a story that linked her career to something meaningful in her upbringing, was brilliant. It was brilliant for two reasons: first of all, stories are easy to remember, and secondly, reaching into your childhood for moments that link to your career interest shows the listener that they're not just hiring someone who woke up and wanted a marketing job; they're hiring someone who has been on a mission since they were a kid, someone who feels a connection to their work beyond the salary it offers or the tasks in their day, and that is powerful. In doing this, we are able to showcase our why, as well as early indicators of our CORE SKILL SET, which ideally aligns with our career interest.

I sat with the words she used to start her pitch: "I grew up with . . ." and immediately got inspired to change my own pitch on the spot: *I grew up in a house where the news was always on, so from a young age, I was exposed to the happenings of the world. My family members on the East Coast were very impacted by 9/11 and I have since been motivated to become a part of the cause to keep people safe.* I wrote this in my journal while the colonel worked his way through the line of students, and kept repeating it to myself in my head.

Do you ever feel cheesy or fake when you plan ahead on what you're going to say in a conversation? As renowned life coach Steve Chandler once pointed out to me, *authentic* has the same Latin root as *author*, and I think it's *authentic* to *author* the things you value in your life, from your elevator pitch to who you are. The alternative? Hope; hoping the right words will come out in the moment that counts the most in your career. It felt right to be intentional about my story. It felt right to give it time and attention and memory. I repeated that story line until it was in my cells. And by having something so ingrained in me, over time I was able to flex and flow with my story every time I was in front of someone. If you don't get intentional, your nerves run the show, and that is *not* the look you're going for. When you practice and get intentional, it's like your nervous system doesn't run you anymore, and you can infuse your intentionality into your communication. My take? Practice your elevator pitch until you're blue in the face. Doing that isn't fake or forced; it's intentional and thoughtful.

So how do we link our history with our pitch? My friend Daniel had just accepted a job offer to be an engineer. I thought about how his story could be about how he used to pull computers apart and put them back together when we were kids. Or my friend Kiera, who ended up becoming a neuropsychologist, helping people overcome brain damage, could describe how she used to advocate for the underdog on the playground when we were kids. My friend Barry Griffin, who is currently running for office in the Bahamas, was often volunteering in orphanages and speaking up against political corruption when he was a kid. What were you like as a kid? How can it relate to your career? All my friends' career choices were organically tied to their individual passions growing up. This created the roots for a powerful story statement at the beginning of their pitch.

Thoughts on "The Cuff"

While Colonel Garrett was captivated and moved by the stories, I noticed that he didn't always offer to help the student unless they did something else, and that was when I wrote down the word *cuff* in my journal. They would drop some sort of authority—they'd do a humblebrag, really—*off the cuff*. What did this look like? One was a star athlete in college, another had good grades and was accepted into Harvard for grad school, or maybe it was their versatile language skills they'd share off the cuff.

This is exactly what a student named Anthony did when the colonel asked him: "Tell me about yourself." Anthony shared a story in the same manner in which Rachel had, only he took a golden second step further, which showed the colonel that he was a top performer, right off the cuff. He said, "I'm really grateful to have spent the past few years here in college as the quarterback of the football team—it's something that's given me a lot of discipline." Upon hearing this, I watched how the colonel sat up and said, "I know some people who are looking to hire interns and employees who have that sort of discipline and ability to execute. What's your email?"

It became abundantly clear to me that if you want to captivate someone and grab their attention, start your elevator pitch with a story. But if you want them to take action and actually help you, share one relevant brag *with humility*. This brought me back to the question, *Is it fake for me to brag like this?* And I came back to the desire to be as intentional as possible about how I was communicating about myself. I had too much self-love to let myself drown in a sea of people at any more networking events. I wanted to stand out, and that meant thinking intentionally about this. I then began to wonder what my off-the-cuff asset might be. What made me interesting? Was it that I was fluent in French, or that I was on the dean's list every single year in college? I didn't know, and that was okay, but I wrote down in my journal: *I'm so grateful that I'm fluent in French, as this is something I plan to bring into my government career.* What if you have nothing to brag about? I'm going to go as far as to say here that you *always* have something to brag about.

Ask friends what you have to brag about; I bet they'll find plenty. Most of all, ask yourself, are you afraid to celebrate who you are and drop a humblebrag? Why?

I've found that there *is* an exception with elevator pitches in this second cuff step: you should never brag to a recruiter in your *cuff* if you think they have some sort of concern around your job application or qualifications. What constitutes a concern?

> Perhaps you're job-hunting to make a career pivot, and you don't have experience in the sort of job you're about to interview for.
> Perhaps you have a gap in your work experience because you needed to take some time off, or you lost your job.
> Perhaps you had your own business, and now you're coming back into the workforce.

These things aren't real concerns in the sense that I don't think they will hurt your career much in the long run, but recruiters will often notice them and experience a lingering question in their mind about you. The problem with this is that they often won't raise the concern with you, giving you an opportunity to address it. That's why I don't recommend using this cuff section to brag if you're feeling like something significant is missing when you're interviewing for a job. When that's the case, I recommend statements like these:

Resume gaps

> "I took some time out of the workforce as I faced a health issue, but I'm so grateful I'm now well and able to fully focus on my career."
> "I left my last job, as it wasn't a fit for what I wanted to do with my career, and decided to travel the world for a while. In that time, I got a lot of clarity that I'd like to transition into [insert career path here]."

Career pivots

> "I loved working in [insert your past job], and I'm so grateful I learned [insert relevant skills here], but what was missing for me was [something this next job will offer you]. Needless to say, I'm excited to be making this transition as it's more aligned with who I am and what I can do best."

> "I left the workforce to start my own business and it was such an amazing experience, and has made me such a better strategic thinker and action taker. That being said, I decided I prefer being in a more stable path, and that is why I ultimately decided that the workforce makes more sense for me!"

I call it a cuff for a reason, friends! Because it's off the cuff, in and out, whether you're taking the bragging route or addressing a perceived shortcoming. Needless to say, there's a fine line between addressing an insecurity and shining a spotlight on it. That's why I keep the bragging quick. If there are any objections they may have in mind, I use the cuff to address them with speed. And, by the way, did you notice that I flipped some of these and turned them into an asset? For example, if you took a year off, or you had to take care of your sick mom, don't worry. Use that and flip it into an asset. Talk briefly about how you took a year off to learn other cultures or languages. Don't feel ashamed if you had to care for a loved one. These moments in life are assets, not liabilities. They show you have heart, and compassion.

You will make an impact with your elevator pitch, and your job history, when you remember that your resume is less about what you've done and more about how you talk about it, both in the words you use and the energy you're speaking from. By the way, that's another reason why memorizing an elevator pitch is so powerful, because it supports you in having more confident energy when you talk about yourself. Think about it: if you know what you're going to say, you can instead shift all your focus onto your energy and your delivery. Practice breeds certainty, and certainty breeds confidence, you know?

Stop seeing moments of transition as gravestones on your resume. The truth is they're stepping-stones. The real issue you face as a job seeker is owning your energy, because the energy you speak from when you talk about these stepping-stones is what builds trust. Life is always challenging you to up your game, so use it.

I didn't know it then during that May class, but years later, these journal notes would become a four-step formula I would teach to thousands of job seekers and continue to use today.

THE FORMULA

1. YOUR STORY: Captivate Your Audience.

Inspire the listener by linking your CORE SKILL SET (or chosen industry) for your career to a story from your childhood. This needs to be one that solidifies your passion or provides context for your career. A suggested start is "I grew up in a house where . . ." or "Looking back, I was always the kid that . . ."

2. THE CUFF: Where You Can Humbly Brag or Address a Concern.

Share your greatness with gratitude. For example, you can start with "I'm so grateful that I . . ." and then share something badass about yourself, a specific asset you can bring to your next job—it could be anything unique or relevant about you, be it a foreign language you speak or a special training you have. Remember: you don't have to come across as bragging; just share something out of gratitude about your greatness. And, of course, if you have an area of concern—a gap on your resume, a career pivot, etc.—you know what to do from the scripts above.

3. SKILL: Know What Skill the Recruiter Wants You to Have.

Every hiring manager is yearning for their next hire to have at least one particular skill that would be a game changer for them to have on their team. Your job is to ask yourself what that skill is, given the job you're interested in and the sorts of people they need to hire. See the following table for examples of skills associated with specific career fields or positions.

Career Field or Job	Skill Set
Intelligence or counterterrorism	Identify patterns in data
Counselor	Ability to listen
Writer	Creativity
Startup or Business Entrepreneur	Innovation
Accountant	Attention to detail

Here's the key. You don't want to share that you have this one skill by touting yourself, like "I'm amazing." Instead, put it in testimonial format. This means instead of saying, "I have a gift for attention to detail," dig in the depths of your past to find someone credible who complimented you on that skill. That can look like, "My boss used to always tell me that I have a gift for [insert ideal skill], and I know this is going to be useful in this position we're discussing." If your boss didn't love you up for the skills your mama gave you, go down the ranks: Did your professors celebrate it? Did your colleagues ever notice it? Worst case, perhaps your friends did. By any means necessary, put the compliment in third-party testimonial format when you speak it.

4. GOAL: Get the Job You Want.

This is the end of your pitch, and it's where you must share why that job, or company, specifically matters to you. That could be because of their mission statement, their processes, their client roster, their corporate responsibility, their culture, their press coverage . . . anything. Your job is to find out why they're special to you, and relay it to them. In a lot of ways, job hunting is like dating. No employer wants to hire you because you just need a job or a salary hike. They want to hire people who want to work specifically for them. It really is like dating, huh? So your goal statement could sound like this: "I'm particularly excited about this opportunity because [insert something special about the company or its mission here]."

Or, let's say you're not interviewing for a job, but you're networking, in which case your goal isn't to get the job; it's for the person to perhaps be of support to you. That could look like, "I'm excited at the moment to be transitioning into a role doing [skill set], ideally in the [put the industry here] industry." You must make it crystal clear what you are looking for. That could sound like: "At the moment, I'm looking for an internship, ideally doing research in the national security arena."

>>•<<

I was so engrossed with all the lessons my impromptu eavesdropping session brought into my life. In fact, I almost missed the colonel as he was preparing to leave because I was seated, taking so many notes on this whole divine elevator pitch download I was getting. It was now or never, I said to myself. This was my shot at talking to him, so I closed my journal and packed up. I was terrified to walk up to him and felt my words slipping from my memory as I prepared to talk to him. Some of the most magical opportunities in life come not from a series of big events, but rather from that one courageous step when you decide you're going to walk up to someone and say hello, or walk into the networking event you would rather hide from.

"Colonel Garrett," I called out as he was about to walk out of the building.

He turned with a friendly, warm smile in his eyes. "Did you write down all of my secrets, or are you looking for more?" *Busted.* Except not really, as I wrote a whole formula for elevator pitches based on what I heard that I liked, and what I didn't, among the students.

Before I could say a word, he continued and said, "Actually, I thought it was a great idea . . . listening to other students ask their questions as a way to soak it all in and learn." *Busted again.* My only option was to own it, so I smiled and said, "I am resourceful like that." He smiled and asked how he could be of service.

In that moment, I went into the elevator pitch I had written in my journal only minutes before: "Well, I grew up in a house where the news was always on, and from a young age I really cared about the happenings of the world. My family was really impacted by 9/11, and I think that really solidified my interest in government, so that I could do something about it . . . That's what inspired me to become fluent in French, and I plan to also become fluent in Arabic . . ."

Then, I stalled. I couldn't remember my four key steps.

Shoot. Story, cuff . . . and, *oh, that's right,* I reminded myself: skill and goal.

After a slight cough to mask my internal dialogue, I continued: "A lot of my professors have told me that I have a knack for writing, so I'm looking to bring that into an intelligence analyst career right after grad school. I actually head to London for a one-year master's program in a few weeks . . ."

LIFE HAPPENS IN MOMENTS OF COURAGE

I gasped for air, nervous, awaiting his reply. He smiled with warm eyes, and it was in that moment that I knew he was going to change my life in some way. I didn't know how it would look, or what he would do to help, but I knew that he was a special person. I thought about how that moment of mustering up my courage wasn't about figuring out what I'd say to him, nor was it about figuring out what he'd say in return . . . I realize now that it was about taking only two steps: finding the courage to say something that sparks a conversation, and trusting myself to let the rest unfold.

Life happens in moments, doesn't it? In those brief little seconds when you decide to say hello to someone, stand a second longer and have that awaited conversation, or get courageous and ask for what you want. Think back on your life: Was there one moment in particular when you got courageous and said hello to someone that made a big difference for you? It was so funny to me, thinking about how often I used to believe life was about these times where we'd get a "big break" when really, it's these little courageous moments that consistently create the big breaks. And it's about choosing, every single time, to show up and create these moments.

Colonel Garrett spoke up:

"I'm going to a dinner at Old Ebbitt Grill with a bunch of people from the Secret Service and the State Department. Would you like to come along?"

The invitation felt intimidating, but I couldn't think of anywhere else better for me to be, so I said "yes" without even blinking. I wondered if I was good enough for such a table full of people, if I'd have anything interesting (at my young age) to add to the conversation, and then I realized my only option was to be myself. Do you ever get anxious at a table of people you believe to be more successful than you are? That was me that night. I thought to myself, if I was able to impress the table with some quick conversation, I'd have to keep that up! But what I didn't have to "keep up," though, was just being myself. In situations where you're anxious about meeting someone or being in a tough social setting, remember that being yourself is underrated.

As we walked to dinner, I thought about my elevator pitch, and how I could talk about myself to those at the table. *Gosh, I needed to impress them. What the heck would I even say? Maybe less was more. Maybe I should stay quiet.* My thoughts ran amok, so when we walked in the door, I excused myself to go to the restroom. I stood in the stall, popped my journal open, and reread my four steps in my notes:

Story: My "Why," or a life story linking to my career skills or interests.

Cuff: Something that makes you awesome or explaining yourself.

Skill: Being grateful for a skill you plan to use in your career.

Goal: What you're looking to do next, where you could need help.

REALLY, DON'T BURN BRIDGES

I was ready for anyone to say, "Tell me about yourself," or any version of a prompt that would bring me into my elevator pitch. I breathed in, breathed out, and walked toward Colonel Garrett's dinner table, surprised to see a familiar face: the mayoral candidate who let me eat his burger that night out with the marine, Collin. He smirked and looked at the colonel. "Good choice of a student to bring to dinner. I know Ashley. She's fun . . . Want to share a burger, by chance?" he asked with a smile, as if it was our little secret. It was in this moment that I truly understood the importance of never burning a bridge, and the smallness of the government world.

The rest of the table looked at me, curious to connect, and asked about my plans for the future. I hung on to my elevator pitch for dear life and watched them all nod. I talked about how I just got into King's College London's Graduate Program in War Studies, and how I was about to start it in just a couple of weeks. Then I just started asking questions about them because I read a book that said people think you're more interesting if you're interested in them. When I got home that night, I refreshed my email in-box and saw more than seven email introductions to contacts in London. The colonel later told me that he gave everyone at the table my email, and asked them all to go through their contacts and see how to help me. Networking isn't a single event, and it doesn't happen only when you throw on a name tag. *It's a way of life.* It's a repeated choice to wake up every morning and create conversations that turn into opportunities.

ALL IT TAKES IS ONE "YES"

All it takes is one yes, I thought. I looked back on all the times I put myself out there only to be rejected (most of the time), and realized that I needed to keep flexing this muscle no matter what. Was it petrifying? Yes. In fact, the thought of choosing a life where I constantly put myself out there made me feel nauseous.

The only thing worse, I decided, was living a life where I left my potential on the shelf, dying with my music or my art inside me. That's what it looks like when you choose to let life happen to you, isn't it? Realize that those tiny moments when you choose to stand on the sidelines of opportunity represent a habit that is robbing you of your greatness. Showing up and putting myself out there, whether it was in my DNA or not, would become a muscle I'd choose to build. I knew there would be a conversion rate of yeses that would happen in my life, if I was willing to face many more noes. Like my grandpa Sol used to tell me, "If you knock on tons of doors, you'll eventually get a 'yes.'" Ultimately, the discomfort of the small, more frequent rejections is simply the price you have to pay to play the game of life. In the weeks that followed, I experienced the magic that came from using my elevator pitch. Every time we had a speaker in class, I would wait to connect with them last, one-on-one, in a more casual way, walking them out. It gave me an invaluable lesson on human interaction.

Just as I began to really settle into my life on Constitution Avenue, it was time to pack for London. The summer rain pelted onto the cab window as I headed to the airport. The driver tried to talk to me, but I was feeling too scattered and nervous about my move to have any real conversation. Leaving DC felt emotional, as though I'd found a part of myself there I was worried I'd leave behind. I looked back at the Washington Monument as we headed onto the freeway, placed my right hand fondly on the window, and whispered quietly to myself, *Goodbye, DC.* I felt the power of the city permeate my system as we drove away, and I was so grateful for all I had learned in those short weeks.

I arrived at Dulles International Airport at 5:45 AM, a couple of hours before my flight. After checking my luggage, I sat in a bagel shop and kept compulsively refreshing my email. A headline suddenly appeared in my in-box, taking the wind out of me: *Welcome to the Mishcon de Reya Human Rights Team.* I must have reread the email ten times, in disbelief that the same law firm that once represented Princess Diana would be hiring me as their intern. My excitement buzz about the internship put me into total exhaustion by the time I boarded the plane.

I slept through all seven hours of the flight, and woke up from a deep slumber, practically drooling on the shoulder of the woman next to me, as we were descending into London.

YOU TURN #8:

DISCOVER HOW TO
craft the perfect elevator pitch

One of the biggest mistakes job seekers make is in overlooking the obvious: how to talk about themselves and their resume. We get so scared that interviewers will ask us crazy questions (which they may) that we tend to forget the basics: How do you talk about yourself? How do you channel your strengths into a page-long resume that shows your power? How do you walk the recruiter through your resume?

This chapter is about a few key concepts: mustering courage in moments when you could choose to let life pass you by, knowing when you're being invited into an elevator pitch, and being intentional about creating an elevator pitch. The prompt could sound like:

> Tell me about yourself.
> What got you interested in [subject]?
> Why did you apply for this role?
> Who the heck are you?

You get what I mean.

Also know that this formula is meant for longer conversations, which could look like a coffee meeting, a nice conversation at a networking event, or a job interview. It's not meant for someone who is a drive-by hello, who isn't showing interest in you. Your elevator pitch is meant to live in conversations, not in emails.

What are some other ways to have a powerful networking conversation, where you're likely using your elevator pitch? One thing I love telling clients in my Job Offer Academy course is to ask a couple of key questions when it comes to informational coffees and networking conversations:

1. Do you have any suggestions for how I can stand out as a candidate? This question tends to inspire people to offer to pass your resume around, because, let's face it: that is how you stand out as a damn candidate. This question isn't geared for job interviews, obviously.
2. Do you have any suggestions of companies I should look into that are perhaps not on my radar?
   This question tends to inspire people to connect you to their friends at other companies. This question is also not meant for job interviews, obviously.

USE THIS NOW

1. What is your CORE SKILL SET you're carrying into the workforce?
2. What is a *story* from your upbringing that demonstrates you using that skill?
3. Start your *story* statement with "I grew up in a house where," or "I was always the kid that" in the space provided after step 7. Don't exceed one to two lines for your *story*.
4. Are you interested in jobs that align with your past experience or are you making a pivot?
   a. If you're aligned, then come up with a humblebrag for your *cuff* statement, one that is relevant for the job.
   b. If you think your interviewer has an objection or concern over your application (e.g., a career pivot or resume gap), write your *cuff* statement explaining yourself in the space provided after step 7.
5. What is the one *skill* your next job really would want to hear that you have (i.e., their biggest need and pain point)? Write down if there's been a time where you've been complimented for it! The

ideal compliment would come from your boss, but if not, then your colleagues would be the next ideal people in ranking order.

6. What is your *goal* statement?

    a. If you're networking, the statement should relate to what you're transitioning into (i.e., "At the moment, I'm looking into communications or marketing, ideally for a fashion brand," or "I'm here in hopes of meeting more people who [state the ideal contact you're seeking]").

    b. If you're in a job interview, the goal is to get the job, so the statement should be why you want to work for them specifically (e.g., "I'm excited about this position in particular because [insert authentic flattery about their mission statement, their corporate values, or whatever moves you]").

7. Study and practice your elevator pitch until you're blue in the face. Know it so well that it's in your cells, and it flows or shifts a bit every time you say it. Write it in full here:

_____

_____

_____

_____

CONCLUSION

Deciding to put myself out there as a way of life is what changed my path the most—moments like the one when I mustered the courage to say hi to the colonel, or when I mustered the courage to say "yes" to dinner with his friends. It's key to recognize when you're being invited into an elevator pitch. It's also key to tap into a moving, quick story about your life that inspires someone to listen to you. Needless to say, mentors are everything. The colonel became a mentor to me, and he helped me in ways beyond my imagination.

Chapter Nine

Have High Intentions and Low Attachment

AUGUST 2, 2010

My dorm room window was cracked open all night. Rain was cascading down from the sky, and the thick air smelled of asphalt and freshly cut grass. I glanced down at my phone and noticed it was 9:07 AM. *Time to get to the airport*, I thought as I jumped out of bed. I threw on a green chunky sweater, and heard my three closest friends—Tricia, Elodie, and Barry—knocking on my dorm room door, all there to help me carry my bags to the tube. As we gossiped about nothing in particular, we moseyed down the wet streets of London. Grad school was over. I could only pay so much attention to our conversation, as I felt uncomfortable feelings attacking me from all sides. I knew it was time to move on, but part of me, the part that yearned for comfort or predictability, wanted to stay in school forever. Do you ever just yearn to go back to college and learn?

GRADUATE DEGREES: A SOCIALLY ACCEPTABLE WAY TO HIDE FROM THE WORLD

It was almost as though I was living in purgatory: reveling in the excitement and fear for the new, alongside my unfinished grief and yearning for the old. While one of my saving graces in life has been my willingness to accept when it's time to move on, this truth was hard to swallow: it was time for adulthood. Paying my own bills. Showing up for work. Reporting to someone. I reflected upon my time in grad school and felt a truth bubbling up inside me. I had used this degree to hide from the world. In fact, it was a socially acceptable, respectable way for me to hide.

But now, real life was coming at me anyway. Unfortunately, when you consider that only 27 percent of graduates get a job related to their degree, it's obvious most people aren't crystal clear about how they plan to use their graduate degree to advance their career.[1] On top of this, getting a master's degree (if it's not well thought-out) can actually hurt your career, as it makes you appear "overqualified" when you reenter the workforce and seek jobs that don't require it. It can make you appear "all over the place" when you apply for jobs that are not exactly related to the focus of your graduate degree. Look, I'm all about getting educated, but in some cases, those who hold a master's degree report a 6 percent pay decrease, compared to someone with a bachelor's degree.[2]

When graduate school is well thought-out, it's intentional and necessary for one's next career step. When it's not, I find it can be damaging, both financially and due to the opportunity cost that comes with leaving the workforce. Have you ever thought about getting a graduate degree? If so, do you have clarity on where you're headed and evidence that it's absolutely necessary? Perhaps you can easily afford to study a topic you love for no other reason but the joy of it. If that's you, party on. But if you're like most of us, your graduate degree is an expensive distraction, and an exit from a world you'll eventually have to face. If you haven't given your degree enough thought, you'll be behind, with a heap of debt and years lost in the workforce, ones where you could have been growing in your job.

Your results in life aren't really about what you "attract," but rather what you are willing to put up with, and the energy you bring with you. I must ask you . . . What are you "putting up with" in your career right now? I walked into London's Heathrow Airport, and waited in line for my chai latte with more thoughts brewing in my mind than there were airport baristas brewing coffee. As my thoughts slowed down, I made a decision: I chose to be excited about my career. My life. The possibilities. Who I was becoming. All of it. I realized what had gotten me down, what robbed my excitement for this next phase, was the fear that my basic degree from a mediocre college or my average grades would mean I would never really amount to anything great. In a way, greatness felt like it was reserved for *other people*, not me. That thought scared me, and oddly, motivated me.

FEAR IS THE ULTIMATE TIME-SUCK

I saw those feelings for what they were: fear. Fear that if I let myself be so vulnerable as to believe life could happen for me, I'd be let down by failures. Fear that I'd make a fool of myself if I really wanted something that was "too good" or "too much" for little old me. They'll tell you, "Don't hold your breath," or that they're "waiting for the other shoe to drop," but you know what? Hope and vulnerability are for the bold. What's your relationship to hope? Do you get afraid something will be ripped away from you, or do you courageously choose to believe that life is working in your favor?

I told myself in that moment: *I'm made of the same damn stuff everyone else is.* My body came with batteries fucking included: the same beating heart, brain cells, and vision that everyone else came in with. So what was with my excuses and my smallness? I decided I would no longer spray fear on my dreams, like an unwelcome residue that robbed me of the life I hoped I could have. Fear made that life seem far away.

I thought about how much time I lost in my life because of fear: the hour-long conversations I'd logged on the phone with friends, the weeks I'd spent creeping on LinkedIn profiles, wondering if I could ever be as interesting as the other person I saw, all of it. How much time have you given up in your life because of fear? I wondered what I'd do with all that extra time back, and realized that this time could be all mine if I stopped buying into fear. I decided that all the mistakes, all the discomfort, and all the failure would be worth it for me, because if I didn't grow a pair of lady balls, I would never get to run my own life; life would run me. I recognized how a lot of the time we feel an energy running through us, one we may decide to call fear. But what if I started to name this crazy energy *excitement*? Think about it—the sensations associated with fear and excitement are really similar: fast heart rate, nerves, energy shifts. As children, we associate all of this with excitement, and then somewhere along the way the label of this emotion shifts to fear. So what if I changed the way I related to that feeling? Was I being delusional or inspired?

I hopped onto the airport Wi-Fi and combed through job postings in Los Angeles. Big surprise: there was nothing in counterterrorism. I slept through the flight and cried when the plane landed. The voice piped into my head: *Party's over, Ash. Time to make minimum wage and duke it out with the recession.* As I went through customs, text messages came in from my dad:

WELCOME HOME WE ARE READY OUTSIDE LOVE YOU
XO DAD . . .

Haha, I can always count on Dad for an entertaining caps-lock text message string. I smiled when I saw him standing in the airport with one of the biggest handwritten signs I'd ever seen, which said "Welcome home, Ashley!" He smiled so big he looked like he'd won the lottery. Man, dads; they just win your heart, don't they?

I slept like a rock and woke up at 6 AM, ready to take on the world. In fact, despite feeling "ordinary," I thought I did everything right to prepare myself for my career: I got the degrees, I learned the foreign languages, and I did the internships . . . You name it. What about you?

Did you work hard to prepare yourself for your career? If you didn't, there is no shame. Know that it's never too late to own it.

HIGH INTENTION, LOW ATTACHMENT

Over the next four hours, I applied for twenty-eight jobs with almost no break. My energy was fueled by possibility as I started to fantasize about myself in different jobs I was applying for. I didn't know it at the time, but as a career coach, I can now tell you that this sort of fantasizing is a form of expectation and job-hunting suicide. Here's my job-hunt mantra, which I got from my time as a student at the University of Santa Monica: *high intention, low attachment*. Look, there's nothing wrong with taking a moment to visualize yourself in a particular job, but that's all you should ever allow yourself: a brief moment of fantasy. Otherwise, be intentional. Put yourself into it; be open to everything but attached to nothing. Why? Because indulging in that makes you attached to something you're not even sure is real. Do you get stuck fantasizing about the life you'd have in a certain job? That, my friend, is an energy suck! Plus, if you have that much time to be attached to a fantasy of a particular job, you're not applying for enough opportunities, truly. To me, a good job hunt means putting yourself out there for so many opportunities that, when you hear back, you *almost* don't even remember the opportunity itself. Remember, life is a numbers game.

Thanks to my jet lag from Europe, I woke up early on the second day and raced to my laptop to check emails. *All this before coffee?* I was obsessed with immediately hearing back from the companies I was targeting. Tapping on the in-box, I was crushed: no emails, unless you counted the one from my local coffee shop offering a sale on their holiday travel mugs. For about two weeks, I slept on my parents' couch and kept the fantasy of what was possible alive—until I couldn't bear the crickets anymore. Have you ever gotten stuck applying for jobs and wondering if anyone ever even sees your application? I see you, my friend, and it is the worst. I felt powerless over my future and wondered if this would become my new normal. I thought about all the friends who landed job offers while I was away in grad school, and how they seemed to be happy with what they were doing, and more importantly, where they were going in their lives. If there's anything I've learned working in personal development all these years, it's that what creates happiness more than anything else is progress. It hurt to feel like I had none, and it felt as though everyone else was passing me by.

"I just have to take what I can get . . . I just need to . . . get my foot in the door. After all, something is better than nothing . . . Maybe it's time I start networking with family and friends," I told my oldest friend, Kiera, over a coffee. I was buying into some of the worst job-hunting myths I'd eventually uncover.

SABOTAGING JOB-HUNTING MYTHS

MYTH #1: THE "TAKE WHAT YOU CAN GET" APPROACH

Trust that job opportunities are everywhere . . . because they are. It's just a numbers game and you've got to play it. Even in the midst of the COVID-19 quarantine, clients would tell me maybe they should "stand down" in their job hunt, but know this: companies were hiring. Plus, the best jobs don't always go to the best candidates; they go to the best job seekers. That means the people who have job-hunting skills will almost always trump the Ivy League resume.

MYTH #2: THE "FOOT-IN-THE-DOOR" APPROACH

Have you ever taken a job, thinking it'll help you get your foot in the door, a foot toward a better, different job? I hate to break it to you, but when you take a job simply to get your foot in the door, you're not priming yourself for the job you actually want, you're pigeonholing yourself in the job you don't want. Remember: the years you spend in that job you took to "get your foot in the door" are years you're potentially investing in a skill set that neither you nor your employer will want to see you have, if you're trying to go somewhere else. At the bare minimum, take a job related to the one you want if you are trying to "get your foot in the door." Taking a job in hopes you'll get a different job out of it is like wishing a salad was a donut. Story of my life, and I promise it won't work.

After all, rarely does someone want to turn their personal assistant into a marketing manager. They want their personal assistant to be . . . drumroll, please . . . *their personal assistant.* Taking a job to get your foot in the door is a quick way to get stuck, and believe me when I tell you that while you have your head down working hard for some job you don't want, your company, at some point, will be hiring for the job you actually want. And they may like you and love your energy, but they will tend to see you as "the assistant" or whatever job you took in hopes you could move elsewhere within the company. If you take a job, take it within the channel you want to work in. If you want to work in marketing, make sure it's on the marketing team. If you want to work in communications, make sure you jump onto a communications team. As I'm writing this, I bet it sounds like common sense to you . . . *and that's because it is.*

Myth #3: The "Networking with Family and Friends" Approach

Another mistake I made during this time was in putting too much stock in the connections of family and friends when it came to networking. I mean, you tell me, when's the last time your friend's dad was hiring for the exact job you really wanted? One that harnesses your CORE NATURE, your CORE SKILL SET, and your CORE VALUES? Probably never. That's because good networking is usually cold networking. It might sound overwhelming, but even cold contacts can become warm contacts if you know how to have conversations and work on your elevator pitch. When you're clear on what you want, and intentional in who you reach out to, magic happens for your job hunt. So stop networking with Becky from high school's mom (even if she's really sweet), and get more targeted in your conversations. I also reiterate that you never know who you're talking to, as I learned the night Benny the cabdriver rocked my world. He ended up hooking me up with a meeting in the White House, by the way.

Myth #4: The "Something Is Always Better Than Nothing" Approach

I've learned that "finding the one," in both love and work, isn't about finding the "right" one. It's about saying "no" to the wrong one. That means there's an opportunity cost to taking a job you don't want to be in. It saps your time from hunting for the job you actually want. And one thing I teach my students in the Job Offer Academy is that you can easily make a full-time job out of applying for jobs. The payoff? Those who focus on my Job Offer Academy Formula usually get multiple offers in just weeks. It's not to say you can't have a beautiful slow burn with your job hunt, but it is to say that the universe will reward your hard work and focus. I know what you may be thinking: *I can't afford to be without a job. I need to make money and I need to make it right now*. Trust me, I've been there, and I get it. Nobody says you can't take a part-time job to cover your expenses while you job-hunt. Too bad I didn't realize this when I was job-hunting at that time, but then again, everything happens for a reason, doesn't it?

At the start of my fourth month job-hunting, an email came through with a subject line that read INTERVIEW OPPORTUNITY. It was to be an administrative assistant at an ad agency, and although I'd never thought about working in advertising, I was excited about the possibility of having somewhere to go every morning—and stuck in that damaging mindset that "something was better than nothing." I replied immediately with my availability and was stunned when they offered me the job on the spot the next day when they had me come in. Who knew I'd be so excited to hardly make minimum wage? I didn't feel worthy of much more.

THE SECRET OF SUCCESSFUL PEOPLE

In fact, I thought I was painfully average. I felt like perhaps my job would validate me or make me feel worthy in the workforce, and I realized later the key would have been to come to the job-hunt table with more worthiness and less desperation. Easier said than done? Yes. But here's the thing I've learned about the world: everyone has a gift. It sounds cheesy—and it is. But it's also true. The difference in someone who is out there, happy, and living their purpose is that they decided not to accept the status quo. They believed it was possible to do something that inspired them and they weren't willing to just "push through" in hopes that happiness would come find them. They also were willing to explore the possibility that they had a gift, that there was something they could do well. They committed to finding out what that gift was, which often looked like declining opportunities that were really a distraction or job-hunting when they knew where they were wasn't working for them. I was certainly not in a headspace where I thought this sort of fulfillment was available for me at that time.

Pulling into the Playa Vista offices for my interview, I have to admit I was immediately impressed. Creative offices and companies have a way of making a great first impression. Does the feel of a building draw you in, too? The truth of the matter is that while some sleek interior design may help your mood, nothing matters more at work (for your long-term career growth) than taking a job that grows your CORE SKILL SET. The outside of the building was colorful, and the lineup of luxury cars out front said that this place was on the move. There was a food court in the middle, indoor trees, a basketball court (yes, really), and beautiful people all milling about with their own sense of purpose.

The next day, the trap was set . . . I began a career in advertising. Walking through the front doors, I took note of the people who held the power in the industry: the creatives, which is what the executives are called at an ad agency. I felt somewhat like a toucan lost in the Arctic, struggling to find sunlight. After studying counterterrorism and learning three different languages, I was disappointed to realize that none of that mattered here. Have you ever worked hard toward a skill that you don't feel is needed in your job? It feels like a loss, doesn't it? In the world of advertising, ideas were king. Not foreign languages. Not top graduate degrees. Creativity won. There was something about this that felt freeing, and intimidating.

The first day of a new job can feel much like the first day of school— uncomfortable. Everyone I met welcomed me with open arms. This made me feel good about my decision, because I had accomplished exactly what I had set out to do—take the first thing that came my way. In other words, I was miserable and I didn't even know it yet.

"Good morning. I'm Donna—lead assistant. I'll be checking in with you, showing you the ropes. You know, making sure you have what it takes to stay, because if you don't, well . . . You know the drill, right?" A moment of silence hung between us as she stared right at me, before smiling and handing me a folder. The president of the company, her boss, walked past us, and I excitedly asked, "Can you introduce me to her?"

Donna looked at me in dismay.

"Absolutely not." She continued, "You're an assistant in a sea of employees here. You're not a creative. My job is to protect her time, and I don't want you to grab at it." I tried to hide my embarrassment, while simultaneously feeling a bit of compassion for Donna's tightness and anxiety. The warm and fuzzy feeling of being part of a team evaporated the minute I met her.

"Here's your list for today's assignments. I'll circle back after lunch, and see how you're coming along."

I grabbed the list with excitement as she walked me to my new desk. I stared at all the supplies on the desk and felt like my cubicle was a sacred safe zone for me. In that moment, it felt like a gateway into adult-hood; I didn't realize that later it'd feel like a prison. I read the list she handed me as she walked away:

> Count all the highlighters and colored pencils in the supply room.
> File travel receipts in order of date, create and print off an expense spreadsheet.
> Edit a PowerPoint deck for the 10:30 am sales meeting tomorrow.
> Pick up coffee for all the creatives' 4 pm meeting.

It was in this moment that I realized the pain of being in a job role that exists solely to pick up the scraps that don't fit on someone else's plate. I existed as an extension of someone else, and there was no space for me to breathe my own creativity or brainpower into anything. Have you ever felt that way, like there's no space for you to contribute what you're actually made of at work? What was worse was that my job felt so useless to the company, almost like the world wouldn't be any different if I didn't show up to work the next day.

THE ROOT OF CORPORATE EMPTINESS

I felt a sense of meaninglessness I'd never felt before. I didn't know yet that I'd eventually move to DC, or become an entrepreneur, and the blankness of what was ahead terrified me. Leaning back into my chair, I thought about how Karl Marx argued the Industrial Revolution was the beginning of the end, because the world shifted from the artist experiencing the gratification that comes with making a full chair, into factories doing it with an assembly line, meaning workers would now just focus on one piece of said chair, such as the leg.[3] For me, I wasn't even responsible for making a leg . . . I was getting coffee for the person who worked for the person who made the leg. My job felt meaningless. I felt meaningless. I started to wonder: If I weren't here, where would I go? It was one thing to hate my job—that I could handle—but what I couldn't handle was the pain and hopelessness of not knowing where to go next.

THE THREE TYPES OF PEOPLE

I've noticed that there are three types of people in the world as it relates to making a change. First, there are the *change-makers*; when they feel the start of their misery as they notice they are lukewarm about something, their lukewarm feelings inspire them to make a change. Secondly, there are the *sleepwalkers*; they're the ones who aren't tuned in to the whispers of their pain, only to wake up out of nowhere feeling miserable, overwhelmed, and urgently in need of a change. Third, there are the *deniers*, the ones who know their pain is there, yet don't feel strong or deserving enough to actually look at it and make a change. That third one was me, and my transition into adulthood looked like learning to love myself so much that I'd choose to become a change-maker, in time. Which type are you? How do you relate to pain and making changes in your life? Do you take action quickly (change-maker)? Do you fail to notice it at all (sleepwalker)? Or do you try not to see it (denier)?

PAY ATTENTION TO WHAT FEELS
GOOD (IN YOUR BODY)

On that first day, I recognized that my freedom hinged on me investing in my future self, by doing something that inspired me and contributed to the person I would eventually become. When all else fails and you're not sure where to go next, it is important to follow what feels good in your soul. Have you ever thought about what inspires you, or more importantly, *who* inspires you? Are you inspired to be around creative people? Are you an inspired part of an effective team? According to Stanford University, 60 percent of your best ideas come when you're not at work.[4] They come when you are in your element, or doing a bunch of nothing. For me, my element meant writing, being in a class-room, working on a project, and yes, going to a hip-hop dance class no matter how tired I was. That was me.

The question now becomes—how do you connect to yourself to even *feel* what *feels* good? In a world of internet trolls, texts, and tweets, the data is officially in: we have become so connected that we have somehow become disconnected. We've heard it all before: "Do what you love and the money will follow," or my least favorite from the self-help movement, "Follow your passion." These expressions are often a fast track to nowhere. But when you actually learn to connect to your body and tune in to what feels good, you have the ability to change your life. When you do what feels good in your body, your purpose is often either right in front of you or residing somewhere on its periphery.

For me, later choosing to move across the country to work in coun-terterrorism felt right. In the process of that, on the periphery, I became an incredible job seeker, which in turn inspired me to help others find their purpose in the form of their ideal job. Then, on the periphery of even that, I stepped into one of my biggest dreams of all—writing this book. In a world of "five-year plans," unnecessary degrees, and climb-ing the corporate ladder, we are collectively striving for an unrealistic goal: perfection. But who you are at twenty-five isn't who you will be when you are thirty-five or even forty-five. This is why it's important to see your career as an experiment that meets you where you are right *now*. This means writing down all of your ideas for where you could go in your career, and paying attention to how your body feels when you think of each one: Do you feel expansion, or contraction? Joy or fear?

Excitement or dread? Suffocation or liberation? Dig deep and listen to the messages of your body and soul.

START A JOY JOURNAL

Have you ever taken the time to notice what lights you up every day? Probably not, huh? That's why one of the most powerful tools I have ever discovered in my career journey was my old therapist Alyssa's recommendation to start a joy journal. When you're feeling disconnected, frustrated, or alone, commit to thirty days of writing down the moment that lit you up the most each day. It doesn't matter if it was a conversation you had in line for the bathroom or that meeting you led at work . . . This exercise is about the joy that you experience while moving about your day. Recognize those moments. Write them down. Then, at the end of the thirty days, search for patterns in your inspiration. Ask yourself: What CORE SKILL SET am I using when I'm most inspired? This is setting yourself up for more joy, more happiness, and, most of all, using the gifts you were born to use. At the end of the day, when you feel connected, you are residing in the truth of who you are.

Since work wasn't a place where I felt my true self, I committed to doing whatever I could to feel more "me" outside of work. My hope was that my inspiration outside of work would leak into my energy throughout the day (which does tend to work!). I signed up for a beginner Arabic class at UCLA. The move felt good, but I wanted more. So I started following hip-hop dance influencers online and, with my headphones on, I would dance to their YouTube videos as a workout. I know it's hard to find inspiration from 5 PM onward if you feel miserable from nine to five. But, believe me, that inspiration is your salvation. It'll give you answers . . . and momentum. According to *Review of General Psychology*, one initial success sparks a higher intensity, frequency, and duration for future successes. Success breeds more success, and psychological motivation.[5] Think of it as a domino effect; a small win of inspiration in hip-hop dance led me to feel more inspired and motivated not only there, but also in other areas of life. As Newton's first law of motion suggests, an object at rest stays at rest, but an object in motion stays in motion. So get moving. Motivation and action-taking are a positive feedback loop.

This exercise started to work. I began to feel like my old self again. And perhaps we can just call it an act of ease and grace, or letting go, that an elegant idea came through me as if it were a channel from the career gods: *I should email my college and ask for a list of alumni who graduated and moved to Washington, DC.* Maybe they would have such a thing. After all, everyone in DC was working in something government-related, and that list could prove to be a gold mine. At this point, I was more scared of what my life would look like if I stayed stuck as an assistant making minimum wage at an ad agency than I was of making awkward phone calls to successful people in DC.

KNOCK ON HUNDREDS OF DOORS, AND YOU'LL ALWAYS GET A "YES"

An hour after asking my university for an alumni list, I got an email back with an attachment of two thousand names and emails of alumni who were living in the district. In between work, taking intensive Arabic at night, and dancing to the hip-hop videos, I made the decision to call every single one, no matter how long it took to work through the list. So there I was, stepping outside for lunch, investing in my future self, making these phone calls. I'll never forget my favorite one:

ME: "Hi! I'm Ashley, I went to University of Redlands and found you on the alumni list. I'm job-hunting in DC and would love for you to pass my resume around."

ALUMNUS: "Fuck you."

I had to laugh as I heard the line go dead on the other end. I guess the guy was having a bad day and wasn't into helping a fellow graduate. And while the call didn't go as I had hoped, it taught me a very important lesson: when you're networking, don't tell people you're job-hunting;

tell them you're "looking to transition." Saying you're job-hunting can feel to someone like you're asking (or about to ask) for a favor. And definitely don't ask them to pass your resume around. Instead, ask them if they have any suggestions for you to stand out as a candidate at x, y, or z company. Usually, they'll offer to pass your resume around if they're nice, because they know that is the best way to stand out as an introduction.

I was able to get anywhere from five to twenty phone calls done every time I took lunch, and eventually couldn't help but notice how we live in a world where people feel violated when you call them out of nowhere. That inspired me to start emailing, and that got me excited because I knew I could just send a lot of emails. But the secret, I learned? Personalize every single one. I wish I had easier advice for you to implement, but this is the approach that works.

OPPORTUNITY IS EVERYWHERE WHEN YOU SEEK IT

Over the next week, I managed to send more than eight hundred personalized emails and heard back from eighty of them. That 10 percent response rate is a perfect illustration of how job hunting is seriously a numbers game. I started scheduling calls and learning for the first time how to talk to recruiters and hiring managers. Most of all, it gave me the courage I needed to believe that there was more out there for me. Courage to take risks. Courage to ask for help. Courage to fail. The best part about all this was realizing how full of opportunity the world is. I started to see opportunities as if they were the air I breathed, all around me, and my job was simply to grab on to them as they floated by, versus hoping they'd somehow land in my lap.

Knowing that most of the alumni contacts were living on the East Coast (three hours ahead of California's time zone), I scheduled my calls for when people were more likely to answer their phones—any time before their workday was over. I even started calling at 8 AM Pacific, before I went into work, hoping that some people in DC would be on their lunch break, available for my cold call. The process was riddled with rejection, but the wins were so worth it. They gave me so much confidence to keep going, and to this day, I have kept some of the friends I made during that time. All this was the result of one elegant idea that flew in when I started doing things that make me feel more myself, and more in my CORE NATURE: asking for this list of alumni. Far too often, we search for one opportunity after another, without realizing that perhaps there is one place we can go that holds multiple opportunities. That alumni list with two thousand names was just that: many opportunities I tapped into through one email.

A couple of weeks later, after calling every number on the list and sending a note to every email address, I couldn't help but notice how often people in DC offered to help me. I once thought I didn't have much to offer people, that because I was just a regular administrative assistant in a sea of others struggling and making minimum wage, there'd be nothing in it for them. I learned in this time of my life that people are innately kind and generous. I also found that people knew in their cells that I was someone on the move. That's the secret right there, to be someone who is on the move. Everyone is seeking that energy of aliveness and career inspiration. Make the pursuit of something that lights you up nonnegotiable, because, wow, people feel it when you're on the rise, and they want to be a part of your journey.

FOLLOW THE NUDGE, AGAINST ALL REASON

That inspired me to take one of the biggest risks I've ever taken in my career: quit my job and move across the country without any money.

"Dad," I said, "I'm moving to DC and joining the CIA. I'm going to use my degree from King's College London and work in counterterrorism."

My father nearly choked on his fried chicken right there at the dinner table. "You're what?" he asked, clearing his throat with the help of his napkin.

Sometimes in life, we have these moments where, against all reason and rational thinking, our soul asks us to take action on something. I've found that my relationship with that internal "nudge" has only deepened over the years. In fact, when someone feels disconnected, it's this little voice or nudge that I believe they struggle to hear. Because of fear. Because of limiting beliefs. Because they've listened to everyone else. My relationship with this voice (or nudge) has given me the innate ability to trust my intuition without questioning it. But then again, it's easier said than done when you are sitting with your parents at the dinner table.

My mom quickly chimed in with a look of terror on her face: "Absolutely not. You're not moving to the East Coast."

I looked at her, filled with confidence and more in touch with my freedom than I had ever been. "Mom, I am going whether you support my decision or not."

I leaned in, looked both of them right in the eye, and finished with, "Guys, I have to do this. I know it sounds crazy, but it's what I have to do. I'm sorry if you don't like it, but I'm giving two weeks' notice at work tomorrow. I would love your support if you want to give it."

My mom cried. My dad smiled. People often tell me I'm a mini version of him, and he loved adventures way too much to stop me from embarking on my own.

Every single day, we make an average of 35,000 decisions. That's a total of 1.02 billion decisions over a life span of eighty years. Isn't the brain incredible? The funny thing about this is that there are only a select few decisions we make in our lifetimes, perhaps ten to fifteen, that drastically impact the course of our lives.[6] According to the research, the top life-altering decisions include choosing your life partner, career path, and whether to have children. What's profound about this is that most of those happen by age twenty-eight.[7]

This moment, this decision, was one of those moments for me. It is these moments that I look back upon fondly, ones when I let a big decision be easy for me, ones when I let my career be an experiment. Do you let big decisions come with a big struggle? What is keeping you from letting them be easy? Tune in to your body and you'll notice that a *yes* or *no* is already there, waiting in your nervous system for you to recognize it. I often used to make my fears mean I shouldn't do something, but I've learned to practice courage. As a coach named Dan Sullivan once said to me: *Fear is wetting your pants. Courage is doing what you were supposed to do . . . with wet pants.*

YOU'RE IN CHARGE OF YOUR CAREER

The next day, I walked into work to quit the world of advertising for good. Donna came over to me with her usual list of menial tasks, and I let her know I needed to talk to her for a moment.

"Donna, I'm so sorry to ask for your time right now, but I, um . . . I want to give you my two weeks' notice."

She looked at me with disgust.

"Do you know what you're doing? This is the top advertising agency in the world. You're just going to up and go?"

I felt shame wash over my heart. Shame for having dreams, or for thinking I was able to achieve something bigger. Against reason, I chose to go with it anyway. Some little part of me, that wise voice inside that we all have access to, knew I was gifted in some way. It knew something bigger was out there for me. I didn't know if I'd find "it" in DC, but I knew I needed to commit to uncovering it, and this would be my first step in the experiment to do so. Plus, my discomfort with moving to DC would never match the discomfort I felt operating on eggshells with Donna.

The president of the company walked over to us midconversation, and looked at me like I was a foreigner, even after eight months at the company.

"Hi," she said with a professional disposition. "What's your name?"

"I'm, um, Ashley. Ashley is my name. I'm glad to meet you. I've always wanted to say hello."

"Well, why didn't you?" she asked me, confused. Donna's anxiety infused the air, and she kicked my foot under the table. Her boss looked at her . . . *caught*.

"Did you just kick her?" she asked.

I interrupted, "I didn't want to waste your time saying hello. I know you're busy. And now I just am giving Donna my two weeks' notice, unfortunately."

"Ah, you should have said hi. I love meeting our young talent. Sorry to hear you're leaving. Where are you headed?"

She smiled curiously as I told her about how I'd studied counterterrorism for the past six years, got a master's degree from a top school, and had been learning Arabic in UCLA's night classes.

"Why did we have you as an assistant? Sounds like you have a lot going on in your brain, and I bet our creative teams would have loved to use it . . . Let me know if you ever want to come back."

Donna steeped in a painful silence as her boss walked away, and it was then that I realized the truth of the matter: no one is in charge of my career but me. No one ever gets to stop me again from being worthy of saying hello. No one is in charge of my happiness but me. And happiness, like clarity, comes from finding out and owning who you are, which starts with your willingness to explore and experiment with your career. Gone were the days of me even thinking about waiting for my career to happen to me, waiting for that annual review where I hope to be noticed, waiting to say hello to that person who may be able to help me—of waiting for life to happen. *Here are the days*, I decided, *where I choose what happens, and where I decide on my career.* Since then, I've had no problem walking up to just about anyone and saying hello. And believe me when I tell you, that simple word, *hello*, opens the door for so much magic.

Part of this means really letting the past be the past. While a part of me wanted to grab on to the president's words, I knew I didn't want to be there in that ad agency. That part of me was my inner safety mechanism, the part of me that we all have that just focuses on our survival in the world. But I didn't just want to survive anymore—I wanted to thrive. I knew that meant really letting go of this path, and not holding on to one ounce of it. Life won't work its magic unless you make space for it. I knew I had to move and create a blank slate so I could make more art out of my career and life.

BIG THINGS COME IN SMALL EMAILS

Two weeks later, I landed in DC, where I rented a room in a row house that was painted red, white, and blue. Does it get more DC than that? It was right by the row house that I lived in for that month before grad school, on Constitution Avenue, and being back in DC after that quick monthlong class when I met the colonel just a year and a half ago made me nostalgic. While I didn't have a job, I was ready to network until I got the job I was meant to have, not a job just to have a job.

I loved being in pursuit of something great and never thought this entire situation would become the basis of launching a career as a podcaster, speaker, career expert, author, and creator of the top-selling job-hunting course on the internet. Who knew that my job hunt to DC would turn into a job-hunting business? When you follow what feels good, your purpose is either right in front of you or on the periphery.

My adventure began with three coffee meetings lined up for the day after I arrived in town. Might seem like a lot of meetings in one day, but after blasting eight hundred emails, I had now amassed at least a hundred invitations for meetings. I went to bed early so that I could wake up and find my way to Georgetown. In fact, I was so excited, I woke up at 5 AM to get ready for my 9 AM meeting. Needless to say, my hair was blown out like nobody's business by 9 AM, and I trotted past the White House ready to make my dreams happen.

SUCCESS IS ABOUT BEING WILLING
TO DO WHAT OTHERS AREN'T

Over the course of six weeks, my eighty meetings turned into two hundred meetings in fourteen coffee shops around the district, thanks to all the kind people who connected me to friends they thought could help me. I was officially the most caffeinated broad in town, having coffee with every Tom, Dick, or Harry in DC, with the thought that no person was too senior or too junior in their career for me to meet with them. I decided to become the exception, not the rule, and to trust that there is always room for me in the world. There's always room for you, too, friend. There's room for greatness and it doesn't have to look like a top university degree, or a fancy job.

In fact, success is just about being willing to do what other people aren't . . . and most people aren't willing to be uncomfortable. But when you're just interested or dabbling in life, you'll keep doing what's convenient for you. It's when you make a decision to be committed that the magic happens, because then you'll do whatever it takes. Greatness looks like having a white-hot desire and running after it. I've found there's a certain level of healthy pain that's needed for fulfillment in life. Otherwise, you're just in your comfort zone, and nothing magical or new really grows there.

WHO YOU ARE ON MONDAY DOESN'T
HAVE TO BE WHO YOU ARE ON FRIDAY

Over those six weeks, I landed three job offers, each of which came in at nearly six figures. It was in this moment I truly realized that success for me isn't going to happen by hoping my managers pay me "what I'm worth," but rather it will happen when I choose to love myself enough to create options. That means deciding I'm worthy of them, despite whatever's happened in the past. I didn't have to come to DC as that admin assistant I was in LA. I could leave her behind, or better yet, I could choose the parts of her I wanted to take with me, and step into who I wanted to be. And who I would become was that new supervisor making nearly six figures running that program I told you about for the Pentagon.

The CEO of the contracting firm looked at me with skepticism and warned, "This job, while it's management level, needs someone who is excited and energetic . . . ready to do *everything*, versus delegate everything. Do you have the energy for that? It's a lot of responsibility, too, you know . . . You'd be managing an eighty-million-dollar contract."

I looked at him like a dog ready to play fetch, as one does when their dreams are on the horizon. *Game on*, I thought, as I spoke to him: "Sir, I will not let you down."

YOU TURN #9:
stop applying for jobs, and start networking

This journey to DC taught me everything I know about job hunting and, most of all, that networking is my golden ticket in life. It's not just something that happens at networking events or conferences; it's what you do in coffee shops, the grocery store, or even on airplanes. In fact, early into my career-coaching practice, I'll never forget landing three new clients while standing in the bathroom line at a diner. Networking means that your mind and your heart are always open to having a conversation. If you are willing to see it as a daily way of life, if you wake up every morning open to having your next conversation, your career will soar. So for those of you who tell me you don't have any contacts . . . My answer is to go make some. Take a walk, hit the grocery store, stand in a bathroom line somewhere. Decide to have a conversation.

USE THIS NOW

Without realizing it, when I moved to DC, I came up with the job-hunting methodology that eventually became the foundation of my Job Offer Academy course.

STEP #1: GO NUTS ON LINKEDIN

If you want to intentionally land a job you want, versus your friend Becky's mom haphazardly handing one to you, come up with three or four keywords: two that align with your CORE SKILL SET (*e.g., communications, writing,* or *speaking,* to name a few in my case!) as well as two that align with the industry or your CORE INTEREST (*e.g., travel, politics,* or *fashion*—in my case!).

Get on LinkedIn's advanced search, and always put two words into the keywords section, or three at most. One word or phrase should always be skill-related (like "financial modeling" or, in my case, "communications") and the other word or phrase should always be interest-related (like "fashion"). Don't pick more than one interest so you can ensure that your search goes deep and is focused.

Start to dig into the profiles that come up and pay attention to who inspires you. *Notice what you notice* about people, and start forming a list of companies or jobs that capture your attention. This is one of my favorite types of career-coaching sessions I tend to do with private clients as a way to clarify their best career options: looking at the profiles they find interesting and asking pointed questions about why.

STEP #2: MAKE A TARGETED COMPANY LIST

After you've nearly hit your search limit and you're starting to feel like a creepy LinkedIn troll, it's time to start making a list of companies you'd love to work for, up to one hundred different ones that ideally align with your CORE NATURE and CORE VALUES. You should have gotten plenty of inspiration from looking at other professionals.

Step #3: Decide Where Your CORE SKILL SET Belongs

Research each company on your list, and clarify which team you'd ideally like to join in the company. This means getting out of the "take what I can get" mentality, or the "something is better than nothing" mindset, and aligning their job title options with your primary CORE SKILL SET.

Step #4: Select Two Key Points of Contact Within Each Company

Once you're clear on what team matches your skill set, get back on LinkedIn to use the advanced search function. In the advanced search, you'll put:

> Each of your one hundred companies **into the "company" section,** one by one.
> **The postal code** you want to work in.
> **A keyword** that allows the search engine to find the people on your desired team within that company.

From there, you'll want to **find two key contacts: HR and your potential boss.** Your potential boss contact should be neither so high up that your email gets lost in their shuffle or is not relevant to them, nor so low on the company totem pole that you're competing with them for their job. Entry-level job hunters should be reaching out to managers as their potential boss. Midlevel manager job hunters should be reaching out to directors or vice presidents as their potential boss. **Write down the name of your potential boss in each company on your list.**

As for HR, that's a bit more of a doozy. For companies with fewer than ten employees, there's probably no HR person. Shoot, even with all these startups preaching the whole "We have no hierarchy," there could be no HR person. So be loose with this, but be aware and intentional—if you can **pick one HR name,** that's sensible. If none appear, the potential boss's name alone is enough.

STEP #5: FIND THEIR EMAIL

If you even think about direct messaging these people on LinkedIn, I'm going to cry. Why? Because you need to contact people where their priorities are. That means realizing LinkedIn is like Twitter, Instagram, or a million other venues that have a login. It doesn't mean they check it daily or care that much about it. That's why I recommend hitting them up in their direct email in-box, the place where their priorities exist—with everything from Amazon deliveries, to work emails, to messages from their significant other. This is where you'll get noticed, whether they choose to reply to you or not.

In the Job Offer Academy, I talk a lot about how to find someone's email address, but know you can do this! Remember: every email address tends to fall into some sort of clear structure such as firstname .lastname@domain.com, or what have you. Find each company's format by googling the following: "email name @ company.com." For example, if you're looking for a contact at Disney and you know their name is Jane Doe, try googling "email Jane Doe @ Disney.com." The spaces in your search allow the engine to generate options that could fill them in. If you don't know someone at the company, use the LinkedIn advanced search tool to find someone in your desired company who works in communications, or, even more ideally, public relations. Why? PR people have their names and emails more commonly listed on the Internet, and their name will bring you closer to cracking the format.

OVERVIEW OF THE STEPS TO TAKE NOW

> Pick two aligned words reflecting your primary CORE SKILL SET.
> Pick two aligned words reflecting the CORE INTEREST you're pursuing in the workforce.
> Type one to two words to reflect your CORE SKILL SET along with one word to reflect your CORE INTEREST into LinkedIn's advanced search, along with the postal code you're job-hunting in. As a reminder, CORE SKILL SET words

include *writing, brand management, finance, engineering, public relations, organizational development, recruiting.* CORE INTEREST words include *fashion, film, cosmetics, politics,* and, of course, so much more.

> Find who inspires you.
> Make a list of one hundred companies (more is better).
> Find two points of contact in each company (HR and your potential boss).
> Find their email addresses.

Don't send any emails yet. Gather this information and then remember that you want a job, but you're not asking for one. Instead, you're starting a conversation, and opening the channel for the Divine Unknown to work its magic.

Writing a cold email is an art. Here are some tips from my Job Offer Academy course to get you started:

1. The first thing the contact will think when they open an email from a stranger is, "How did they find me?" Open the cold email by letting them know how you found them.
2. Follow this up with a light apology for reaching out. Why? Because sometimes showing up in their personal in-box can feel intrusive, even if it's just networking, something so many of us tend to, and should, do.
3. Offer a little authentic flattery, because we have to admit it, everyone loves a compliment. Tell them what it is about their work that you think is inspiring, and keep it short—one kind sentence will do the trick.
4. Move forward by outlining your current career status to align why you are reaching out to them with where you are currently.
5. Finish this by making your ask, whether it be to schedule a phone call or to meet in person for a cup of coffee.
6. Be sure to attach your resume, and make note of the attachment by saying "attached is a copy of my resume so that you have an idea of

my background." When you say it this way, you come off less like you're asking for a favor in your job hunt and more like you want to connect.

Reaching out to strangers may feel intimidating at first, but with practice, it becomes much easier. I am rooting for you!

CONCLUSION

Do you feel like networking or "making an ask" is a form of taking? I've been there, and I get it. But know this: networking is the highest form of giving, for all parties involved. Plus, the more people you know, the more people you can help. Many people won't get it when it comes to networking, but the people who do, the ones who say yes to connecting with you, will understand the value of helping you as you tap into the workforce. They understand that you will rise in the ranks of your career and that your eventual success will contribute to their success. Smart networkers will see a relationship with you as an investment of their time as you're on the way up. Hundreds of people lent me a helping hand while I was networking my way into the Pentagon, and I must tell you, many circled back and asked favors of me just a few months later. I happily obliged because that is the circle of networking. Needless to say, be willing to help as you're on your way up. Always make sure to ask: "How can I help you in return?"

Networking is not taking . . . It's giving; it's simply the science of how information is now spread. So start now, because the worst time to start is when you need something. Make it a way of life. Have a conversation every day. See it as an ongoing journey in your life, because it doesn't have to be as big as we make it out to be.

Chapter Ten

Successful People Are Simply Willing to Do What Others Aren't

SEPTEMBER 7, 2013

We've heard it all before: *when one door shuts, another will open* . . . Or my least favorite statement people use to soften the blow of heartbreak: *everything happens for a reason.* While that all may be true, it doesn't make the space between *goodbye* and *hello* less intimidating. Some people embrace change like a warm blanket on a winter night, while others will do anything to avoid it. Change is the only constant in life, right?

That's why, as with anything, how you view these pivotal moments matters. What you make the change mean about yourself, or your life, matters. In the end, you are the maker of your own reality, and your own happiness. The days of saying "I'm upset because . . ." and making your dismay a result of something outside of you have expired. If you're saying that, you're just not in touch with your freedom, my friend. Allow me to remind you of your most necessary *You Turn* in life: the return to who you are. Allow me to remind you how you came into the world: free as a bird. If you're living in a reality that feels anything less than that, you've simply forgotten your true nature.

Sometimes we muster the courage to make a big change in our lives, and yet the process of transformation looks wobbly. It looks like saying "yes" to what we want, and then slipping back to our old ways, going back on our decisions as we would with lovers we know aren't good for us. In my case, I courageously left the Pentagon, only to accept another job doing intelligence at home in Los Angeles. Do you judge yourself when you have slipups on the way to your goals?

I was hard on myself about this "misstep" of taking yet another job in national security, but would eventually note that some goodbyes are a process, not a one-time event. Taking one more job in national security wasn't necessarily a slipup; it was just another step in my goodbye process, just like old lovers go through when they keep breaking up and getting back together. Every little breakup in their journey becomes a part of the process on the road to saying goodbye and truly parting ways; getting back together becomes a small form of goodbye, too: it's a way of making sure that they need to feel the pain of the goodbye that's coming so they can work up to acceptance. Eventually, we all get to our final breaking point where we've had enough. We finally become more afraid of continuing the misery we're experiencing in our current situation than we are of the unknown. Our "slipups" can be important, necessary steps on the road to goodbye, over and over again, until we *You Turn* into saying hello to our next level.

YOUR NEW LIFE WILL COST YOU YOUR OLD ONE

Holding that gun on the military base weeks ago looked like my goodbye to national security, but it was only the beginning of my process. My real goodbye came on my next intelligence job, where I was traveling for forty-eight hours in Istanbul. I wove through a busy alleyway at 9:45 AM on a humid Monday. The dull hiss of a crowd kept getting louder, until I turned a corner, and, just like that, I saw tanks driving into a sea of protestors. The government dispersed tear gas into the crowd. My eyes stung, and tears rolled down.

I wondered amongst the screams if I'd ever get the courage to actually leave national security, to really say goodbye—after all, it was a career that paid me well, looked good on paper, and suggested a lot of "promise" for my future. The thing about giving yourself permission to explore what's possible is that it becomes Pandora's beautiful box, because once you start dreaming bigger, you crave it everywhere else in your life. I don't even know if I was more scared of my goodbye to this path, or my hello to a new one.

And, most of all, I wondered if I'd summon the courage to leave my old self behind. The girl who was willing to set goals and work for them, whether she actually wanted them or not. The girl who looked great on paper and had financial security in her job. The girl who would have gotten married to that one "safe" and sweet guy she dated for years, just because it was the "next step." I was *that girl* who had a beautiful life meant for someone else. *Man, that girl would be hard to say goodbye to . . . Would I forever grieve for her and miss her?*

In times of unbearable stress and fear, we tend to compartmentalize our lives, or make excuses to keep ourselves stuck where we are. What excuses are you making about your career or life that are keeping you stuck where you are?

My heart broke in Istanbul as I watched those tanks plow through people, knowing that there would be casualties. I couldn't help but think about my own mortality, because inside, I was dying. I steeped in my spirituality, wondering how so many souls were perhaps floating in the sky, waiting to come down and play here on this magical planet. I thought about how temporary my time would be in the world, and decided that life was too short to keep chasing some vision of success that perhaps wasn't meant for me.

WHAT MOTIVATES YOU: INSPIRATION OR FEAR?

I knew my career could take one of two pathways: fear or inspiration. It was my choice. I could keep pursuing goals out of the fear I wouldn't be able to have a life I loved, or I could choose a path where I was motivated purely by inspiration.

Which energy are you leading with in your career right now: fear or inspiration? The girl I was crying over, *the old me*, was living in fear. She wouldn't be the one who could build an empire. She wouldn't be the one who could stand onstage with stories to tell the world. She couldn't be the one who could write this book you're reading now. And even though she was an amazing job hunter, she wasn't yet the one who was strong enough to ask for what she truly wanted.

That was when this *You Turn* really landed. I would choose a new standard for myself, a new way of being in my career: inspiration. This would mean that I'd have to say no to a lot of options I used to say yes to out of FOMO (fear of missing out) or worry that I couldn't just keep chugging along, or survive, without that dreaded "yes" to anything and everything. One of the biggest and sneakiest forms of distraction can often come as opportunities. What would you have to give up today if you chose inspiration as the catalyst and standard for your career? What would you do differently?

In that moment, I decided to become who I really wanted to be in the world: an entrepreneur and career coach full of purpose, drive, impact, and inspiration. I realized I could never be that person unless I was courageous enough to fully step away from my old self and the entire life I'd built around that identity. I also realized that I didn't have to say goodbye to all of me. I could keep the parts of myself that I liked, like my ambition and my grit . . . Those parts of me could come with me on my more inspired path. This was just another layer in the grand experiment of the *self*: taking what works and leaving the other stuff behind.

As the tanks in Taksim Square turned and headed toward me, I bolted. With tears and snot running down my face, I pushed through the Turkish spice bazaar as I felt a slew of text messages buzzing in my tote bag. The texts were from a DC area code:

> Hi Ashley, it's Sarah Hillware, we met at the awards ceremony in DC! I have you confirmed for a TEDx talk at UC Berkeley in a few months. I hope you can do it. They just need your speaking reel today or tomorrow, if you can.

BE AFRAID AND DO IT ANYWAY

The moment was something out of a Matrix movie, as time seemed to stand still. All I heard were prayers echoing loudly in Arabic from the mosque up the street and the beat of my own heart. I read the text again as sweat dripped down my face, just to make sure I'd read it correctly. I wondered: *Was this some sort of prank? Me? A TEDx Talk?* I had never spoken publicly before, and to think I would kick off my entrepreneurial journey with a TEDx Talk for a live audience of four thousand paid attendees felt like a divine act of encouragement, and synchronicity. These tears marked my surrender ... into inspiration ... into the truth of who I was.

Just thirty-six hours prior to this, I was in Washington, DC, at *Diplomatic Courier* magazine's Top 99 Under 33 Foreign Policy Leader award ceremony, where I met Sarah Hillware, the angel who sent the text message. She was there to accept an award for her work in supporting girls' education, and I was there to accept an award for my work for the Pentagon. Leaving the event that night, I had no idea that my admiration for her during our conversation about her TEDx Talk at the UN would turn into her recommending me to do one. As we parted, I remembered shrugging at her and saying, "Maybe one day I'll do a TEDx talk, too ... That would really be something." She climbed into her cab, smiled, and affirmed, "I bet it's around the corner."

Her teeth practically sparkled as she said it, as though we were both living in some sort of a cartoon that has an upswing at the end of the episode.

After twenty minutes of rereading her text message, I finally got to my hotel room so I could quickly send out an intelligence report covering the protest. I then grabbed my phone and sent a text back to Sarah: "THANK YOU—I am so grateful and I'm on it!" I feel forever indebted to her for this sort of generosity. A few minutes later, my in-box chimed with a welcome email from the TEDxBerkeley curator. Reading the email was exciting, because I had always dreamed of an opportunity like this, but when I read the closing line—*Please send me your speaking reel as soon as possible*—I freaked. I had never spoken publicly before, so I didn't even know what a "speaking reel" was.

POWERLESSNESS IS POWERFUL

I popped my laptop back open as I sipped a Turkish coffee, and quickly googled *what's a speaking reel?* The humid Mediterranean air seeped through my hotel window and my body began shaking, as if it were saying, *You're not ready for this.* These moments in life, when we're offered a ticket into an opportunity that feels like the big leagues, are critical. We can run away from them and self-sabotage, buying into the belief that these big moments are "meant for other people" or that "we're not ready," or we can choose to rise up, lean in to it, and become the person who is up for it. That's what life is, a journey of becoming. I took a few deep breaths and reminded myself that I wanted this, that my fear was just an innocent voice in my head that kept me from risking a failure. What does the voice in your head tell you about yourself when a big opportunity arises? I listened to the scared thoughts swirling around in my mind, telling me that I needed more experience, that I'd embarrass myself in front of the audience or all the other speakers, and that I wasn't cut out for it. I decided I would let those thoughts be there, *and* I wouldn't operate from them anymore. I wondered: Can I simply put my fear on the shelf and just get into action? This question has guided so much creation for me.

With a few more calming breaths, I sat down and began to write an outline for a two-minute talk, knowing all too well that the other speakers probably didn't make their fancy sizzle reel on their iPhone, propped up against an ice bucket in their hotel room. I watched the final presentation that would become my sizzle reel, totally overcome by self-loathing. I cringed at the brightly colored Turkish wallpaper behind me, the faint background screams of street protestors, and my shaking voice. Have you ever watched yourself on camera? It can be sobering. I immediately deleted the video and started over. And over. And over. On something like the seventh take, I decided this was as good as it was ever going to get.

The next morning, I woke up to two very interesting emails: an official invitation to speak at TEDxBerkeley—*what a trip*—and one from Don, my boss at the intelligence firm. Don let me know that one of our clients wanted to hire me as a full-time employee. I always loved talking to Don and appreciated his mentorship, so I called him to ask what my options were as I headed to the airport. He was candid: if I accepted the job with our client, I'd have to move to a small town in Middle America. But, if I would pass on their offer, he would offer me a promotion that would put me in New York City. I interrupted him: "Wait, so there are no opportunities that would keep me in LA? What about my team?"

He sadly replied, "I'm sorry, Ashley, but there are no options left for you in LA. We'll be reassigning your analysts to other teams since the client is closing out this contract. If you decline this opportunity from us and the one from them, you'll be unemployed and you can choose an intelligence analyst for us to consider for the New York promotion." He went on to say if I chose to leave, my last day would be in three months. With a quick look at my calendar, I noted that this day would fall just a couple of days before my TEDx Talk at Berkeley. This couldn't be a coincidence.

The more you say "no" to a life you don't want, the more you will find opportunities that appear in support of the life you actually want.

This isn't some woo-woo shit; it's just common sense. You will only experience the magic of your new yeses if you're not busy tending to your noes. This requires a choice to reroute.

LIFE IS FRIENDLY

Right up until that moment in Istanbul, I didn't really trust that life was friendly. This experience taught me a critical element of the pursuit of success, one I never thought about or even considered: *grace*. I reflected on all the years I spent feeling powerless in my career, buying into the belief that I'd just have to take certain steps to survive in the world, whether I wanted to take them or not. In fact, life always felt heavy, like it was all on me, that there was nothing but hard work and willpower required to get everything I wanted. But it was in this moment that I observed that powerlessness is so . . . *powerful*. Because when you feel a sense of powerlessness, you are only left with one opportunity, really, and it's to surrender. And in surrendering, you make yourself available to grace, a force that is so much bigger than all your choices.

I thought about all of the most important things in my life: my parents, my best friends, my career opportunities. All the best things had come from grace, not from plans, and not directly from a choice, either. Think about the most important people in your life. Did you connect with them because you tried to find them, or was your meeting an act of grace? It's freeing to really accept that while we can make choices that empower us, ultimately, we aren't in charge of everything. Some refer to this as synchronicity—those magical moments when life lines up, or opportunities arrive at the most convenient and opportune time.

TRUST LIFE AGAINST ALL REASON

Grace and synchronicities don't always make sense on the surface. They can often be categorized as beyond reason, but are always infused in our lives if we're willing to simply trust in the concept of it all. That means we need to stop living in FOMO or the belief we should be somewhere else. Grace looks like trusting that who you're talking to at that party is who you're meant to be talking to. Grace means trusting your hand of cards in life. Grace means trusting that where you are is simply part of the puzzle for who you will be and where you are meant to go. Grace doesn't allow for comparisons, because you are on your own journey.

It was no mistake that my TEDx Talk was calendared a few days after my job would ultimately end. Playing it safe is easy. Making a leap of faith in order to live the life you want isn't. Growing hurts, but for me, I knew it was time. I decided that living in the status quo of life is nothing more than a trap. We are, as life continues to show us, ever evolving and growing. For me, I knew it was time to take the leap. So, leaning into my courage, I thanked Don for the promotion opportunity, and then declined his offer and gave my two weeks' notice.

As with most pivotal, life-changing moments, I began to question my decision to leave the corporate world behind. Have you thought about leaving the corporate world behind? It's not for everyone! I experienced more sleepless nights than I can remember, breathing heavily as I fell asleep each night, with my mind anxiously picturing the red circle I'd stand on at TEDxBerkeley months later. In fact, I had so much imposter syndrome running through my veins that I even wondered if the event curators would email me any day leading up to the talk, telling me that they needed to rescind my invitation because they changed their minds about me, or had found a better speaker for the event.

Do you ever experience imposter syndrome? It's defined as that intense belief that you don't deserve your achievements, as well as the intense feeling you'll be exposed as a fraud. According to research, 70 percent of the US population has experienced imposter syndrome in their career.[1]

LIFE IS THE ULTIMATE COACH

At night, I'd stew in my own insecurities, wondering: *Do I have what it takes to be a real entrepreneur? How will I create money out of thin air? Can I really support myself on a consistent basis?* What was the worst that could happen? I fail and go back into the workforce? So be it. When I looked at it like that, entrepreneurship didn't feel as risky as I thought it was.

Whenever fear would come up, I reminded myself this: life will teach me more than the workforce ever could. In fact, experts on the "future of work" are saying soft skills are what matters most—the ability to communicate, navigate through tough situations, and negotiate a solution. Those skills come from life in general. As such, I knew it was time to share my message with the world.

Far too often, we catastrophize and think about the worst-case scenarios without actually asking ourselves, *What is the worst that can happen?* Usually, we can simply course-correct, and keep chugging along. It continues to amaze me how many people choose to live lives of silent desperation, never pursuing their dreams for fear that they'll fail if they do, or because they don't want to do the work to make them happen. Life isn't guaranteed, friend, but your dreams are always worth it. I remembered the words of my dad years ago, how he said successful people are simply willing to do what a lot of people aren't. If it were easy, everyone would be doing it. The reason people become independently successful is because they have a high tolerance for risk. It's not that we are better than a person holding down a salaried position for a Fortune 500 company, either. It's just that we see the fear for what it is—misguided attention—and do it anyway. So I asked myself: Am I willing to do a ton of shit most people won't, for the sake of my dreams? I heard my heart say yes, and that was enough.

If there's anything I've learned about success, it's that it's all about managing your nervous system. In my case, I learned that practicing my TEDx Talk would create certainty for me, certainty that the final performance would feel like yet another practice round, versus some big moment. That's why, for the next three months, I wrote and rewrote my TEDx Talk at least thirty times. I practiced three to four hours a day without fail, worrying that I'd look like an amateur alongside these top-notch speakers. I practiced until the talk felt like it was in my cells.

WHY BE NERVOUS WHEN YOU'RE JUST EXCITED?

On the day of my talk, I woke up a nervous wreck. When the feeling didn't subside, I pulled on my running shoes and went for a jog. I hyperventilated while running around the track at UC Berkeley, scaring the runners beside me. I got sick of feeling afraid, so I decided to call this fiery energy running through my body excitement. I shakily walked over to my hotel room, where my mom looked at me. "You okay?" she asked.

"Yep," I affirmed, "just excited." Oddly, this helped. This shift in my self-talk seemed to help me see my way through it.

THE NERVES (OR EXCITEMENT) NEVER END

After a run-through of the lineup, everyone welcomed me as the youngest speaker in the room. I met Guy Kawasaki, a renowned investor and previous chief marketing evangelist of Apple, as we stood in line to get mic'd up.

The curator let me know Guy was opening the event, and I'd go onstage after him. *Holy shit. Guy Kawasaki, and then ... me.* Talk about a tough act to follow—this guy was brilliant. I looked around the room at the other speakers, though, and realized they were all as terrified (or, should I say, excited?) as I was: highly successful CEOs, well-known researchers, and even an Olympic athlete. Their panicked faces were profound for me to see, as I realized that no matter how successful I become, the nerves never end. When push comes to shove, no matter what our age or achievement level, stepping onto the stage made us all feel like toddlers, crying for our blankies.

Watching Guy onstage was intimidating. The audience roared in laughter, and he looked as though walking onstage was just another day in the life. This was clearly easy for him. I stared in awe. But let's check ourselves before we wreck ourselves: never compare your day one (or first public speaking event) to someone else's day ten thousand (or someone's one-hundredth public speaking presentation). Everyone needs to put in the time for mastery. There are no shortcuts. This later inspired me to create my Business Launch Mastermind online course so that I could help clients establish that foundation for their business to take off.

I kept rehearsing my talk as he was speaking, and then, my moment came: "May we please welcome to the stage, counterterrorism professional turned career coach, Ashley Stahl." I forgot my first words for a moment, glanced down at my speech papers, threw them in my pocket, and walked onstage. This moment was a true reflection of my choice to reroute my career, and to notice the TURN SIGNALS that had been begging for my attention all these years. It was so worth it.

I've since spoken on at least one hundred stages by now, and let me confirm: the nerves never end. It's just that, as with anything in life, your repeated experience of counting on yourself starts to help you realize that you'll perform despite the terror you feel. Nine minutes and thirty-three seconds later, I walked offstage having finished my talk, "Three Questions to Unlock Your Authentic Career." To say I didn't remember what I said would be an understatement. I completely blacked out, but the words came out of my mouth. By the way, this still happens for me as a professional speaker. I don't remember what I said, nearly every time, when I walk offstage.

My mind was racing. *Did I cover everything? Did I smile? Was I engaged with the audience? Did I stumble?* These thoughts of judgment raged on, until I heard a stagehand walk over and say, "Wow, that was one of the best talks I've ever heard. You looked so . . . natural."

As she escorted me over to the sound engineer to remove my mic pack, I turned to her and admitted, "I am really grateful I came and got to do this, but let me tell you: nothing about that was natural to me. In fact, I have been preparing so hard for this that I memorized every word of a script to do it."

She smiled and told me that my feedback was comforting to her. Shoot, it was comforting to me, too, realizing that so many people in the world who look badass in front of the crowd probably feel just like I did: horrified and committed to doing it anyway. *This*, I told myself, *is living . . . It's growth, and I want to do more of it.*

Landing back in Los Angeles, I felt awake, aware, and inspired for what might come next. I was ready to make my business dreams happen. Nobody was going to stop me . . . including, and most importantly, myself. No, that would be the old me. This new me was *on fire* with intentional gratitude and more scared of what her life would look like if she didn't pursue her dreams.

Have you ever felt more alive because of a dream you're pursuing? For all the times I've been lacking energy, I've noticed it was actually that I was lacking in purpose. Having a purpose, feeling fired up about something, is the ultimate life-giving force at work. I bought my domain, ashleystahl.com, and hired a programmer to make a career-coaching website for me for two hundred dollars on fiverr.com. I then began researching networking events for career-driven people. I told myself that life was a numbers game, and that I would find clients no matter what. I posted the idea on Facebook, letting people know I was offering free career-coaching packages in exchange for some honest website testimonials about the impact my coaching had on them after our sessions were concluded. People shared my post, and I woke up to fourteen direct messages from people who were excited about my free coaching. Most of them were from young women who were looking to figure out what they wanted to do with their lives or wanting help with their job hunt.

YOU LEARN TO LOVE YOURSELF THE
MOST WHEN NO ONE ELSE WILL

Who am I to be doing this? That voice would pipe up, and in these moments I would remind myself of an anecdote about Picasso:

The story goes that Picasso was in a restaurant and started drawing on a napkin for a few minutes. A man walked up to him and said, "Wow, can I buy that napkin from you for a hundred dollars?" He was excited to frame it as a Picasso original! Then Picasso looked at him and said, "A hundred dollars? No way. This napkin will run you at least a hundred thousand dollars."

The man said, "What? But it only took you a few minutes!"

Picasso responded, "No, it took me my whole life."[2]

Know that you've been working on your art your entire life—however it looks.

We don't tend to know how much we love ourselves until life pushes us into the fire. That fire can look like a breakup, a loss, or the fear of starting your own business. Perhaps we lose the person who validated us nonstop, or the family member who always reflected our greatness back to us. Whatever it is, in those moments, you take charge of reminding yourself of your own greatness. That, my friend, is a dialogue of self-love. When life gives you flames, you only have one choice, and it's to love yourself. Instead of standing and burning down in the flames, you get to choose to walk through them.

I turned my dream of being a career coach into a plan, and it was now undeniably real. I admit it was scary at first, but I knew deep down that my own job-hunting failures and successes would be valuable to other people. In moments of self-doubt, I developed a two-step affirmation to squash my lingering self-doubt:

1. **I'm responsible *to* my clients, not *for* my clients.**
   This can apply to anything in life where people are expecting something from you, especially at work. Know this: being responsible *to* someone is about integrity. It means only saying yes to clients (or

opportunities) when you feel confident that you can deliver. Being responsible *for* them means taking on the weight of their results, which is just a form of over-responsibility. Know that everyone is in charge of getting what they want out of a situation. Do you ever feel responsible for someone else's results or experiences? As a career coach, I always remember that no matter how much I prepare a client for their job interviews, I will never be able to go into the job interview for them. This realization freed me up and gave me the power to say no to a potential client when I debated if I could or couldn't help them. My business became a lot more fun when I only took on clients I felt certain I could help.

2. **Whenever I felt nervous about how I looked, I realized I was quite literally *out of service* to my greater good.**
   What does this mean? During this period of my life, being of service meant focusing on the other person, really being present with them. Being out of service meant focusing less on them, and more on myself, obsessing about how I look or whether I'm doing a good job. When you are too much in the business of thinking about yourself and not in the business of serving your client, *you are out of service.* Do you ever get stuck like that at work, worrying too much about how you look versus doing the job at hand? You can't change lives when you're obsessing on your own stuff. See your self-preoccupation as an alarm to get back into service for someone else. This mindset works as much in business as it does in your career and personal life.

Over the weeks that followed, I looked for speaking gigs and adopted a mindset of "anywhere, anytime" when it came to grabbing (and creating) opportunities. If the situation put me in front of people, I knew that's where I needed to be. I didn't feel like an opportunist with an agenda or anything; I just felt abundant and aware of what's possible. If there was an upcoming job fair, a corporate conference, or a college recruiting event, I wanted to be on that stage to share my message.

When I look back, doing this was perhaps one of the boldest moves I've ever made. I noticed that when you decide to call yourself something, and you believe in it, other people believe you. It is just about the most mind-blowing secret to becoming who you want to be. Just like I did with job hunting, I emailed everyone. It was bold because I didn't have any content prepared for the talks, but I had a no-fear attitude. I knew that success wouldn't knock at my convenience and that I was in charge of making it happen. I heard friends talking to me about how it takes "years" to build businesses, and yet, I'd see people online building theirs in what seemed like weeks. Have you heard people talk about business in that way, saying it'll take years of struggle to create it? I decided to be the exception, not the rule. You can make a *You Turn* into that thinking, too.

ALWAYS BE "IN THE AREA"

I soon found a series of networking events happening in Southern California and bought tickets to all three locations: Los Angeles, Orange County, and San Diego.

First up was San Diego. During my three-hour drive there, I noticed an uncomfortable, familiar feeling in the pit of my stomach. Walking into that bar, dressed in a new suit, I felt more naked than I had ever felt for any job interview. It was a raw and exposed feeling, because I was my own product; for the first time ever, I was selling me. I put my name tag on with a heart full of hope, duking it out with the voice in my head screaming, *You're unsuccessful; people are going to laugh at you; you're going to make a fool of yourself.*

These moments when we feel completely exposed and vulnerable can either be used as fuel, or consume us. Thinking of the Picasso story, I told myself, *I* am *worthy,* and *I* do *have something valuable to share,* communication skills inside me that I'd been cultivating at least as far back as the second-grade spelling bee. I forgave myself for buying into the belief that I was not successful. The truth, I reminded myself, is that

I made an impact in the workforce, and I wanted to help people with what I have learned. I forgave myself for buying into the belief that people would laugh at me for choosing to be a career coach at my age. The truth, I decided, was also that I was courageous and could be proud of it.

While I was silently forgiving myself for these limiting beliefs, I noticed a woman walking straight toward me. She looked like one of my college professors, and introduced herself, leaning in to read my badge.

"Wow, you're a career coach? You look like you're in your early twenties. Do you even have experience with this?"

Boom. I froze, feeling shame trickle through my body as if it were laced in the blood pumping through my veins. I forgot all the affirming thoughts I had been selling myself on and tried to regain composure. This is what it's about when you run your own business, really standing in those moments of fire and owning what you have to bring to the table.

"Thanks for asking." I smiled, bitter as hell. "Yeah, I used to manage an eighty-million-dollar contract for the Pentagon in DC. What I loved most about the workforce was my experience job-hunting, so I decided to start teaching it to clients. Why? Do you need help finding a job?"

She asked me where I got all my clients, and I couldn't tell if she was asking from curiosity or trying to patronize me. Such is often the case when we feel insecure about something, right? We are already sensitive, and our mind is shopping for reasons to prove our story that we're not worthy. But not me. Not this time. I was stepping the hell up. I thought about all the free clients I was coaching and how I just posted my services to my Facebook page, having signed on four new clients. Regardless of whether they were paying me, I decided that a client is a freaking client. I looked at her fiercely and said, "Well, I just posted to Facebook last week and signed four private clients from that, plus word of mouth. People need this sort of help, you know?" I handed her my card and smiled with sass.

Fast-forward three weeks, and that same woman called and hired me as her coach with the goal of getting clarity on her next career move and landing a job offer. All of this was because I was willing to "be in the area" in San Diego, conveniently ready to meet whoever wanted to work with me, and I refused to make excuses for myself in our conversation.

Think about your life. Where should you conveniently go to make your dreams happen? Is there a place or person you should happen to "be in the area" for, like that white goose waiting to be caught in the winds of opportunity? Put yourself in the area.

CREATE A PRESS AVALANCHE

With her signed up, I now had six online client reviews. Six weeks after that, my TEDx Talk was posted online—and it went viral; today, it's exceeded one million views. The thing about getting your name out there and establishing personal branding is that the media likes momentum. When it comes to press, you really want to invest in creating an avalanche. That means once you get one bite (or win), you must use it as a tool for your next win. For me, that looked like sending the TEDx link to online editors "fresh off the press," and asking if I could write blogs for their website.

Know this: most writers you see online, and even people who win awards, reached out to platforms or editors themselves, and asked for the opportunity to write on their platform. They didn't just get contacted because they were wanted, or they had won awards.

So why not you, too? Like I said, if you want an opportunity, don't wait for it to come to you. What online platforms align with the work you do? Have you ever thought about blogging for them as a way to brand yourself as a voice in your work arena? Do your future self a favor and grab for it.

Here are a few steps to becoming an online blogger:

1. Search for the contributor guidelines of your favorite online content platform. This could be any platform, from a small mom blog to *Forbes*.

2. Contact the editor (or submit through the guidelines page), letting them know what sort of content you'd like to write for them, or

attach a sample blog post. If you haven't heard back two weeks later, find the editor's email and kindly send them a note checking to see if they're planning to use your attached piece, and letting them know you plan to submit the sample for usage elsewhere if they're not interested. That tends to get you a reply.

3. Write a sample article that aligns with who you want to be as a business owner or as a career professional. Personal branding is necessary for both entrepreneurs and corporates. If you're pivoting in your career, use your content creation as an opportunity to brand yourself as a voice in that new space. Think to use your past and take it into your future . . . For example, if you're moving from a role in technology to a role in entertainment, write about the intersection of those two arenas as a way to pivot and brand yourself in both.

Know that, eventually, in a sea of unanswered email pitches and flat-out rejections, you'll get one golden *yes*. *That* will be the beginning of your press avalanche.

The best personal brands are those that become omnipresent. If you look me up, you won't stop finding blog posts online. Saturation is the name of the game! Know that you want to be in as many outlets as possible, which means writing a few more posts once you get approved with one online platform, and making sure to use those as links in your pitches to other outlets where you can write. I don't recommend going too deep on one platform as far as submitting too many articles, unless they're paying you to write for them—especially if they own your content and don't let you repost it in other places, like your LinkedIn profile or your Medium account (anyone can create content on those!).

If you don't want to write, pick a social media platform that feels exciting to brand yourself. If it's Twitter, start creating content and networking on there by retweeting people you like and celebrating them. By the time you slide into their DMs asking for a conversation, they should be familiar with your face or handle, in a good way. That is the way to network, through celebrating and supporting other people online. If you're inspired by Instagram, look at other accounts that embody your ethos and take note of what posts went the most viral. Use those posts as inspiration for your own content creation. Become an observer of what's performing well on platforms, not just a user.

I sent my TEDx links to media outlets like *Forbes*, the *Muse*, Buzz-Feed, and even Mashable, hoping to land roles as a contributor or a guest expert to be quoted, or even garner enough exposure to secure a speaking engagement. Each website had its own set of rules on what it took or what I needed to submit in order to become a writer or speaker there. The *Muse* was my first *yes* in 2013. From there, I began writing blog posts for them on a weekly basis about finding your best career path and job-hunting. Other sites would soon follow, and, before I knew it, my weeks were filled with writing blog posts on career coaching and serving clients. All of this was thanks to my TEDx Talk.

So remember: all you need is one win. Once that's in your pocket, others will soon follow, if you choose to grab for them. Momentum breeds more momentum. In physics, momentum is the product of mass and velocity.[3] Think of your press avalanche as the result of generating more media (mass) with more speed (velocity), and watch it spread.

Six months into my career-coaching business, I was on track to eclipse six figures for the year. What I didn't know then was that, in my second year, I'd generate more than $5 million in revenue over the span of two months. What happened next was something out of a nightmare, because as quickly as it arrived, it went crashing down.

First it all hurt, but later it would transform me.

YOU TURN #10:
TAKE STEPS TO
create your personal brand

If you want to win the lottery, you must first be willing to buy a ticket. While you may have previously assumed that all the authors, speakers, and experts you see online were sought out for their content, chances are they pitched themselves to editors again and again until the opportunity was given to them.

When you see people on the internet, on a stage speaking, or with a large social media following, it isn't because their brilliance is simply craved by an audience of people; it's because the person put their shingle out on the internet and asked for people to show up. That could initially look like email pitches, paid advertising, and much more.

A personal brand is the same. It isn't something that happens because you are interesting; it's something that happens because you put yourself out there to cultivate your audience and credibility.

Plus, press is not usually about generating sales—it's about getting credibility . . . and yet, *credibility pays*. If you're a business owner, building a personal brand and having industry presence will kick the teetering client off the fence about you. If you're a corporate professional on the job hunt, having an online presence is key for standing out in your interviews and landing job offers. It's also leverage for your negotiation.

That means the majority of hiring teams and human resource departments are going to be searching for your name on the internet. Instead of having them find Facebook photos of you raging with your friends over margaritas in Cabo in 1997, use the media to build your brand. Imagine how impressive it will look when a hiring manager googles your name and finds quality content about your workplace focus . . . *everywhere*.

Since you build a brand through securing press, here are a handful of outlets you can establish yourself on:

> **LinkedIn**—Everyone should be posting valuable content here, since there is no barrier for entry, but make sure the content you use (if you have it posted elsewhere online) is allowed to be reposted, given that some online platforms will own your content after you submit it. Creating a niche group of professionals on LinkedIn, and engaging with them almost daily, is also a pro move.

> **Twitter**—Make this a place to tweet content and articles relevant to your workplace focus, and as we discussed, make this a place where you can connect by celebrating and supporting others.

> **Instagram**—This platform is ideal for creatives whose primary CORE SKILL SETS are *beauty* or *words*! A great place to gain industry recognition.

> **Facebook**—The days of using the "likes" function on this platform to stand out are over, so I recommend this platform less than others, but make sure you create privacy settings on here so recruiters don't see your nightclub pictures from last Saturday night. That being said, one way to create authority, or a business, on the platform is through creating a high-value Facebook group.

> **Podcasts**—Look at what shows align with the people who work in your arena, and pitch yourself as a guest expert. *Friendly reminder: you are an expert at what you do.*

> **Television Interviews**—This is also a game of pitching. Find out who the assistant producer is for the shows you want to be on, and pitch yourself as a guest.

> **Newspapers and Magazines**—Find out who the editor is and email them a list of topics you'd love to write about for them, attaching a high-value article sample.

> **Industry Publications and Conferences**—Email event managers to pitch yourself as a speaker or panelist on a topic you love.

> **Local and National Networking Events and Organizations**—You'd be surprised how many organizations need a free speaker. Brownie points if you land a speech and ask to bring a videographer to record your footage!

> **TEDx and Other Speaking Engagements**—Know that TEDx curators go to each other's events. Find one and network with them. Make sure you've got your elevator pitch formula from chapter eight on lock before you converse with them. As for other speeches, you can work to create a sizzle reel (a

three-minute video clip highlighting your speeches and your message) or simply look for event managers who need a speaker!

> **Blogs**—You get it by now.

I suggest starting with blog posts, as you can use them as a foundation to drive future press opportunities, such as interviews or public speaking events. And don't be frightened: it's okay if you're telling yourself you're not a writer. You can always work with ghostwriters (Yep! That's right! People who will write in your voice *for* you) or a publishing house (like the one I founded, CAKE Publishing) to help support, write, and edit your content. If you are a decent writer, but want to appear even more polished, hire a freelance editor to review and proofread your content prior to submission and publication.

CONTENT CONSIDERATIONS

There are some things to consider when you start blog posting to build your brand. Some outlets will want to outright own your content, as I said, meaning you can't publish it anywhere else. Some platforms require you to submit blogs to an editor for review and approval prior to publishing (like *Inc.* or Thrive Global), while others allow you to publish directly (like *Forbes*) once you have been brought on as a writer. Some will want original content from you, while others will accept content you've posted elsewhere. Some will pay you; most will not.

There are nuances to each site and it's important that you understand them fully before emailing, applying, or submitting work. More than anything else, remember to follow up on your email pitches after two weeks. Once you start writing for a platform, be sure to know the style guidelines of the publication. Before you submit a piece, make sure it meets their unique rules like minimum word count, header formatting, and even numeral structure. It would be a shame to write a powerful piece of content only for it to be rejected since you wrote the four as "4" and capitalized each word in your subhead.

DON'T LET THE REJECTIONS GET YOU DOWN

Don't make meaning of the unanswered emails, and keep working toward that one "yes" that starts your avalanche. Know that the internet world needs content, and you are a gift to these editors. Some of the most successful stories of our time were rejected: the Harry Potter and Twilight book series were rejected by dozens of publishers before finally being accepted, and *Chicken Soup for the Soul* takes the cake, having been rejected 144 times before being published. Imagine if they had stopped after the first, second, or 143rd "no." Just because one person says no doesn't mean someone else won't say yes (or that that same person will say no again later).

Even if you don't want to be a writer, you have a voice—you have something to say, and it is time you start sharing it!

USE THIS NOW

Do the following to create a credible personal brand for growing yourself as a leading expert within your corporate niche:

1. When it comes to sharing content and establishing your personal brand, ask yourself clarifying questions:
   > What do *you want* to speak about?
   > What does *your industry want* to read?
   > What do *your clients* (if you have them) *want* to read?
   > What do you get excited to tell others about?
2. Create a list of online outlets (e.g., *Forbes*, *Inc.*, BuzzFeed) that align with your industry and job.
3. Rank the list of platforms from easiest to hardest in terms of reachability.
4. Make a spreadsheet of platform names, the proper editors, a hyperlink to their contributor guidelines, their email addresses, and highlights on all information to submit yourself as a writer, such

as whether they require you to email an editor, or submit a sample blog post on a specific website page.

5. Reach out to the easiest platforms to start publishing on, so you can work your way up your list.

6. Create a list of blog post topics that you think your industry, or clients at work, would be searching for or reading.

7. Commit to a list of ten to fifteen article titles you know are of high value.

8. Schedule three to four writing days over the next month. If you don't want to write alone, you can also use that time to hire a ghost-writer. My company CAKE Publishing does this, as do freelancers on upwork.com, fiverr.com, or reedsy.com.

9. Start emailing editors your blog post sample and pitch (or uploading them to the platform contributor submission page!).

10. Two weeks later, follow up with the editor via email to ask if you can use the post elsewhere (if they're not going to use it). This puts a fire under their ass to say yes.

CONCLUSION

You can either leap into the unknown with an eye toward adventure or suffer the debilitating consequences of *I wish I would've at least given it a shot.* Like motivational speaker and author Jim Rohn said, "Discipline weighs ounces while regret weighs tons."[4] In that space between our goodbye to one career path and hello to another, we tend to make our pain mean that we should question our decision. After all, if goodbye hurts, should we go back to where we were before? I've learned that with every new choice or belief I step into about who I am or what's possible, my personal brand has created a foundation for me to stand and pivot on. Branding yourself online is a project, but well worth it in the long run, whether you are starting a side hustle or establishing yourself as a leading expert in your new or existing corporate career.

Chapter Eleven

Rock Bottom Is Sacred

DECEMBER 1, 2017

A shley, this is your private banker at American Express Business. We've been trying to get a hold of you. This message is to notify you that you're four days late on paying your outstanding bill of $296,413. Please call us back, and make payment as soon as possible to avoid late penalties."

The phone rang again. And again. And again. I listened to my next voice mail from an unknown number, hoping it would be someone more uplifting.

"Hi, Ashley. It's your dentist, Lauri. Can you possibly pay the rest of your dental bill? We're pretty far past the deadline."

It was pouring outside in West Hollywood, and the rain was leaking into my living room. I lay in my pajamas, with my cheek pressed on the hardwood floor, sobbing into a puddle of tears and raindrops. With every sob, I wondered how I'd ever get out of this mess. I thought of my friend Anna, who started a business that went under. Her investors lost $400,000, but she walked away clean. I thought about my friend Jen, whose father gave her $97,000 to invest in a product. The product didn't take off, and Jen simply got a new job in the workforce without having to pay off the loss. And then I thought about myself: I maxed out my American Express card on Facebook ads, was nearly $300,000 in debt, and had no backup plan. Have you ever felt cornered because of money? It can be the ultimate buzzkill for your creativity, right?

I went through five stages in my business to get to this moment. First, I struggled and hustled to build my private practice and create an online course and a free webinar presentation that would sell it and introduce it to new customers. This first stage lasted a long time and probably burned me out. Second, my hard work paid off, and I ended up bringing thousands of new clients into my programs. From there, the third stage was rapid growth and scrambling to service thousands of clients, fast. Fourth, I hired and trained new people to accommodate the influx of customers and my newfound success, and tweaked my course content. The fifth stage was the hardest, and represents what so many people don't know about entrepreneurship: once your shiny idea works, you then have to sustain it. This is where my fear crept in. This is where I self-sabotaged.

I met my financial success with utter exhaustion. This is unfortunately because with success comes great responsibility. Since I was so burned out, and gave all of myself to the process of succeeding, I didn't have any fuel left when it finally arrived. From there, I started making business decisions out of exhaustion and overwhelm. This burnout, and my fear, is what led me into extreme financial loss and credit card debt.

THERE'S NO SUCH THING AS A SAFETY NET

For 99 percent of people in the world, there is no "safety net," let alone one where someone could spare nearly $300,000 . . . and I was no different. I could sit in an energy of "poor me" or I could let go and begin the next chapter of my life, but I still found myself feeling envious of Anna and Jen. Have you ever felt jealous of people who have easily dodged a crisis that you feel stuck in?

Anna and Jen, I thought to myself, *had a safety net.* I felt like I was right back in that same old place I had been after the Bearded Man attack on the military base: exhausted, lost, and . . . alone.

Oftentimes, when we're going through something difficult, we feel like no one will understand, or we simply feel alone. I thought I had learned how to navigate this painful feeling of separateness from the world, but sometimes you need lessons to show up more than once in order to learn them. With every ring of my cell phone, I felt more alone in the realization that no one was going to rescue me.

Over all these years of my entrepreneurial risks, I bought into the misunderstanding that there might be some sort of safety net to protect me. I never realized how much I operated out of feeling that sense of magical thinking around financial risk-taking. Eventually, I'd realize that safety isn't about money or anything I can "get" outside of me, but rather it's an inside job, a feeling that would come from a mindset I'd cultivate, and a knowing that I can handle anything that comes into my life path. This sort of safety is what I'd cultivate through this experience.

The phone rang again, and I picked up this time, for whatever reason, deciding to face reality.

"Ashley, this is a debt collection agency. We've been assigned your account through American Express, and we're on a recorded line. Can you please confirm that this is you? State the last four digits of your social security number."

I paused, and then I surrendered and started talking. About three minutes into the conversation, I got the news. If I didn't come up with $296,413 by the end of the month, the debt collectors affirmed that American Express had the right to repossess all my assets: the small house I bought as an investment, my car, and whatever else they could find.

"Let me see what I can do," I told the debt collector, and hung up.

LETTING GO IS A PROCESS, NOT AN EVENT

My abdomen ached from sobbing, and I had no tears left. It was time for me to throw my hair up, grab a latte, and clean up my mess. This was my choice: fall apart or pick myself up and move on. I thought about my father from years back with newfound compassion and admiration. He had made the very same decision I was about to make. It was a decision to let go, embrace a new life, to go on and not let any one event define you. It takes courage. And in the midst of falling apart, I found the courage like my father did to go on.

It was 10:15 AM. My staff meeting was going to start in two hours, and my entire team of eight had no idea that my company was on its way out. I started writing emails to close friends who I knew would want to hire people from my team, with notes that looked like: *Sarah, shit is hitting the fan in my company, and I need to let people go. Do you need a business manager or a virtual assistant? I can link you to mine.*

This would mark the beginning of me letting my team go, of letting my business go. In retrospect, letting go, like saying goodbye, is a process. When I really look back, I let go of my business a little bit in every moment leading up to this, when I would see that the revenue wasn't much exceeding the company's expenses. With every hope, with every attempt at fixing my ads, with every split test, I said a little prayer wishing that my sales would pick back up . . . and each time they didn't, a part of me resisted the possibility that I'd have to let go of my business. Where in your life are you not wanting to look at the reality of a situation, and instead just hoping it will somehow fix itself?

I was in so much fear of losing it all that, as I watched my corporate accounts dwindle down into nothingness, I'd mentally check out and go into denial, a denial so deep that it cost me dearly—financially, emotionally, spiritually. As my revenue went down, I would fear having to let go of a team that I loved working with so much. I slowly let go of all the customers I knew I could help. And the hardest part—I had already begun defining myself as the CEO, the boss, the thriving entrepreneur. I feared that this identity I loved so much was coming to an end. My success was such a warm place to hide, and I felt naked without it. This fear created a desperation, and denial, inside me that translated into some really bad choices. When do you allow things to go on far too long before taking action? When do you make decisions out of fear instead of a sense of groundedness? What identities do you hold on to in your career? It was at this point that I would stop holding on to my vision and choose to accept the reality of the situation. I was finally free, *even with my pile of debt.*

After this call from the debt collector, choosing to step out of fear freed up a lot of energy for me to be resourceful. Even though there were so many things in my life that I loved, I was able to make decisions about what was important to me, versus what wasn't. While I loved my designer handbags in the closet, I decided they weren't important, and I'd throw them up on eBay. While I loved my sports car, it wasn't important. While I loved my beautiful apartment and independence in West Hollywood, I decided it wasn't important. They were just material things; they weren't who I was. I gazed longingly at my beautiful living room and peered through the window at my Porsche . . . And under my breath, I started whispering goodbye.

I refreshed my email an hour later, and saw that four friends replied with a capital YES to hire members of my team. My team gave my company its spirit, and they were going to be okay.

OVERNIGHT SUCCESS TAKES YEARS

I also saw an email from my Facebook ads guy, Derek, with an attached invoice for $45,000, for his monthly 10 percent fee for running my advertising. To say I was financially drowning was an understatement. These invoices and phone calls marked an unceremonious end to what otherwise looked like a glamorous year.

How did I get here? Well, I put every penny I made into the online marketing for my job-hunting course, now called the Job Offer Academy. Suddenly, after six years of work, the company had skyrocketed into profitability and generated more than $5.5 million in sales in two months. That meant we brought in more than five thousand customers off one e-course, in just weeks. The revenue was coming in so quickly, with up to $50,000 arriving each day, that it almost felt like the financial faucets of the divine would forever keep pouring down on me.

While that success *looked* like it had come in overnight, I had actually worked for four years on it, believing against all reason that the course would take off. After all, there was no other millennial woman online offering a job-hunting course, and my content was completely original. The system in the Job Offer Academy gave me more than job offers; it gave me freedom. Freedom to know I could create my own career options in the workforce. Freedom to leave any job that didn't work for me. Freedom to make the living I wanted to make. I wanted the world to experience it, and I believed in it with every fiber of my being. Freedom is one of the CORE VALUES that many people, especially entrepreneurs, value, and this course allowed me to offer it to everyone.

What I didn't know was that my success would evaporate just months after it showed up. This would be the chapter of my life where I got to know rock bottom and cultivate a sense of equanimity and trust in life. What was your last rock bottom? What did you learn because of it?

I heard voices outside my front door and rushed to clean my tears off the floor. I threw a black rayon dress over my head and put my hair into a bun. I covered my eyes with my nerdy Harry Potter–looking glasses as my team knocked on my door.

Everyone walked in, excited about the day, with their Ashley International notepads ready in hand. My chief career coach, Melonie, pulled me aside while everyone fixed themselves coffee in my kitchen. Melonie was making six figures at my company, working part-time from home, privately coaching clients on how to get clarity in their career.

"Ashley, I need a raise. I don't feel valued by the company with the amount of work I'm doing . . ." She wanted to continue, and I interrupted her, kindly, to let her know this conversation may not make sense for today.

We both walked back into the living room, and I'll never forget my COO, who looked at me to say, "Ash, is everything okay? It feels . . . sad in here."

I was impressed with her intuition. Pain is palpable, isn't it? I asked everyone to sit at my marble table, and, when they settled in, I threw my hands up: "So do you all want the good news, or the bad news?"

I heard a few of them murmur that they wanted the good news, so I feigned a smile and spoke up: "The good news? Okay, well, the good news is that I got you all new jobs . . . Umm, so that takes us to the bad news. The bad news is that I'm closing all of our programs."

My team looked into me, and I say "into" because that was how it felt. Every part of me was exposed, and I couldn't hide.

"What happened?" they all asked. From there, I don't remember much about what I said. I vaguely remember how I spoke about what a joy it was to give this company six years of my life, how I believed in my job-hunt and clarity courses and tried everything to make them work. Yet revenue wasn't justifying our expenses.

I told everyone when their last day would be, and then was desperate to be alone so I could begin crying again. It's interesting that when you feel so alone, sometimes all you want is to be just that . . . *alone*.

Now I knew what my father meant when he said money was going to kill him . . . I felt like I was suffocating, and I didn't know how I was going to get myself out of this mess. On top of that, I was completely burned out, running on fumes, trying to find energy to fix everything that I worked so hard to build. Did you know that there are four root causes of burnout: a lack of (1) power, (2) sleep, (3) community, or (4) purpose? Have you ever suffered from burnout due to the extreme lack of one of these?

I started my business with plenty of community and purpose, but I was low on sleep and power. By now, I felt a lack of agency, or power, over my business. As it grew, I got more sleep and felt good in all four categories. Then, as the business started to fail, I moved into desperation, and lost my inspiration, my purpose, my power, and sleep. This left me descending back into my original wound: scarcity, working to survive, and more. In fact, I started questioning the entire idea of going at a career on my own. I started questioning myself.

The rest of the afternoon, I sat on my living room couch going through the motions: emailing my landlord my thirty days' notice, texting a friend to see if he wanted to buy my Porsche, writing emails to sell a new course (the Career Clarity Lab) to my email list, and notifying my brother that the house we co-owned could be taken by American Express. As I wrote my text messages and emails, I sat with the question my team had asked me: Where did it all go wrong? That sent me into a flashback to the year before I met my ad guy, Derek. He changed everything, for better and then for worse.

Eighteen months before the day I met Derek, I was scrolling Facebook aimlessly, page after page, until I noticed something that made my fingers stop: an image of a woman in designer clothes, all made up, looking happier than ever, with a caption that read, "I quit my minimum-wage job, and three months later, I was earning more than $1M a year as an entrepreneur . . . Click below to learn my steps you can take to do this, too." This represented two concepts I'd never seen on Facebook before: paid ads and a free webinar.

I signed up for this woman's webinar with the mindset that I'd study what she did. For the hour-long presentation, I was captivated: she gave incredible business tips on how to land new clients (which was just about the last thing I needed at the time), and at the end, she sold a business course for a discount that would be granted as long as you bought it before the end of her presentation.

I started searching for free webinars on how to job-hunt and found none online. *There's gotta be a need for this . . . I can do this*, I thought. *Imagine all the job offers people could get through my Job Offer Academy course.* I felt such a connection to the idea of helping more people through an online webinar.

To give you some context on where online coaching was at this time, webinars and Facebook ads were considered the "new" thing in online marketing, and the idea felt so right. Looking back, I have learned that when ideas feel so right, it's usually because they were often already sprouting inside you and just hadn't found their way out yet.

YOU DON'T KNOW WHAT YOU DON'T KNOW

Facebook had just started offering paid ads, so I took it as a sign to act, which is exactly what I did. In the eighteen months that followed, I invested every dollar of my private coaching income into my online course, now called the Job Offer Academy, which became the ultimate experiment of my career.

It was messy. First, it meant learning how to sell products through webinars. Second, it meant a ton of trial and error when it came to using various technologies. Picture eighteen months of late nights, with me trying to troubleshoot technology, days of broken web page links to which I was sending hundreds of dollars in ads, and unnecessary websites that I thought I needed, just to name a few obstacles. That's the thing about starting a business: *you don't know what you don't know.*

I could have sidestepped some of those expenses if I would've simply hired the right mentor, coach, or advisor (business or financial) in the process. In total, I spent more than $128,000 to make it happen. I still can't decide if that was an act of insanity or inspiration. In many cases, I felt like an octopus desperately reaching out for answers or services I didn't actually need, hoping they'd be the "magic bullet" that made it all happen.

How do you operate when you want to make something happen? Do you invest in yourself? While I spent a lot of money on it, I am so grateful I was willing to make an investment in my best asset . . . me.

I mean, let's face it, when you take risks like this, there is no promise that it'll happen. But what I've learned over the years is that risk-taking is a muscle. We should expect failures along the way. In the end, the calculated risk-takers always win. The winners do two things most people won't: (1) they don't give up, and they eventually win, and (2) they tend to have a better conversation going on in their head about success and failure. And then, of course, we have the magical thinkers, who tend to think things will work out without actually putting the effort into logistics or having the mindset it takes to succeed. In my case, I decided I would keep trying things until my webinar worked. I promised myself I would win, because I wouldn't give up.

FEEL THE SUCCESS BEFORE ANY SIGN OF ITS ARRIVAL

What's interesting in retrospect is that before my success came crumbling down, when I was in the trenches working hard, some part of me knew the truth: that it would work. This webinar I spent years building, my job-hunt course I poured all of myself into, I knew in my bones would work. In fact, I remember, during the early, lean years of my business, I'd be jogging through the streets by my apartment in Santa Monica every day for a focused thirty minutes, visualizing the webinar generating revenue, and all the clients I would help through the course with finding their purpose at work and landing job offers. Have you ever felt like you're winning before you win? It is such a wonderful self-fulfilling prophecy. I didn't know what I was doing at the time, but I was fully in alignment with the laws of attraction and manifestation, feeling success even when my life showed no evidence that it was coming.

There's a science behind it. When you clearly visualize your goals, you are convincing your brain that they are already happening or have already happened. This makes it easier to complete the tasks required to reach the goal without as much fear. Research has revealed that when you follow mental practices of visualization, you become as effective as if you physically practiced.[1] This has proven to be powerful for professional athletes like Tiger Woods and Muhammad Ali, who combined physical repetitions with visualization.[2] It's also important to note that if you're living in fear and you visualize your worst nightmare happening, you're contributing to it becoming a reality because, as you know, those fear-based visions influence the way you behave. In fact, I think part of my business's demise was a result of all the fear and nightmares I experienced as a result of my limited money mindset, back when I started financially succeeding.

The business model was simple, but it took a lot of work to perfect it: paid ads about job hunting and a landing page online inviting people to sign up for my free webinar for an hour, which gave the user fifteen minutes to claim a discount on my course shopping cart. In fact, I learned over time that success in online marketing doesn't come from creating; it comes from tweaking—fixing every little detail that could boost your sales, be it the subject line of your email or your wording in your webinar. It was so ironic to me that one hundred hours of my time went into creating the Job Offer Academy, while the rest of my year would be all about selling it. And such is business: you better believe you need to have a good product, but most of your time will be spent on optimizing your marketing and sales.

Despite my credit card debt and lackluster results, I believed in the Job Offer Academy so deeply that I did the live webinar presentation online more than ninety-one times over the course of one year. Ninety-one times! I recorded my results for every webinar. Let me tell you, that was painful. For the first thirty-five presentations, I spent $2,000 on ads and tended to make nothing back. For the following twenty presentations, I started reading books on copywriting. That got me to break even on my advertising budget and sales. I still couldn't find my way to profitability—until I discovered Derek.

SUCCESS LIVES ON THE SAME
BLOCK AS FAILURE

On one particular Monday morning about sixteen months into my webinar adventures, my initial ads specialist, Annabelle, called to apologize to me after coming home to a slew of my text messages that came in while she was off the grid camping over a three-day weekend. While she was away, the link to my webinar registration page wasn't working, which meant I was sending $300 worth of Facebook ads to the broken page each day, where people should have been able to register for my free webinar. I had no idea how to fix it, so I just sat there, watching my credit card get charged throughout the weekend. With almost $130,000 in credit card debt invested in marketing my online course, I was coming to the end of the road. Something had to give.

Annabelle called right when she saw my texts on Monday night: "Ashley, I am so sorry . . . I just fixed the page now, but that doesn't make that $900 down the drain feel any better. What can I do?"

I just sat on the other side of the line, completely checked out, at my wits' end, telling Annabelle that maybe this was just a sign it was time for me to give up. I mean, let's face it, when you're in the mood to jump ship, you can easily make anything a sign that it's time to quit, right? The truth of the matter is that your mind can go shopping in the world for proof of just about anything it wants to find. Her voice shifted on the line, and she insisted that I try one more thing, that she wanted to make this up to me.

"I'm going to refer someone to you, but it has to be confidential that the referral came from me," Annabelle said. "Don't ask me why."

To this day, I still don't know why I couldn't tell him the referral came from Annabelle, but she gave me an email address and told me to contact a man named Derek to help me. I couldn't find the guy anywhere online, but I was desperate for this business to work and blinded by hope. I emailed the guy saying someone gave me his name, and he replied, setting up a call with me for the next morning.

Rent was due in three days and I somehow needed to make $2,500 and find the funds to hire this Derek guy, who would eventually become my business coach and ads specialist. Those of you who know online marketing know it's a *huge* conflict of interest to have one person play both of those roles. Why? Because your business coach should be advising you on what's best for your business, while an ads specialist's income is usually tied to how much you scale your advertising online. That can sometimes block them from seeing what's in your best interest, but I didn't know that at the time. When you're heading into burnout territory like I was, your brain's neural circuits become altered. This results in the struggle to see clearly, think creatively, or reason well.[3] I was burned out and losing hope, and needed something to work.

On our call, Derek told me it would cost $3,000 a month to work with him, and every fiber of my being was convinced that working with him was the magic bullet I had been waiting for. I told him I didn't have the money, and he told me that my business inspired him so much that he'd give me a week to find the cash.

Next, I called my mom, telling her I needed to borrow $3,000 because I was out of cash and my rent was due. She always believed in me, telling me ever since I was a kid that she thought I could do anything I wanted to do in the world.

"If this is for your rent," she continued, "I'll give it to you, but if this is to hire another coach or marketing person, I can't lend this to you, Ash. *Enough is enough*. I believe in you, but you're in so much debt. Perhaps it's time to start thinking about getting a job again, at least part-time or something."

"Yep, this is for rent!" I said. That marked the first and perhaps the only time I ever lied to her as an adult.

My mom's $3,000 showed up in my personal account the next morning, and I sent it straight to Derek via PayPal. I was high on possibility for our first coaching call, as we scheduled a full workday for him to come to Los Angeles and teach me everything he knew about copywriting, e-courses, and selling online. The great news is that, with his genius support, I would go on to become an expert in copywriting, sales, and coaching, in addition to having created courses that generated millions of dollars online. And that's the funny thing—that, sometimes, things really do happen for a reason. If my webpage hadn't broken over the weekend, I might have never heard of Derek. Think about your life: Has something really awful, a crisis of sorts, caused you to discover something else that was really great? Chances are you'll find something, or someone, really important for you on the periphery of your crisis.

ONE DAY WILL ALWAYS BE YOUR "LUCKY DAY"

The lesson I learned from my own losses was to always stay open to what is trying to emerge, to trust life. In fact, I used to roll my eyes when friends would say things like, "Oh, you're in a breakdown? That just means the breakthrough is coming!" I thought: *People who say this are the same ones who convince themselves that when a bird shits on them, it's good luck.*

News flash, friends: it's not good luck when a bird shits on you, because a bird shit on you. But the truth is, you never know what tomorrow will bring, and while it may not be likely that every tomorrow will be your "lucky day," you better believe that life is aimlessly embellished with unexpected gems and moments of opportunity. This means one day will be your "lucky day," and usually that day starts and feels just like any other, right? One day will be the day you meet your ideal romantic partner in the peanut butter aisle of the grocery store, or one day will be the day you're sitting on an airplane right next to the person who can hire you for your dream job. Your work, my friend, is to look up, get present, and stay receptive to this magic. Keeping your eyes and heart open to life's serendipity is an ongoing practice in a world of stimuli vying for your attention.

In the twelve weeks that followed hiring Derek, everything changed. "We're just one small tweak away from success!" he would say, and I believed him. I read seven books that he suggested on copywriting and gave my webinar presentation nineteen times. Each week, we added something new to test on my webinar script. We looked at the data after every single presentation: How much did I spend on ads leading up to the free webinar? How many people registered for that free webinar? How many people actually showed up? How many people bought my job-hunting course from that presentation? These steps and pieces of data represented my "sales funnel," which constitutes the sales steps that start from when a customer discovers you (likely through some free content) all the way down to when they buy something from you.

In December 2015, something shifted. It was my nineteenth live webinar presentation under Derek's watch. Having spent $5,000 on Facebook ads to fill the online presentation seats, it was yet another opportunity to test out a marketing strategy. After I presented my online course to the viewers, I exited the presentation, and, as per usual, looked at my sales dashboard: $40,000 in sales. Yep, that's right. I spent $5,000 to fill that hour-long webinar and sold $40,000 worth of my Job Offer Academy course. My body didn't even know how to register the success, mainly because I was so conditioned to a state of always being broke. It was as if I had been conditioned to struggle and not succeed. Until now. That night, I called my parents, crying, telling them I could finally take care of them later in life because my business model was working.

"*Great!* Ashley, now it's time to scale, scale, scale! We need to spend $50,000 in ads for the next one . . . *Imagine* all the customers you'll get!" Derek spoke as if he were on drugs, and he even went on to offer to do my advertising himself.

I was so high on the possibility he was promising that I didn't realize how vulnerable I was. Vulnerability is beautiful for relationships with established trust, but when it's not mindfully used, it creates a false sense of trust. Similar to how cult leaders attract wounded people to become members and heal,[4] I experienced business healing through Derek's guidance. That made me trust him.

DON'T GET ADDICTED TO HOPE

I thought this webinar was another example from the universe of how I was on the right track with his guidance, but boy, was I mistaken. My vulnerability and my hope blinded me to some red flags I didn't want to notice. For one, if he knew all these surefire ways to make money, why was he only teaching them and not practicing them on his own site? And why was he living in Alaska? Did he have a troubled past? Something about him felt illegal, but I couldn't put my finger on it. Plus, there were times where friends would comment, saying, "That Derek guy, it felt like he was kind of . . . hitting on you. Do you ever feel that, Ash?"

"Derek?" I'd ask in shock. "No! He has three kids and a wife at home. Why would he do that?" I wanted my dream to happen so badly that I pushed away the confusing feelings and pressed on.

I was so committed that I woke up every day at 5 AM to work on my webinar, and to add content to my Job Offer Academy course. On many days, I would work until 2 AM, promising myself I wouldn't go to bed until my to-do list was complete.

How do you treat yourself when you have a heavy workload? I was a work machine and addicted to the possibility of making this webinar a success. I *needed* it. Badly. I told myself I just wouldn't stop until that dream became my reality. And eventually, it did.

SUCCESS CAN BE LONELY

The following night, I had dinner with my friends from college, as I did every Wednesday. Only this time, I was carrying the shock of success along with me. What I didn't realize at the time is that having that kind of money felt lonely for me, almost as if it alienated me from other people. I mean, for *years*, friends would ask about how my "webinar thing" was going, and they got used to hearing me talk about my failures (and debt) with it. What would I say now? *Um, things are great; I just made $40,000 in an hour and am now doing that every single week.*

No. Would they still love me? Would they still feel like I was one of them? Would they talk poorly about me? Would they be jealous? The limiting belief was: *If I make money, people won't like me*, and it soon became, *If I lose all my money, who will still be my friend?* Do you have any beliefs about what would happen with your relationships if your money situation changed drastically? It was a game of mental ping-pong that would ultimately prove to be exhausting. In retrospect, I had so many limiting beliefs about money and what having money or not having money meant about someone. Those must have held me back for years and I didn't even realize it.

Within two weeks of my big win, we decided to automate my webinar presentation. Our conversations were peppered with my worry about how scaling an ad on Facebook is not something many ad specialists have done, and how it was a risk to trust someone to do it. Derek called within a few days of all the technology changes getting implemented and said, "Ashley, I have been thinking of you, and want to offer you something that, really, is crazy for me to offer, because it's just *so* much work on my behalf to do. And, you know, I wouldn't do this for just anyone, but . . . I am willing to manage your Facebook ads for you."

I mentioned this idea to a couple of business coach friends, and they let me know that was a huge conflict of interest. After all, he'd be making money off me scaling—10 percent of my ads budget, to be exact—and this could blind him from giving me quality advice. For example, what if it wasn't in my best interest to scale? Or what if my ads weren't performing? Would he be willing to take the financial loss on that?

I pressed on, choosing to ignore the signs, and signed an agreement for him to both coach me and scale my advertising online. For the next month, we bought Facebook ads and automated the webinar presentation. That meant, instead of a weekly date and time for a live webinar, it would be available all day and all night, whenever a person found the landing page.

Soon, my business started to feel like a literal ATM. Some days I would clear $20,000, and on other days, my good days as I called them, I'd clear $50,000 in revenue. It felt as though money were falling from the sky, rewarding me for all my hard work. I paid off my $128,000 in credit card debt in twelve days' time. I paid my mom back the $3,000 I had borrowed and confessed about lying to her. She let me off the hook, not just because I was making money, but because she was my mom.

Through a lot of tears, mostly my own, I began to take responsibility for myself. It would prove to be a pivotal moment in my own personal development, a lesson in forgiveness. This made me think about the girl crying herself to sleep because she didn't know if she could pay her rent. I forgave myself for all my previous mistakes and found a way to love myself for the girl I had been, and the girl I was becoming. I loved myself for trusting my instincts and leading a visionary life.

On February 1, 2016, we were spending $2,500 a day on Facebook ads. That created more than $350,000 in revenue that first month we tried to scale, which was chaotic, because I needed to make sure my customer service reps were trained to handle the incoming customers, of which there were *a lot*. By March 1, 2016, we were spending $5,500 each day on ads, which meant we were making more than $900,000 in revenue that month. By May, we were close to $5 million in sales from my Job Offer Academy course.

"You're on fire! You're making at least $20,000 to $30,000 in profit every day. I have yet to see a webinar and course do so well!" Derek yelled during our coaching call. He continued, "You can buy your dream house in Malibu! Retire at age twenty-eight!"

Oddly, I wasn't on the same page.

My mindset hadn't yet caught up with my bank account, and let me tell you, today's customer won't wait more than twenty-four hours for an email response . . . and I can't blame them! I felt as though the clients and emails were coming in faster than I could serve them. This sounds like a good problem to have, but I got so overwhelmed I started to feel powerless. *How can I keep this up?* I wondered. I was so busy training new customer service employees and hiring new career coaches to help with the program that I didn't feel one second of my success. In fact, I was the most stressed out I'd ever been, and it wasn't because of how busy I was . . . It was because of my limiting beliefs: I was scared that I would lose it all. I began operating from a place of fear, not inspiration. Making decisions, having conversations, and living each day from a place of fear is not enjoyable.

SELF-FULFILLING PROPHECIES ARE REAL

In fact, I was so scared of losing my money that I called my lawyer, Jenny. I set up an appointment in her office to let her know of the news, and knew she'd be floored since she, too, was used to me failing in my sales. When I walked into her office, she smiled as I spoke.

"Jenny, I am making so much money. Like up to $50,000 per day. I mean, I wake up and money is just flying into my bank account, and I . . . I . . . I don't want to lose it all, you know? What I'm hoping you could help with is, um, looking at everything, all my content, and making sure I'm following the rules."

Next, Jenny began to ask some hard questions, and gave me the news: "There are *a lot* more rules than you realize to this online thing. I suggest you slow down on your advertising spending and let me look into all your content: your webinar, your email sequences, your course content, and your landing page. All of it."

My relationships with Jenny as my lawyer and Derek as my business advisor often were rooted in my own lack of self-trust. Instead of trusting my own wisdom about my market, or my own awareness that I was playing by the rules, I would abandon my own mind and buy into whatever vision either of them had. This lack of self-trust looked like a lot of extremes. Scaling through the roof, or turning everything off. My disconnect from my own intuition barred me from residing in a much-needed middle ground. My biggest mistake was automatically putting *all* my trust in others without really collecting all the information I needed to make a good decision. Where have you done this in your life?

"Okay, then, um, I'll shut it off until then." I decided on a whim, totally overwhelmed. What's interesting about this was that she never quite told me to shut off my ads; that conclusion and decision came straight out of my own fear.

Leaving her office was an absolute 180 from the way I felt going in. I got into my car and began to question everything. My fear told me to do all I could to prevent myself from losing everything, so I might as well take her advice. What I didn't realize then was the Facebook algorithm was currently favoring me and my ads. If I shut off the ad spend, would it stop giving me good lead costs altogether? The answer may sound obvious now, but back then, ads on Facebook were a new thing. Why should I turn off something that was proving to be a fountain of revenue? Because I wanted to be aligned with the law, and most of all, I was scared I'd lose it all if I didn't hire someone to look at it. Plus, I told myself: *I did it once, I can do it again. I'll just turn this thing back on after Jenny gives me a green light on my assets*—which she eventually did. The irony here is also that Jenny didn't really find anything wrong, and yet my ads didn't work when I turned them back on. In retrospect, I sabotaged myself out of fear and made decisions from a place of fear and extremes because I didn't trust myself.

THE "UPPER LIMIT PROBLEM"

I also think I hit what *New York Times* bestselling author Gay Hendricks calls "an upper limit problem." Hendricks argues that most people subconsciously have a limit on happiness, an internal set point they feel comfortable with. He outlines four fundamental limiting beliefs that explain why most people maintain this internal upper limit on their happiness: (1) feeling fundamentally flawed or not good enough, (2) a fear of disloyalty and abandonment if they become successful, (3) the belief that more success will only bring a bigger burden, and (4) the fear of outshining and making others feel bad.[5] Do you have an upper limit problem? Which one do you resonate with most?

On my spiral downward, I felt fundamentally flawed (#1), and as a result, I sabotaged my business. We accept what we think we deserve, and the flip side of that is we will sabotage whatever is beyond the limits of what we think we're worthy of having, and we become the instrument of our own destruction. With this realization and Jenny pumping my brakes, I worked up the nerve to ask Derek to pause my ad spend. Here's the thing about pausing ad spend, though: it takes mastery as an advertising person to scale an advertising account. I don't just go from spending five dollars a day in ads to ten thousand a day in ads. It takes tact, and for me to turn it all off meant we'd have to undergo a risky process, hoping the algorithm would treat us well again, if we ever turned them back on. Needless to say, I did not understand this at the time.

"Turn off ads?" Derek asked in a rage. "Are you insane?"

He could have coached me in that moment to see my own extreme thinking—how I was all or nothing, with my ads scaling all the way up, or my ads completely turned off—but I don't think he could see past his own interests. After all, Derek was making a profit off my ads, and my decision to turn them off was a financial loss for him. In retrospect it's hard to determine whether he was looking out for me at any point, or simply focused on his own financial profit off me. I justified my extreme, fear-based decision to turn everything off to myself and him, explaining to him that, as someone who worked in counterterrorism (the apex of justice), I valued my integrity, and that part of this meant having lawyers look at all my assets and program agreements before I kept scaling.

He was so upset and turned off my ads with a frown on his face. That meant the faucet would also turn off on his ads earnings from me.

Over the next two months, I sat by and waited as Jenny and her legal team pored over my platform, making sure all my online assets were abiding by all the laws surrounding online marketing, consumer promise, and so on. The reason for this was because the internet was filled with online scams and get-rich-quick schemes. I knew it was better to be safe than sorry, so I waited. And waited. I spent that period reviewing my content and training new employees, which was a total full-time job. Eight long weeks later, Jenny gave me the green light to turn the Facebook ads back on, saying that my program was in line with integrity and in compliance with all the laws governing online marketing and consumer promises. I called Derek immediately.

"Derek! *Big news!* The webinar is ready to be turned back on. We can start advertising again. Jenny had a couple of important tweaks to my emails and program agreements, but said we could party on."

He was excited and let me know ads would start again tomorrow.

Rising the next morning, hoping to see a throng of sales, I quickly saw that our profit margin was cut in half. The advertising wasn't performing the way that it used to. I called Derek, and he informed me that the Facebook algorithm had changed, and that we may no longer be profitable . . . I couldn't let myself believe the news to be real. I spent thousands of dollars on lawyers, coaches, technology, and consultants on the belief the cash would just keep flying in. I was in denial, and somewhat felt as if I were starting all over again.

I asked Derek if there was anything we could do, and he replied: "There's a lot of things: we can film new videos for your ads, we can change the wording on the ads, and test a bunch of new sets. All we need to do is keep testing . . ."

He grew quiet, and I could sense thoughts swimming in his mind. He continued: "There is one thing we could do, that I know would work . . ."

My ears perked up.

"It's actually quite simple, but, Ashley, you have to trust me and do exactly what I tell you to do."

I nodded without questioning him. After years of working on this webinar and e-course, and a quick taste of success, I was desperate. *What would it be?*

"The thing about the algorithm," he continued, "is it favors the spenders. That means that if you're willing to pump a ton of money into your one ad, Facebook will eventually lower its lead costs for you. You just have to push really hard. Then your profitability will pick back up. Tell me, how much do you have available on your American Express?"

"We can put about $400,000 into ads over the month before they call me," I said.

"Great. I'm starting that tomorrow. If you don't see immediate profit, don't worry." And then he said the words that would become my downfall: "Just know it's all going to happen if you hold on."

There will come a time when, regardless of your career, you will have to make a large decision. Whatever the decision is, having clarity on your CORE MOTIVATOR is a major part of knowing how, why, and when to make the call.

DECISION-MAKING: ARE YOU WOUNDED OR INSPIRED?

He went on to say things that I would later look back upon and examine to this very day. Deep down, I know that I ignored my better judgment. My decision to press on against all reason came from a wounded place, a place of fear and desperation that I'd "lose it all," or that I couldn't "make it" again, or that I had made a "fatal error" by shutting it down, versus from an inspired place, one that was motivated to press on and make it happen. If I had been inspired in my decisions, I'd have probably chosen something less desperate or extreme.

What drives your career choices? Are you choosing your job right now because you're inspired by what it means for you or what impact you're making? Or are you wounded, choosing it because of how you look to the outside world, or out of scarcity that there is nothing else out there for you? Take a look at these statements in the following table and ask yourself which side you lean toward most.

If you feel wounded thoughts come up often for you, it's time to make a *You Turn* and shift into inspired thoughts and actions.

Wounded Thoughts	Inspired Thoughts
I'm taking this job *for the money*.	I'm taking this job because it excites and inspires me.
I'm taking this job *because I'm afraid* no other opportunities will come my way.	I'm taking this job because it's what I want. Opportunities are everywhere.
This job title will *make me look good*.	This job aligns with my purpose.
I will stay in this job for two more years so my *resume and LinkedIn profile look good*.	I am choosing to stay in this job because it is helping me learn and grow.

Derek stepped on the gas. We spent $100,000 on advertising the first week in and made only $27,000 back in revenue. My mom, Debbie, is an amazing bookkeeper and tracked my numbers voraciously. She called and said, "Ashley, it's not working." She told me what I already knew but couldn't face—the return on the ad buy investment wasn't breaking even . . . not even close. This is a red flag in business. Shit, it's Business 101. I wasn't here to brand my online business. I was here to sell. If your ads aren't working, the prudent thing is to stop all campaigns. Immediately.

I called Derek to voice my concerns and how I thought we should stop. He retorted: "You said you'd trust me on this, and it takes time, Ashley. When the algorithm favors you, it gives you better costs per lead, and you'll soon double your profit margins. You just have to trust me. I know what I'm doing."

When I hung up the phone, my higher self, the part of me that I wasn't willing to listen to, chimed in with a question: *Why did he keep saying to trust him on this when there were no results?* But I didn't trust myself enough then. I trusted his expertise more, partly because I wanted to. After all, if I chose to trust myself first and foremost, a part of me thought that meant I was alone, really. Alone in my decisions, and alone in my success; so much aloneness. I was willing to risk it all in the hope that it would all work.

Then $100,000 on ads became $200,000, and then $300,000. I called every week, letting him know it wasn't working, and was met with insistence that it would. In retrospect, it's easy for someone to encourage a risk when they're not going to pay the price. But I would, quite literally, be paying the price. Despite that truth, I didn't step into my power and put a stop to all this until American Express called, letting me know I was late on my payment. In total, with Derek's guidance, $450,000 of Facebook ads made their way onto my American Express card. And we only got $100,000 in revenue back from it. I was $300,000 in debt; not to mention, I'd soon get Derek's invoice for $45,000 . . . his 10 percent of my ad spend. How was this happening?

Then it hit me. He was burning my cash to raise his percentage. He knew, no matter what my return, he would make 10 percent on the ad buys. I sat there, without words, feeling the weight of the world landing on my shoulders like, well, the massive debt that it was. Of the $5.5 million we had earned before the stoppage from my legal team, I had spent $2.2 million on Facebook ads; more than $1 million in team overhead and on consultants to "save" me; lost $1 million in customer refunds, which apparently is normal in online business (20 percent of customers took us up on our thirty-day, no-questions-asked guarantee, and, conveniently, 78 percent of those refunds were requested on the day of the deadline, after the customer had watched all the content); $400,000 was lost in failed customer credit card payment plans, which apparently is also normal; and I personally blew through $450,000 myself (a new car, a house, and all the material trimmings because I assumed my broke life was over)—which left me at *zero*.

I was broke. And, even more so, I felt broken, like there was nothing left inside me to give. No more inspiration. No more hope. No more trust in Derek. And, worst of all, no more trust in *myself*.

Just when I thought it couldn't get any worse, it did. Jenny called to walk me through what bankruptcy would mean for me, and as I heard her go on about it, I decided I wouldn't claim it. Some part of me was wounded about it, afraid of being labeled by the word *bankruptcy*. Another part of me was inspired by it and wanted to show myself that I could clean up my own damn mess and pay my way out of it. I stared at myself in the mirror of my bathroom and envisaged the word *bankruptcy* floating across my forehead. My body shrank into my oversized sweater, trying to hide. I faintly heard people's voices outside, having fun and on their way to a night out. But not me. I wouldn't be going out. I couldn't afford it anymore, and I had a huge mess to clean up. Not just the mess of today, but the mess of the mindset I'd cultivated over time. Thoughts like *money is tough, money is easy to lose,* and *money is hard to make* permeated my being in the world. Those beliefs created a rough reality and I knew that I needed to change from the inside out, no matter how long it would take. So I decided to let go.

YOU TURN #11:
KNOW YOUR PRIMARY AND SECONDARY
core motivators

Over the years I spent in my career-coaching practice, I developed practices that killed my well-being. For one, I promised myself I wouldn't go to bed each night until my insurmountable to-do list was complete. Some nights I'd finish at 1 AM; other nights I'd be going until 4:45 AM. Tonight was no exception. I closed my eyes at the kitchen table, with a tired body and an active mind. I heard my body talking to me: *Ashley, please, stop. You can't do this anymore. You need sleep. I need you. Please.*

The thing is, your body deserves listening to, but I didn't love myself enough then to honor it. Now, I take these signs and listen to myself. Yes, some nights I am still up pretty late, but if that does happen, I counter it with a self-care day or an early night in.

According to many experts, the fundamental two CORE MOTI-VATORS for why people do what they do in life are to (1) avoid pain or (2) receive pleasure. At this point in my life, I was clearly falling into the "avoid pain" category and needed to make the switch, the *You Turn*, from a place of pain and wounded mentality into a life of pleasure and inspiration. After researching countless studies on motivation, I have come to believe there are ten CORE MOTIVATORS when it comes to your career, and that usually people operate out of one or two primary motivators. I got fancy with the acronym of MOTIVATESS:

1. Meaning
2. Optimal Health
3. Time
4. Impact
5. Visibility

6. Accomplishment
7. Training
8. Ease
9. Spending
10. Self-Expression

Let's unpack this!

1. **Meaning: Doing work that aligns with a spiritual purpose.**
   This could look like aligning your CORE SKILL SET and CORE
   VALUES with a sense of personal mission. It's different from impact
   because it's more self-focused. You could do something with personal meaning that does not make an impact in the world.

   > *Wounded: I am doing this because it will make my life mean
   > something.*
   > *Inspired: I feel called to do this because I light up when I do—
   > and that means the most to me in my career.*

2. **Optimal Health: Work that supports your health or physical
   wellness.**
   This could look like something that is easy on your body if you're
   not well; it could also look like something that challenges your body
   to be stronger.

   > *Wounded: I am doing this because I'll look good.*
   > *Inspired: This career helps me feel well, and that means the most
   > to me in my career.*

3. **Time: Work that allows you time, freedom, or flexibility.**
   This is a career that gives you a sense of control over how you're
   spending your time.

   > *Wounded: I'm doing this so I don't have to work that much.*
   > *Inspired: I thrive as a person and creative when I have space on
   > my schedule, and that means the most to me in my career.*

4. **Impact: Work that you know is changing the world or making a difference.**

    This is a career where someone is committed to a cause or mission, above all else. This is different from meaning because meaning is all about your personal calling (the self), and impact is all about contribution (the other).

    > *Wounded: I'm doing this so that other people see value in me.*
    > *Inspired: I'm doing this because this cause means a lot to me.*

5. **Visibility: Work that grants you prestige or recognition by others.**
    This is a career that grants you prestige and validation. It is often wounded if not checked.

    > *Wounded: I'm doing this so that I am important to the world.*
    > *Inspired: I'm doing this because I have a message to share, and I know the world needs it.*

6. **Accomplishment: Work that grants you a sense of completion.**
    This is a career that often has deadlines and is a fit for someone who likes the dopamine hit that comes with achievement. It gives them a sense of motion, and the completion gives them gratification.

    > *Wounded: I'm doing this because the more I do, the more I'm worthy or valuable.*
    > *Inspired: I'm doing this because I love feeling a sense of completion, and I'm inspired by the journey of execution.*

7. **Training: Work that allows growth, learning, and expansion.**
    This is a career that consistently presents you with opportunities to grow, be it through challenges or adventures.

    > *Wounded: I'm doing this because I want people to think I am valuable and need to prove my value to myself.*
    > *Inspired: I'm doing this because I light up when I am learning.*

8. **Ease: Work that allows you comfort, which means it helps you avoid shame, fear, failure, anxiety, and physical or emotional pain.**

This is a career based on simplicity—doing work that you feel competent doing, without much challenge to your growth.

> *Wounded: I'm doing this because I am not capable of doing other things.*
> *Inspired: I'm doing this because I value simplicity.*

9. **Spending: Work that supports you in making money, saving it, or keeping it.**
   This is a career that pays you well.

   > *Wounded: I'm doing this because money is everything.*
   > *Inspired: I'm doing this because I enjoy the achievement of earning and am stimulated by my work.*

10. **Self-Expression: Work that grants you the freedom to channel your emotions and ideas to come to life.**
    This is a career that leads with creating through your feelings and ideas.

    > *Wounded: I'm doing this because I need attention and love.*
    > *Inspired: I'm doing this because when I express myself, I become more alive.*

USE THIS NOW

1. What is your primary CORE MOTIVATOR when you're wounded?
2. What is your primary CORE MOTIVATOR when you're inspired?
3. Do you have a secondary CORE MOTIVATOR?
4. How does your CORE MOTIVATOR align with, or permit you to experience, your CORE VALUES?
5. Is your career currently rooted in your CORE MOTIVATOR?
6. Are you experiencing any symptoms of burnout?
7. If you are experiencing burnout, what is your most likely root cause?
8. Have you ever self-sabotaged something great?
9. Do you have what Gay Hendricks calls an "upper limit problem"? How is it showing up in your career right now?

10. When in your career right now are you addicted to hope that something will "eventually" change or get better?
11. When in your life right now are you addicted to hope that something will "eventually" change or get better?
12. What is the maximum level of income or success you think is possible for you?
13. What belief or situation do you need to let go of?

CONCLUSION

In life, we choose to lead with either a wounded CORE MOTIVATOR or an inspired one. When I am wounded, I'm driven by spending and visibility. My need to grow a business that would provide a massive amount of wealth was driven not by the inspired joy of accomplishment, but rather by the wounded mindset and belief that money is everything. We all know where that came from: the little girl in me who suffered from heartbreak in her family when watching her hardworking dad struggle to support his family in the wake of huge financial loss. On the flip side, when I am in my true nature, my primary CORE MOTIVATOR is time, and my secondary one is self-expression. Why? Because time is the gift that allows me the space to create. You can see here how this authentic CORE MOTIVATOR feeds into my CORE VALUES, as one of my deepest CORE VALUES is creativity. Look back on your CORE VALUES to see if the same is true for you.

PART *four*
THE HIGHWAY TO HAPPINESS

Our salvation, our aliveness, rides on our ability to stay real when we are being met with illusions.

—You Turn Podcast
Episode 62: "Thoughts on How to Be Authentic"
with Me, Ashley Stahl

Chapter Twelve

You're Never Actually "Starting Over"

MARCH 17, 2019

t's time. It's time. It's time. The voice inside my head wouldn't leave me alone.

There it was, that voice of inner wisdom, that knowing that we tend to hear in the back of our minds when we get really quiet. Michael Alan Singer's international bestseller, *The Untethered Soul*, speaks directly about this voice, saying, "In case you haven't noticed, you have a mental dialogue going on inside your head that never stops."[1] We can use this internal dialogue to be empowered or defeated; how you proceed is up to you. The question is, are you able to create an environment in your life that grants you access to this voice with a clear mind and centered heart?

Now, the funny or ironic thing about that screaming voice is that it was happening right in the middle of an otherwise peaceful breath-work class I was in with two friends: Sarah Pendrick and Natalie Ellis. It kept repeating itself, over and over again, until I rolled over into Natalie's unsuspecting arms, wailing and sobbing unabashedly. I screamed: "Not again. Not again. Not again." I felt embarrassed, thinking *This is a breathing class, not a crying class.* Another upheaval was coming . . . *an upheaval of the truth.*

WELCOME IN YOUR NORTH STAR

The realization that I was on the precipice of change was overpowering. Have you ever experienced that? The knowledge that massive change is coming? I felt like a little girl, standing on the beach, watching a tidal wave coming directly at her. It would either wipe me out or make me stronger . . . and would I even remember how to swim?

I remember you, I thought. *You're the voice who told me to break up with that perfect guy who wasn't meant for me. You're the voice who told me to leave the Pentagon, even when it seemed like a crazy idea. You're the voice that burns me up in flames so that I can reemerge as the woman I am supposed to be. You are the voice that broke my heart a few times in the past, but also the one who sewed me back together so that I could become the next version of myself. You're the voice of the truth, the kind that will unforgivingly unravel my life so that I can become better.* Despite the pain this voice has brought into my life, I decided to see it as my best friend, and my guru.

It's time, the voice kept saying.

"This is going to hurt!" I said, in tears, as Natalie began to rub my back and tend to my heart with her nurturing energy.

"It's okay," she said as she leaned in, comforting me. "It's okay, Ash. It's always going to be okay . . . even when it doesn't feel like it."

The wise voice in my head agreed with her and told me something I'd never forget: *Stop going against yourself. Be you. All the way. And watch life work for you.* This voice, my intuition, has become my North Star in life.

THE UNKNOWN IS AN EXCITING PLACE TO BE

I didn't want my rock bottom to be my final destination. No, I would look at it for what it was — a brief layover on this tropical vacation we call life. In fact, every New Year, I choose a word I want to embody more of, and in 2019, my word was *equanimity*. To me, that meant allowing ease and grace. It meant allowing myself to fully feel everything I was going through — the joys, the wins, the pains, the losses, the heartbreaks, and most of all, forgiving myself for judging myself as smaller or unworthy of greatness.

It's time. It's time. Stop fighting me, the voice continued.

In the middle of the class, crying into Natalie's arms for a good forty-five minutes, I felt the familiar wave of fear wash over me. I began to think about all that had happened: getting rich, going broke, and of course, when I worked in counterterrorism, traveling to some of the darkest corners of the world . . . I thought about it all. It was a rush of feelings, as if the toxins from those thoughts or experiences were being purged from my soul.

YOU MUST LET GO TO RECEIVE

The minute I decided to write this book, I mean literally from word one, I was grieving the recent death of my big sister, Stacie. She passed away unexpectedly from a fatal stroke (triggered by drug use) just weeks before my book deal came in, and I'm pretty sure she was the only person in my family who truly understood all my thoughts and feelings. It was a true moment of yin and yang, where one minute I was burying my big sister, and the next I was celebrating this book deal.

When I began writing chapter three, I got rid of my Porsche and moved out of my beautiful West Hollywood apartment. I swallowed my pride and moved back in with my parents so I could pay off the last of my debts.

In the middle of writing chapter four, William, a family friend I've known since I was five years old, stopped by the coffee shop where I was writing, saying he wanted to catch up. In that moment of seren-dipity, I realized I never noticed how funny, insightful, or handsome he really was. I spoke to him about the book, we laughed, and I swear, in that moment, we fell in love. Life is funny like that. The truth of the matter was this: he had always been there in my life, and yet, I wasn't ready to see him until now. In fact, we know each other because our moms have been best friends for decades, and we've gone on a joint annual family trip since I was young. With him, things were different. *It was different because I was different.* It wasn't until I was honest with myself about who I truly was that I would finally be able to choose the person I wanted to spend my life with. I write these final words to you after having spent the past week moving into a house with him and get-ting a German shepherd puppy named Jupiter.

I feel reborn, as though I'm finally lifting off in life. And just when things couldn't get any better, I was offered a huge consulting job that will pay off the last of my debts. For good. I knew I would never go back to the way things were because right now is what I have been look-ing for all my life.

I poured my heart onto these pages and had no idea how much the process would change me . . . for the better. Writing a book isn't easy. I can't blame anyone who starts and never finishes. In my case, writing this book has been a big part of my healing. These words and experiences have weighed heavily inside me, waiting to come out onto these pages since I was a little kid. I am grateful for every moment that has brought me here to you, wherever you are reading. This book has cleared me out so that the new can come in, and it has reminded me of who I truly am. I hope it's done the same for you.

BECOME AN EXPERT IN NEWNESS

What I know for sure about life is this: it's always moving. Know that the joy of completion or the pain of rock bottom is . . . transient. It is always followed by the same opportunity: the experience of newness, and the experience of growing. As a career coach who has helped thousands of people find clarity for their best career path, land job offers, and start businesses, I am an expert in "newness." And here's the thing about newness, or as my grandma Lorraine calls it, the Divine Unknown: usually, it trips people up. Seeking newness for the sake of newness can also be referred to as running away. But newness from a place of authenticity? That, my friend, is a *You Turn*. It's a spiritual awakening fueled by the power of the universe. Some call it fulfillment; others call it the purpose of life. Because when you are in the flow with what rests inside the deepest parts of your soul, you get to experience your wholeness.

The fear I felt while in Natalie's arms was simply that: a friendly awakening, newness that was tripping me up. Some people will get excited to make art of their blank slates, while others will slip into feeling afraid or completely stripped by their new beginnings, buying into the belief that they're totally "starting over." For me, none of this has ever felt true. We never really start over; who we are right now is made by the ingredients of our past experiences and emotions. We are *always* carrying the thread of our past with us into the future of our careers, relationships, and lives, whether we want to see it that way or not. We can choose to hold the new with lightness.

THE "WRONG" PATH LEADS YOU TO THE RIGHT ONE

It will never cease to amaze me how many people will opt out of the right path for them because they invested ten years in the wrong one. Who decided that we should know from a young age what we're meant for? How has this become threaded into our society? What so many fail to realize is that that "wrong" path is part of a necessary process, and it has led them to this moment—or, in this case, the right path.

Did you ever realize that you needed that "wrong" path in order to get to the right one? You *need* the wrong to learn the right. In fact, studies reveal that the regrets over what you *could have done* weigh so much heavier on the soul than the feeling of what you *did do* "*wrong*."[2] Are you holding yourself hostage on a career path just because of the years you invested in it? Don't allow your past "wrongs" to stop you from doing things you wish for in the future. Your degrees and years worked are here to serve you; you're not here to serve them.

Anjali, my client who spent years working as a doctor, was upset because if she honored her heart and pivoted her career into fashion, she felt like she would be "starting over." Even though she didn't like being a doctor, she felt she would be abandoning all the years she put into medical school and the years she put into developing her practice. That's not true. If anything, she's *finally* moving forward because she is honoring her heart. Look, the world smiles back at you when you decide to be who you are, and usually that requires a *You Turn*. If you're meant to be a doctor, go be one. If you're meant to be a sailor, go be one. If you're meant to be a filmmaker, do it. Also know that who you are, and what you're meant to be doing, changes.

After months of coaching, Anjali finally left her medical practice behind and took a job as an assistant at a top fashion brand. Perhaps it looked like she was "moving backward" or as though her time as a doctor was "wasted," but a short three years later, she emailed me, in charge of Fashion Week for the company, asking if I wanted to come to their show in Paris. If you are wondering how she was able to ascend so quickly, it's because of her "wrong" path. She carried the grit and attention to detail she learned while acquiring her medical degree into her new job in the fashion world. I would always look her in the eye and remind her that backing up in her career, making a choice to reconfigure her life, did *not* have to mean she's backing down. Backing up is not always a form of backing down. Period.

One's ability or work ethic is a skill set that never goes away because nothing is ever lost. In fact, what *was* becomes a part of what *is.* If Anjali stayed in her role as a doctor, she might have sleepwalked through another ten years of her life, all while feeling the same way about her current career and her dream job. When I encouraged her to go for it, I gave her the best advice I could. I admire the trust she gave me in listening to my coaching. But in the end, it was Anjali who made her dreams happen because she decided to trust herself. Trust yourself, and life will start working out in your favor. Life will be your friend if you let it.

MAKE ART OF YOUR LIFE

I thought about that Picasso anecdote, of him spending his whole life working on his art, which eventually translated into his ability to create that quick, masterful scribble on a napkin. If we really think about it, we all have that capacity. To be a genius in our own right. In fact, we are all Picasso. We are all making art of our lives and underestimating how much wisdom and magic we carry with us as we embark into undiscovered opportunities.

"SELF-LOVE" MAY LOOK LIKE MOVING IN WITH YOUR PARENTS

I think a lot about how taking responsibility for yourself—your wishes, your messes, your progress—is the ultimate vehicle for self-love. For me, it looked like accepting the reality of the present moment when my book deal came in: moving back in with my parents so I could grieve my sister, paying off my debts, writing this book, and learning how to budget (*finally*).

It isn't always pretty on the outside, but it gave me something that we all may not realize makes us come most alive: progress. I've had clients who are stressed out over a home they can't afford, who have stayed in a bad relationship or even married the wrong person for them, in the name of forward motion, or "progress." Staying on a path that isn't in alignment with who you are, or being with the wrong partner, is sneaky, because it may be disguised by society as a step forward, when it's not: it's a self-destructive step backward.

Progress begins when we love ourselves enough to accept ourselves for who we truly are, what we actually want, and the person we aspire to become. Real progress is built on the ability to be honest with yourself, even when you know it's going to hurt.

THE WORLD NEEDS *YOU*, NOT THE PERSON YOU THINK YOU SHOULD BE

All my thoughts came to a pause and I brought my mind back into the room of the breath-work class. I looked up to see my friends sitting on the floor, looking at me. Actually, they were looking *into* me. They were seeing my most vulnerable self and emanating unconditional love. I stared back into the eyes of Sarah and Natalie and all I could do was smile, because in the middle of my soul's upheaval, I knew how fortunate I was to call them my friends. To the world, they are seen as business rock stars. To me, they're my lucky stars.

Before the class, they were talking about their business models, and all the magic they wanted to create in the world. Sarah talked about having larger live events for her women's empowerment company, Girl-Talk Network. Natalie talked about expanding BossBabe beyond their already two million followers on Instagram. Amanda, my dear friend, who is a spiritual business and life mentor, talked about writing a business book on authenticity and social media. I couldn't help but notice that, on paper, my business looked just like theirs did: an extensive email list, a podcast with thousands of downloads, blog posts all over the internet, and Instagram followers. I knew I had a lot to be grateful for, but I also knew in my heart that I didn't feel the same joy they did toward the future of this path as an online coach or guru . . . *That* was the confusing part. The unknown.

I went through a mental checklist of the steps one would take, that most of us took, in our businesses:

> ❯ *Fill my one-on-one career and life-coaching practice.*
> I did this in 2014, and ever since, I have had a waitlist.

> *Launch group coaching programs.*
> I already accomplished this in 2015.
> *Scale an online course.*
> We all know how that ended in 2016, and these courses are still available online to this day.
> *Host large seminars.*
> Accomplished in 2016.
> *Have a high-end coaching group.*
> I thought about it and couldn't pull the trigger.
> *Create a highly downloaded podcast.*
> Hello, *You Turn Podcast.*

My friends lit up as they spoke about these steps: their sales funnels, their new e-courses, and their large-scale live events. But not my soul. Mine told me *no.* I felt a certain exhaustion in my cells—not the kind of exhaustion from simply being tired, but rather the kind you get when you are going against the grain of being who you are.

I had spent years trying to make it into the CIA, only for that voice to tell me to leave as soon as I was on the brink of a big break. I spent years learning about online business, building email lists, and gaining "followers"—only for this voice to now tell me that even though I finally had cultivated an audience, I wasn't meant to be an influencer on the internet. *I need a break,* I thought to myself, remembering that when you live with purpose, you tap into wells of endless energy.

Just do it, my ego said, desperate for me to grow the parts of my business that didn't align with my heart, all so I could feel as though I was safe in the world, or I had a plan of sorts. An unforgiving, fearful voice flew into the winds of my mind: *You know the steps . . . Just create a bunch of lead magnets and get rich online.* But I heard my soul reply: *I won't let you do it that way—you're gonna do it your way.* Have you ever heard such a message from your soul, a big whopping no, in the face of what looks like an easier path? That message is an invitation for not only a new beginning, but a new level of commitment to your true self.

I looked at the girls earnestly, knowing that this book you're reading would mark a new beginning for me, where I'd own who I genuinely was in my career. With disappointment, I admitted: "I'm not a Sheryl Sandberg. I'm a Shel Silverstein."

They looked back at me, confused, so I unloaded: "I've worked so hard to get to this point of my career, so why can't I just keep on being an online marketer guru thing? It would be *so easy*. Making money this way, I can do it in my fucking sleep. But that's not me. *Ugh*, that's not me. I fucking *wish* it was. If I'm being really honest with you guys, writing this book felt *so good*. The kind of good that means I need to keep writing, even when it's done. And I hate that. I hate that I'm not meant to be a businesswoman like you guys are. I'm meant to be a poet . . . so now what? Do I write a little collection of weird coffee-table poems? *Why* does this have to be who I am? I don't want this to be what I want."

"But the world *needs* the Shel Silversteins," Sarah whispered, "so that's exactly what you'll do." Sarah and Natalie nodded in agreement. I needed to hear their words, but part of me (a big part of me) wanted to reject them.

"That's cute, a poet," I said as I began to cry again. "But nobody will pay me to write fucking poetry. Let's be honest. No one. After finishing *You Turn*, I'll have to be *someone else,* that businessy person that does well in the world, in order to get by."

Sarah smirked. We both knew I was lying to myself. *She knew that I knew better. I knew that I knew better.* But the truth is, I was *scared*. What followed was completely unexpected: we all started laughing, *hard*. It was the kind of laughter that doubles you over with release. For me, it was surrender. Isn't it crazy how we can so quickly laugh about the hilarity of our rock bottoms? Isn't it great to notice how temporary they actually are? According to research, we physically experience our emotional feelings for an average of only ninety seconds.[3] And yet, we can spend *weeks* avoiding those painful ninety seconds, living at a slightly lower frequency, limited by the pains that sit unmet in our hearts.

Know this, my friend: you're not designed to live at rock bottom. It's simply a place that shows us who we are, and who we are not. It's a place that gifts us with a blank slate to begin anew, often because we have no other choice. It's a place that teaches us to make friends with the Divine Unknown. The minute we do this is the minute we begin to lift off so we can take flight into our new adventure. Do you identify as an artist, or a businessperson? Some part of you knows the truth, whatever it is. The world needs both. The only thing harder than being yourself is resisting it.

Crying in Natalie's arms, I decided I would devote the rest of my career to my own creativity and self-expression; a lot of that meant I wouldn't lead with business or money. It meant moving forward with my show, *You Turn Podcast*, whether it makes money or not. It meant speaking on stages around the world, and sharing my message about life purpose, rock bottom, confidence, and leadership. Most of all, it meant doing the most vulnerable thing I could: be who I am in a world that has so many messages about who we *should* be. That meant writing the poetry book I was always supposed to write. That meant letting my family read all my feelings here in this book, and facing my fears that perhaps they'll judge me for being "too emotional" or "too" . . . *something*.

Will my editor laugh at me behind her computer screen when I send my next book proposal for a poetry collection? Will my agent tell me that being a "poet" after writing a career book is literary suicide? I don't know. But I am embodying what I think life is really about, my most courageous *You Turn* to date: choosing to be myself. The little girl who, at age five, announced to her preschool graduation audience that she'd be an author, mother, and poet . . . one down, two to go.

Life's a trip, huh? But most of all, it's an experiment and a game. If you choose to see it this way, the winner, the one who is actually moving forward, is the one who finally decides to honor the voice of their heart. Not later. Not when it's convenient. But now. Today. This means tuning in to your intuition, seeing your life for what it is, and taking action. In times of stress, fear, or anxiety, the most common piece of advice we hear is: "Just be yourself." But did anyone ever sit you down and tell you how hard that could be?

Throughout all my years of career-coaching others, I've learned that people become stuck for two simple reasons: the first is they are buying into the belief that they need to push through the misery of being on the wrong path. This keeps them stuck for life. The second is they haven't chosen to connect to themselves, to tune in to that wise voice and discover who they truly are. They are scared, intimidated, or buying into the belief that they aren't worthy of being happy. This is a lie against the soul, a lie of the mind.

We are all made of the same stuff. The same science. The same art. We also come from the same divine place, wherever that is. Everyone has a gift, a God-given CORE SKILL SET, but not everyone chooses to harness it. Everyone also has a distinctive CORE NATURE that creates an imprint in any room they enter. Have you properly set aside the time to discern yours? The only difference between you and that person out there doing the thing you want to do is that they decided to listen to the voice and follow the nudge of their soul. Your *You Turns* are your birthright. Take them, even when they're embarrassing, even when they're inconvenient, even when they're messy.

That's what personal development really is: walking the bridge between who you're being now and the voice of your heart that's telling you who you're really meant to be. Are you willing to walk that bridge? Today. Right now. I think you are ready, because you're reading this book. The bridge can be long, painful, and arduous; it can also be a whole lot easier than you think. The great news about this journey is that it can start at a moment's notice. From there, you can change on a moment's notice. You get to change whenever you want, however you want. It doesn't have to be long. Never forget that where you are today has nothing to do with where you can be by next week.

What is that voice in your heart telling you about what you are meant for? If you don't hear it chiming in, realize that's the work you need to do right now, the work of simply connecting to yourself. That starts with creating the circumstances in your life that would grant your mind the stillness it would need to hear the voice of your heart.

But there's no shortcut. There's just doing the work. So you do this by paying attention to what lights you up. Explore how you feel to others when you walk into a room (your CORE NATURE). Know and cultivate your CORE SKILL SETS. Use your CORE VALUES as a filter for your life choices in your career and dreams. Commit to discovering your MONEY BLUEPRINT by exploring the traumas or memories you've picked up and carried with you about money. As part of your healing, investigate your limiting beliefs and learn to BEFRIEND YOUR BLOCKS.

When you do this, you are better equipped to notice when your body is in a state of yes or no, expansion or contraction, to the opportunities that are flowing into your life. This is where you get to tune in to your intuition.

There's something powerful about paying off half a million dollars of debt. The experience changed me. It wasn't about the money; it was about the humility of it all. It was about realizing that life moves, and the game is about showing up and meeting life right where it is meeting you. That humility created a message inside me that I look forward to sharing with the world and my journey to *You Turn*.

YOU ARE SO MUCH MORE THAN YOUR OUTER RESULTS

In the three years since my rock bottom, I have had the privilege of viewing myself in many different lights. From a successful entrepreneur to broke and moving back in with my parents, I have developed an overall sense of knowing in my bones. This knowing is a deep-seated awareness that I am so much more than my bank account, my business results, or my image. My spirit is infinitely bigger than all my fears. The game of life, the real work, is in the meaning you make of yourself when you're both on the highs and on the lows. Never rob yourself of the dignity of your rock bottom, and always face the inconvenience of the truth. Who you are is so much bigger than all of it.

Last week, I went to see Tycho, one of my favorite bands, play at the Greek Theatre in Los Angeles when a moment of euphoria hit. Goose bumps covered my entire body and a smile unlike any other came across my face. I listened to their music every single day as I wrote this book, and there I was, within a few weeks of my deadline, dancing to their melodies and laughing with my friends beside me. For the first time in my life, I felt truly whole. I thought about how I would be going to bed that night with my favorite human and my love, William. I thought about how I am now finally debt-free. I thought about how that little five-year-old girl who lost her home is finally moving into a house and becoming the poet she was always meant to be. I marinated in a sense of energetic harmony with the world, feeling more in flow than I ever have before. Not because of everything that was happening in my life, but because of who I had become along the way. That's the real *You Turn*, isn't it?

So as you make your way over to your next *You Turn*, of which there will be many, the good news is that today can be a new day. Yesterday's done, so be done with it. Today is an opportunity to step into the new you, the true you . . . It is another opportunity to *You Turn* into your greatest yet-to-be.

The good news is that, you and I, we're only getting started.

ACKNOWLEDGMENTS

I walk around the world feeling a constant, invisible force field of support around me, my community, and I channel it into everything that I do. Thanks to my friends and family who empowered me not only in the writing of this book, but in my repeated choice to be myself along the way. I am forever indebted to you. Below are just a handful of many amazing people in my life who I would especially like to recognize.

To my loving family: **Stacie Stahl**, my sister, whom I will forever miss. You are the person in my family who understood me the most and I am so grateful for all the conversations we had. My dad, **Alan Stahl**, you are the most entertaining human I have ever met . . . The most fun parts of me come from you. My mom, **Debbie Stahl**, thank you for being the ultimate listener. My brother **Joshua Stahl**, for showing up when it's inconvenient and no one else will. **Robert Stahl**, thank you for your nonjudgmental ear, for calling me no matter how much I tell you I'm allergic to the phone, and your depth. My sister-in-law, **Andrea Stahl**, you are sacred to me.

To my true love, **William Haddad**, thank you for showing me what right feels like in my heart.

I want to thank the women who I chose as sisters in this lifetime: **Nicole Nowparvar**, my best friend and travel partner, thank you for helping me edit the pages of this book and for giving me the constant experience of effortless connection. **Sarah Anne Stewart,** you have become home to me. Thank you for always picking up the phone and rooting for me. **Alyssa Nobriga,** my lifelong teacher, student, and forever friend, thank you for helping me discover my freedom. **Gina DeVee,** thank you for your "fabulousness" and your endless help with editing and ideas. We go so many lifetimes back in history together. Our friendship is so unique, profound, and divinely timed. **Kenzie Woods,** my oldest friend, you weren't just helping me edit this book, you were helping me stay true to myself. **Amanda Bucci,** thank you for your pure heart and wisdom. **Jessica Winterstern,** thank you for reminding me what I am capable of. You are so insightful and I am so grateful for the journey we've been on. **Natalie Ellis,** you lead by example with empowering women. I am so lucky to call you my friend. **Sarah Pendrick,** our bond is deeper than words. **Samantha Skelly,** thank you for bringing the crazy fun out in me. **Lara Conovaloff,** thank you for being the friend who always says "yes" to having fun, and for helping me come up with this book concept. **Chelsea Krost,** our conversations fill me up and you keep me grounded in such a special way. **Brenna Moore,** for cheering me on so fully since I was a kid riding the school bus. **Elodie Garson-Besançon** and **Tricia Chan,** you both made me into a citizen of the world and expanded my understanding of myself—I love you. **Kiera Himsl Fillerup,** for being my oldest friend who always gives me full permission to celebrate who I am.

To the men who empower me: **Jason Goldberg,** thank you for making it safe for me to share my dark and my light, and for your ability to laugh your ass off with me. **Barry Griffin,** I will never forget our endless late-night conversations in London about our dreams—your support has been a catalyst for mine.

To my writing team: **Eric DelaBarre,** thank you for your wisdom. **Kirsten Trammell** over at CAKE Publishing, thank you for helping with copy edits, and giving me feedback. You have so much follow-through and I appreciate it so deeply. **Lauren Kinney,** your copy edits took this book to another level. **Greg Brown**, for understanding me, polishing this book, and validating the messages I had to share. **Giles Anderson**, thank you so much for believing in my book and being my agent. You made this possible for me, and I am forever grateful for the enthusiasm you had when I sent you the proposal. **Glenn Yeffeth** at BenBella Books for completely supporting my vision and helping me get this out into the world with so much love. **Debbi Molnar**, thank you for reading the sticky chapters and helping me make sense of them both in my mind and on the page.

RESOURCES

→ *You Turn* **Book Readers Private Facebook Community**
Do you have questions about your career, or the book? Let's talk about your *You Turns*! Join my *free* Facebook community, *You Turn* Book Readers, to get support as you make your *You Turns* in life. This private group is here to support and elevate you along the way.

https://ashleystahl.com/FBgroup

→ **FREE QUIZ: What Is Your Actual Dream Career? (It's Not What You Think It Is!)**
Visit my website for a free quiz that helps you determine your most ideal career fit. You'll also be added to my weekly email list, where I will consistently share free resources with you, from podcast episodes to free online courses. No spam ever, and I rarely message more than once per week.

ashleystahl.com/freequiz

→ *You Turn Podcast*
Your transformation is a process, not an event! That's why I hope you'll join me every single week on the *You Turn Podcast*, where I host incredible experts who will transform your mindset, in both work and love. Every month, I also drop a solo episode on a *You Turn* I'm working

through and learning from, so we can grow together. Other than this book, my podcast has been the ultimate passion project!

https://youturnpodcast.com

→ **FREE ONLINE COURSE: How to Land Your Dream Job**
Register for this free one-hour course preview of the Job Offer Academy, my flagship job-hunting program with more than ten hours of content that's helped more than six thousand job seekers land offers they're excited about!

Free mini course preview: https://youturnpodcast.com/job

Full course: www.JobOfferAcademy.com

→ **FREE ONLINE COURSE: Get Clarity on Your Best Career Fit**
Register for this free one-hour course preview of the Career Clarity Lab, my flagship clarity program with more than six hours of content that's helped thousands of job seekers discover their best career fit.

Free mini course preview: https://youturnpodcast.com/clarity

Full course: www.CareerClarityLab.com

→ **FREE ONLINE COURSE: Launch Your Service-Based Business**
Register for this free one-hour course preview of the Business Launch Mastermind, my flagship business program with more than six hours of clarity content that's helped thousands of job seekers discover their best career fit.

Free mini course preview: https://youturnpodcast.com/biz

Full course: www.BusinessLaunchMastermind.com

→ **Contact**
To hire Ashley as your MC, spokesperson, or keynote speaker, visit www.AshleyStahl.com/Speaking.

For private coaching, or any other inquiries, please contact support@ashleyinternational.com.

→ **Social Media**

Instagram: https://www.instagram.com/ashleystahl/

Facebook: https://www.facebook.com/ashleystahlcoaching/

LinkedIn: https://www.linkedin.com/in/ashleystahl/

Facebook Community: https://ashleystahl.com/FBgroup

Twitter: https://twitter.com/ashleystahl

Text message us: (818) 917-3857

NOTES

Introduction

1. Ronald and Mary Hulnick, *Loyalty to Your Soul: The Heart of Spiritual Psychology* (Carlsbad, CA: Hay House, 2011).

Chapter 1

1. Bureau of Labor Statistics, "Employment Status of the Civilian Noninstitutional Population by Age, Sex, and Race," Labor Force Statistics from the Current Population Survey, August 14, 2019, https://www.bls.gov/cps /cpsaat03.htm.
2. Catalyst, "Quick Take: Women in the Workforce—United States," Catalyst: Workplaces That Work for Women, August 19, 2019, https://www .catalyst.org/research/women-in-the-workforce-united-states/.
3. Chip Conley, "How Do We Combat Ageism? By Valuing Wisdom As Much As Youth," *Harvard Business Review*, Generational Issues, June 21, 2018, https://hbr.org/2018/06/how-do-we-combat-ageism-by-valuing -wisdom-as-much-as-youth.
4. Center for American Women and Politics, "Women in Elective Office 2018," Eagleton Institute of Politics, Rutgers University, August 14, 2019, https://www.cawp.rutgers.edu/women-elective-office-2018.
5. Dong Won Oh, Elinor Buck, Alexander Todorov, "Revealing Hidden Gender Biases in Competence Impressions of Faces," *Psychological Science* 30, no. 1 (January 2019): 65–79, doi:10.1177/0956797618813092.

6. Don Pettit, "The Tyranny of the Rocket Equation," NASA, May 1, 2012, https://www.nasa.gov/mission_pages/station/expeditions/expedition30/tryanny.html.

7. John Murphy, "New Epidemic Affects Nearly Half of American Adults," MDLinx, January 11, 2019, https://www.mdlinx.com/internal-medicine/article/3272.

Chapter 2

1. John Levya, "How Do Muscles Grow? The Science of Muscle Health," BuiltLean, December 31, 2018, https://www.builtlean.com/2013/09/17/muscles-grow.

2. J. B. Furness, B. P. Callaghan, L. R. Rivera, et al., "The Enteric Nervous System and Gastrointestinal Innervation: Integrated Local and Central Control," *Advances in Experimental Medicine and Biology* 817 (2014): 39–71.

3. World Health Organization, "QD-85 Burnout," ICD-11 for Mortality and Morbidity Statistics, August 19, 2019, https://icd.who.int/browse11/l-m/en#/http://id.who.int/icd/entity/129180281.

4. Steve Nguyen, "The True Financial Cost of Job Loss," Workplace Psychology, January 9, 2011, https://workplacepsychology.net/2011/01/09/the-true-financial-cost-of-job-stress/.

Chapter 3

1. "Preventing Adverse Childhood Experiences," Violence Prevention | Injury Center | CDC. Centers for Disease Control and Prevention, April 3, 2020, www.cdc.gov/violenceprevention/childabuseandneglect/aces/fastfact.html.

2. Ryan Hart, "What Percentage of Lottery Winners Go Broke? (Plus 35 More Statistics)," *Ryan Hart*, August 21, 2019, https://www.ryanhart.org/lottery-winner-statistics/.

3. "From the Goal Line to the Soul Line," YouTube video, 4:47, posted by "University of Santa Monica," https://www.youtube.com/watch?v=NDO4AM1BlG8.

4. Amir Levine and Rachel S. F. Heller, *Attached: The New Science of Adult Attachment and How It Can Help You Find—and Keep—Love* (New York: Tarcherperigee, 2012).

5. Stephen Chbosky, *The Perks of Being a Wallflower: 20th Anniversay Edition* (New York: Gallery Books, 2019).

6. T. Harv Eker, *Secrets of the Millionaire Mind: Mastering the Inner Game of Wealth* (New York: Collins, 2019).

7. Ashley Stahl, "MINDSET: How to Have a Millionaire Mindset with Leisa Peterson," *You Turn Podcast* 100, https://ashleystahl.com/podcast/how-to-have-a-millionaire-mindset-w-leisa-peterson/.

8. Napoleon Hill, *Think and Grow Rich* (New York: Fall River Press, 2019).

9. Ashley Stahl, "MINDSET: How to Uplevel Your Money Mindset with Chris Harder," *You Turn Podcast* 39, https://ashleystahl.com/podcast/how-to-uplevel-your-money-mindset-w-chris-harder/.

10. Ashley Stahl, "MINDSET: 6 Steps to Upgrade Your Relationship with Money with Morgana Rae," *You Turn Podcast* 61, https://ashleystahl.com/podcast/6-steps-to-upgrade-your-relationship-with-money-morgana-rae/.

11. Lynne Twist, *The Soul of Money: Reclaiming the Wealth of Our Inner Resources* (New York: W.W. Norton, 2017).

12. Ashley Stahl, "MINDSET: How to Get Out of Debt with Ashley Feinstein Gerstley," *You Turn Podcast* 58, https://ashleystahl.com/podcast/how-to-get-out-of-debt-ashley-feinstein-gerstley/.

13. Barbara Stanny, *Overcoming Underearning: A Five-Step Plan to a Richer Life* (New York: Collins, 2007).

Chapter 5

1. "What Is Chaos Theory?" Fractal Foundation, August 28, 2019, https://fractalfoundation.org/resources/what-is-chaos-theory/.

2. Douglas Bremner, "Traumatic Stress: Effects on the Brain," *National Library of Medicine* 8, no. 4 (2006): 445–61.

3. Masaru Emoto, *The Hidden Messages in Water* (Hillsboro, OR: Beyond Words Publishing, 2004).

4. Nate Heim, Boneva Maloney, and Reeves Jones, "Childhood Trauma and Risk for Chronic Fatigue Syndrome: Association with Neuroendocrine Dysfunction," *National Library of Medicine* 66 (2009): 72–80.

5. Joseph Goldberg, "Mental Health and Dissociative Amnesia," WebMD, August 29, 2019, https://www.webmd.com/mental-health/dissociative-amnesia#1.

Chapter 6

1. ManpowerGroup, "Millennial Careers: 2020 Vision," World of Work Insights Resource Library, September 1, 2019, https://www.manpower group.com/wps/wcm/connect/660ebf65-144c-489e-975c-9f838294c237 /MillennialsPaper1_2020Vision_lo.pdf?MOD=AJPERES.
2. Patricia Chen, Phoebe C. Ellsworth, and Norbert Schwarz, "Finding a Fit or Developing It: Implicit Theories About Achieving Passion for Work," *Personality and Social Psychology Bulletin* 41, no. 10 (October 2015): 1411–24.

Chapter 7

1. Lauren Weber, "Your Résumé vs. Oblivion," *Wall Street Journal*, January 24, 2012, https://www.wsj.com/articles/SB10001424052970204624204577 178941034941330.
2. Wendy Kaufman, "A Successful Job Search: It's All About Networking," NPR, February 3, 2011, https://www.npr.org/2011/02/08/133474431/a -successful-job-search-its-all-about-networking.
3. Ethan Kross et al., "Social Rejection Shares Somatosensory Representations with Physical Pain," April 12, 2011, www.pnas.org/content/108/15 /6270.
4. Nathan C. DeWall et al., "Acetaminophen Reduces Social Pain: Behavioral and Neural Evidence," *Psychological Science* 21, no. 7 July 2010, 931–37, doi:10.1177/0956797610374741.
5. Tim Askew, "The Remarkable Power of Simply Telling the Truth," *Inc.*, August 17, 2015, https://www.inc.com/tim-askew/lies-damn-lies-and -entrepreneurship.html.

Chapter 8

1. "Could Being Boring Cost You Your Job?" Scribd, blog.scribd.com /home/being-interesting-job.
2. Summer Allen, "The Science of Awe," Greater Good Science Center at UC Berkeley, September 28, 2019, https://ggsc.berkeley.edu/images/uploads /GGSC-JTF_White_Paper-Awe_FINAL.pdf.
3. "The Secret Structure of Great Talks," video, 18:03, posted byTEDxEast, https://www.ted.com/talks/nancy_duarte_the_secret_structure_of_great _talks?language=en.

Chapter 9

1. Brad Plumber, "Only 27 Percent of College Grads Have a Job Related to Their Major," *Washington Post*, May 23, 2013, https://www.washington post.com/news/wonk/wp/2013/05/20/only-27-percent-of-college-grads -have-a-job-related-to-their-major/.

2. Elka Torpey and Terrell Dalton, "Should I Get a Master's Degree?," US Bureau of Labor Statistics Career Outlook, September 30, 2019, https:// www.bls.gov/careeroutlook/2015/article/should-i-get-a-masters-degree .htm.

3. Karl Marx, *The Communist Manifesto* (Chicago: Pluto Press, 1996).

4. May Wong, "Stanford Study Finds Walking Improves Creativity," *Stanford News*, September 6, 2019, https://news.stanford.edu/2014/04/24 /walking-vs-sitting-042414/.

5. Charles Dotson, "Psychological Momentum: Why Success Breeds Success," *Review of General Psychology* 18 (2014): 19.

6. Joel Hoomans, "35,000 Decisions: The Great Choices of Strategic Leaders," *Leading Edge*, March 20, 2015, https://go.roberts.edu/leadingedge /the-great-choices-of-strategic-leaders.

7. Alice Hughes and Andrew Gilpin, "Life's Biggest Decisions Revealed— from When to Get Married to Quitting Your Job," *Mirror*, September 30, 2019, https://www.mirror.co.uk/news/uk-news/lifes-biggest-decisions -revealed-married-16047685.

Chapter 10

1. Jaruwan Sakulku, "The Impostor Phenomenon," *Journal of Behavioral Science* 6, no. 1 (2011): 75–97, doi:10.14456/ijbs.2011.6.

2. Charles Chu, "Picasso's Napkin and the Myth of the Overnight Success," Fee, September 9, 2019, https://fee.org/articles/picassos-napkin-and-the -myth-of-the-overnight-success/.

3. The Editors of Encyclopaedia Britannica, "Momentum," *Encyclopaedia Britannica*, September 9, 2019, https://www.britannica.com/science /momentum.

4. "A Quote by Jim Rohn," Goodreads, www.goodreads.com/quotes /209560-we-must-all-suffer-from-one-of-two-pains-the.

Chapter 11

1. V. Ranganathan, V. Siminow, J. Liu, et al., "From Mental Power to Muscle Power—Gaining Strength by Using the Mind," *Neuropsychologia* 42 (7): 944–56.

2. AJ Adams, "Seeing Is Believing: The Power of Visualization," *Psychology Today*, December 3, 2009, https://www.psychologytoday.com/us/blog /flourish/200912/seeing-is-believing-the-power-visualization.

3. Alexandra Michel, "Burnout and the Brain," Association for Psychological Science, September 16, 2019, https://www.psychologicalscience.org /observer/burnout-and-the-brain.

4. John Curtis and Mimi Curtis, "Factors Related to Susceptibility and Recruitment by Cults," *Psychological Reports* 73, no. 2 (1993): 451–60, doi:10.2466/pr0.1993.73.2.451.

5. Gay Hendricks, *The Big Leap: Conquer Your Hidden Fear and Take Life to the Next Level* (New York: HarperCollins, 2010).

Chapter 12

1. Michael Alan Singer, *The Untethered Soul: The Journey Beyond Yourself* (Oakland: New Harbinger Publications, 2007).

2. Susan Kelley, "Woulda, Coulda, Shoulda: The Haunting Regret of Failing Our Ideal Selves," *Cornell Chronicle*, May 24, 2018, https://news.cornell .edu/stories/2018/05/woulda-coulda-shoulda-haunting-regret-failing -our-ideal-selves.

3. "Emotional Mastery: The Gifted Wisdom of Unpleasant Feelings," YouTube video, 15:17, posted by "TedxTalks," September 23, 2016, https:// www.youtube.com/watch?v=EKy19WzkPxE.

ABOUT THE AUTHOR

Ashley Stahl is a counterterrorism professional turned highly sought-after career coach, *Forbes* blogger, and author on a mission to help job seekers step into a career that lights them up. Ashley is a creative writer, modern-day entrepreneur, and content creator, and more than 516,000 job seekers have subscribed to her free trainings, while her online courses have helped thousands of job seekers in thirty-one countries unlock their best career fit, land job offers, and upgrade their confidence.

Follow Ashley on Instagram @ashleystahl, or visit her website at ashleystahl.com.